PARATEXTUALITY IN ANGLOPHONE AND HISPANOPHONE POEMS IN THE US PRESS, 1855–1901

Interventions in Nineteenth-Century American Literature and Culture
Series Editors: Christopher Hanlon, Sarah R. Robbins, Andrew Taylor

Available

Liminal Whiteness in Early US Fiction
Hannah Lauren Murray

*Carlyle, Emerson and the Transatlantic Uses of Authority:
Literature, Print, Performance*
Tim Sommer

*Crossings in Nineteenth-Century American Culture:
Junctures of Time, Space, Self and Politics*
Edward Sugden

*(P)rescription Narratives: Feminist Medical Fiction and
the Failure of American Censorship*
Stephanie Peebles Tavera

*New Perspectives on Mary E. Wilkins Freeman: Reading with and
against the Grain*
Stephanie Palmer, Myrto Drizou and Cécile Roudeau

*Paratextuality in Anglophone and Hispanophone Poems in the
US Press, 1855–1901*
Ayendy Bonifacio

Forthcoming

Melville's Americas: Hemispheric Sympathies, Transatlantic Contagion
Nicholas Spengler

The Aesthetics of History and Slave Revolution in Antebellum America
Kevin Modestino

Gossip in US American Literature and Culture, 1850–1920
Katrin Horn

The Asian American Literary Renaissance: Encounters Across Time
Mai Wang

www.edinburghuniversitypress.com/series/incal

PARATEXTUALITY IN ANGLOPHONE AND HISPANOPHONE POEMS IN THE US PRESS, 1855–1901

Ayendy Bonifacio

EDINBURGH
University Press

Edinburgh University Press is one of the leading university presses in the UK. We publish academic books and journals in our selected subject areas across the humanities and social sciences, combining cutting-edge scholarship with high editorial and production values to produce academic works of lasting importance. For more information visit our website: edinburghuniversitypress.com

© Ayendy Bonifacio 2024, 2025

Edinburgh University Press Ltd
13 Infirmary Street
Edinburgh EH1 1LT

First published in hardback by Edinburgh University Press 2024

Typeset in 10/12.5 Adobe Sabon by
IDSUK (DataConnection) Ltd

A CIP record for this book is available from the British Library

ISBN 978 1 3995 2349 3 (hardback)
ISBN 978 1 3995 2350 9 (paperback)
ISBN 978 1 3995 2351 6 (webready PDF)
ISBN 978 1 3995 2352 3 (epub)

The right of Ayendy Bonifacio to be identified as the author of this work has been asserted in accordance with the Copyright, Designs and Patents Act 1988, and the Copyright and Related Rights Regulations 2003 (SI No. 2498).

CONTENTS

List of Figures	vi
Acknowledgments	viii
Introduction: Poetics of Paratextuality	1
1 Poetess as Paratext: The Contextualizing Influence of Lydia H. Sigourney and Alice Cary in the *New York Ledger*	25
2 Reprint Poems in Francisco P. Ramírez's *El Clamor Público*	65
3 The Reprint Lives of "Panic Poetry"	90
4 The Epitextual Sites of Cholera Poems	124
5 Gertrudis Gómez de Avellaneda in Puerto Rico's Partisan Press	154
Coda: "In Defense of Newspaper Poets"	181
Bibliography	190
Index	201

FIGURES

1.1	"Pete, The Scout, Triumphant," *The New York Ledger*, January 24, 1857. Public domain.	43
1.2	"The Scout and the Indian Sentinel," *The New York Ledger*, February 21, 1857. Public domain.	46
2.1	*El Clamor Público*'s poems: an interactive map. Google My Maps. Map data © 2023 Google.	73
3.1	Front page, *The Evening Post*, October 2, 1857. Library of Congress. Public domain.	94
3.2	"Lessons from the Times," *The Evening Post*, October 2, 1857. Library of Congress. Public domain.	98
3.3	Fire insurance ads, *The Evening Post*, October 2, 1857. Library of Congress. Public domain.	98
3.4	"Panic Poetry," *The Wheeling Daily Intelligencer*, November 3, 1857. Library of Congress. Public domain.	100
3.5	"Second Stock of Fall & Winter Goods," *The Wheeling Daily Intelligencer*, November 3, 1857. Library of Congress. Public domain.	101
3.6	"Panic Poetry," *Plattsburgh Republican*, October 31, 1857. Library of Congress. Public domain.	105

3.7	"Assorting Brokers," *The Anti-Slavery Bugle*, October 24, 1857. Library of Congress. Public domain.	107
3.8	"Lines Written on the back of a Protested Note," *The Liberator*, December 11, 1857. Library of Congress. Public domain.	108
3.9	"Hard Times," *Edgefield Advertiser*, October 14, 1857. Library of Congress. Public domain.	114
3.10	"Hard Times," *Edgefield Advertiser*, August 12, 1857 (left) and October 14, 1857 (right). Library of Congress. Public domain.	115
4.1	Robert Seymour, "Cholera 'Tramples the Victor and the Vanquish'd Both,'" *McLean's Monthly*, October 1, 1831. National Library of Medicine Digital Collections. Public domain mark 1.0.	135
4.2	John Leech, "A Court for King Cholera," *Punch*, September 25, 1852. Licensed under the Creative Commons Attribution 4.0 International (CC BY 4.0).	137
4.3	"Map Showing the Localities Where the Pestilence First Appeared in 1832" and "The Districts Where the Cholera Raged in 1849," *New York Herald*, July 23, 1866. Library of Congress. Public domain.	140
5.1	*La Gaceta de Puerto-Rico*, May 14, 1861. Library of Congress. Public domain.	162
5.2	*La Democracia*, October 2, 1901. Library of Congress. Public domain.	170
C.1	*The New York Times Magazine*, December 31, 1922. Newspapers.com. Public domain.	183

ACKNOWLEDGMENTS

Because it takes a village, there are so many people to thank for the manifestation of this book. I want to start with my partner and best friend, Joey Sue-Kyung Kim; thank you for reading every word I've ever written. Your unyielding support and generous spirit keep me going. I deeply love and respect you. Finding you through this journey has been the joy of my life. I am grateful to the Edinburgh Interventions in Nineteenth-Century American Literature and Culture series editors, Christopher Hanlon, Sarah R. Robbins, and Andrew Taylor, for cultivating and believing in this project. Thanks are also owed to my Edinburgh University Press editors—Elizabeth Fraser, Emily Sharp, Eliza Wright, and Fiona Conn—for your help in shaping my manuscript into a publishable monograph.

I am beyond indebted to my family, closest friends, and colleagues for their continued support of this project. Their wise words, kind ears, and unconditional love have been a source of motivation throughout the years. Sincerest thanks to my teachers, mentors, and life gurus who helped me along the journey of writing: Elizabeth Renker, thank you for your insight and mentorship and for guiding and challenging me. Thank you, Beth Hewitt and Jared Gardner for believing in this project when it was a dissertation. Thank you to The Ohio State University's Department of English faculty for helping me realize my scholarly potential: Pranav Jani, Aman Garcha, Fredrick Luis Aldama, Molly Farrell, Jake Risenger, Marcus Jackson, Clare Simmons, Koritha Mitchell, Ethan Knapp, and Jim Phalen. Your exemplary pedagogy, research, and activism have shown me how to exist both inside and outside of academia with consistency and persistence. Thank you, Carol Oliver, Rex Nobles, and the Ronald E. McNair Scholars Program for providing underserved communities and people of color a path toward a doctoral education. I don't know where I would be without this life-changing program.

Thank you to my wonderful friends and colleagues at the University of Toledo—Joey Kim, Dustin Pearson, Joey Gamble, Kim Mack, Parama Sarkar, Andrew Mattison, Tina Fitzgerald, Ben Stroud, Dan Campora, Tyler Branson, Tim Geiger, Natalie Bullock, Mel Gregory, Karie Peralta, Charles Beatty-Medina, and Charlene Gilbert. You have all pushed me to be a better writer, thinker, and educator. I am grateful for your support and collegiality. Thanks to all of my students, especially those who show enthusiasm and openness to my lessons on nineteenth-century newspapers and print culture. Your energy and curiosity are daily reminders that the world of nineteenth-century print is important and fun. I can't forget to thank all of the students, staff, and community members at the UToledo Student Recreation Center for providing me with a space for play and joy. Evenings in the weight room and basketball courts have been therapeutic for my mind and body, true oases that allowed me to get out of my head.

Thank you to the generous and amazing mentors, teachers, colleagues, and collaborators who have guided me along the way: Lorgia García Peña, Ana Castillo, Ilan Stavans, Maria Cristina Fumagalli, Erika M. Martínez, Eduardo C. Corral, Jewon Woo, Eric Gardner, Rodrigo Lazo, Jesse Alemán, Elisa Sampson Vera Tudela, Kenya Dworkin, Carmen Lamas, Robert McKee Irwin, Jean Lee Cole, Bernadine Hernández, Karen R. Roybal, Mark Noonan, Kelley Kreitz, Adam McKible, Jesse W. Schwartz, Daniel Worden, Trent Masiki, Justin Mann, Emily Hainze, Travis Foster, Brigitte Bailey, Renee Hudson, Maia Gil'Adí, Sarah Salter, Jim Casey, Michael Dowdy, Janet Neary, Red Washburn, and so many others. You have all shaped my thinking, reading, and writing in significant ways. Thank you for motivating me to keep writing and rewriting a lot of this book.

My Brooklyn, East New York family, you will always have my heart because you raised me with love and encouragement. Joseph Familia, Ruben Cedeño, Mark Cedeño, and Mike Loubriel, Jonathan Santana, Cesar Rodriguez, Rudy Luciano, Stephanie López, and Francisco López, thank you for always having my back and believing in me.

I am appreciative of my family, Jessica Bonifacio, Estarly Bonifacio, Isaura Bonifacio, Ángel Bonifacio, Isabella Bonifacio, Ramón, the Ulloa brothers, Jennifer Kim, Victor Pham, Adeline Pham, Sophia Pham, Christine Kim, Jonah Gold, and Esther Kim, Drs. Hyo Kim, and Jin Kim. Your continual care and guidance enable me to pursue my writing and art with grace and humility. I am blessed to know all of you.

ACKNOWLEDGMENTS

Finally, thank you to my grandparents in this realm and the next: Mamá Flora, Papá Victor, Mamá Carmita, Papá Chepe, and Papá Agustin, you will always live through every word I write. *Mis Padres*, Ana Peralta and José Julian Bonifacio, when we first immigrated to the US from our natal Dominican Republic, English was a superpower that we did not have. For years, this language eluded us, at times made us feel like permanent visitors in our own home. Let this book be proof that we belong here and that this language, this superpower, is ours too. Thank you for your courage, for it is from there that I draw strength every day for every word. Our family is the root of my experience, the inspiration for all that I create.

For Evie

INTRODUCTION: POETICS OF PARATEXTUALITY

Today, we routinely encounter poetry in online and print versions of books, anthologies, and literary magazines, but rarely—if ever—in national and regional newspapers. This was not always the case. Throughout most of the nineteenth century, readers encountered more poems in newspapers than in any other medium. With the rise of the penny press in the 1830s came changes to the production and dissemination of verse throughout the century. Editors printed, often without the authorization of authors, popular songs and poems alongside news, advertisements, and editorials. By the mid-nineteenth century, the US had produced more newspapers and newspaper poets than any other modern nation. This moment of mass poetic production presents a unique occasion to study the cultural, social, and material phenomenon of the newspaper poem, inviting a serious reflection on the poetics of newspaper poems and the function of the elements that surround and contextualize them.

Paratextuality in Anglophone and Hispanophone Poems in the US Press, 1855–1901 is about the seldom studied parts of US nineteenth-century poetry: the unoriginal, the imitated, and the ephemeral. These parts amount to lesser and unknown poets, poems, editors, and periodicals; correlations between news and poetics, serial, and verse; and the newspaper poem as a genre. Via structuralist print culture readings, cultural critique, historical poetics, and translation, in chapters that move from poets, to editors, to high-impact episodic events, to a single author, this book provides multiple and interconnected frames and methods for reading and contextualizing newspaper poems. These frames and methods set newspaper poems within their original publication context, and in some cases de-anthologize them from their authoritative place in the tome. In this book, newspaper poems are not simply cultural or material examples. Instead, they make up a remarkably complex archive of languages, assorted genres, writers, editors, and periodicals, which enabled public intrigue, infodemics, celebrities, data, and sustained the identities of certain social groups.

Drawing examples from over 200 English-language and Spanish-language newspapers and periodicals published between January 1855 and October 1901, *Paratextuality in Anglophone and Hispanophone Poems in the US Press, 1855–1901* ultimately argues that nineteenth-century newspaper poems are inherently paratextual. By paratext, I am referring to the location of newspaper poems on the page, their links to surrounding textual items and discourses, their editorialization through circulation (the way poems were altered from newspaper to newspaper), and their association and disassociation with certain celebrity bylines, editors, and newspaper titles. These various contexts enabled contemporaneous poetic value and taste that, in the mid- to late nineteenth century, were not only sentimental, Romantic, and/or genteel. Rather, poetic taste and value were also determined, I argue, via arbitrary consequences of circulation, typesetting errors, and editorial intervention, what I call a poetics of paratextuality.

I make this case in archival detail in five chapters that delineate the complex social and cultural functions newspaper poems and reprints played in the everyday lives of Anglophone and Hispanophone readers. The opening chapter makes a case for how newspaper poems fed the celebrity status of poets like Lydia H. Sigourney and Alice Cary, two of the most popular "poetesses" of the mid-nineteenth century. Chapter 2 shifts from the East to the West coast, and from English to Spanish, recovering transamerican Spanish-language poems in Francisco P. Ramírez's *El Clamor Público* (1855–59), the first Hispanophone newspaper published in California after the US–Mexico War. Chapters 3 and 4 excavate the robust but largely unknown archives of newspaper poems circulating across the US concerning the Panic of 1857 and the New York cholera epidemic of 1866.[1] The final chapter takes a necessary turn away from the mainland US toward Puerto Rico to conceptualize a poetics of paratextuality at the margins of the US before and after the Spanish–American War. While many literary critics understandably argue that the material circumstances of a newspaper poem's publication, circulation, and reception impose considerably upon efforts to critically understand them paratextually, the many contextual and historical implications of the paratext have gone generally unremarked.

Poetics of Paratextuality

Essentially, I am interested in an understanding of poetic taste and value through what Gérard Genette labels the "paratext." Genette posits that the paratext is "[m]ore than a boundary or a sealed border, [it] is, rather, a threshold, or [quoting Jorge Luis Borges] a 'vestibule' that offers the world at large the possibility of either stepping inside or turning back."[2] For Genette, the text "rarely appears in its naked state."[3] It is reinforced and accompanied by prefaces, illustrations, authors' names, and titles, which surround and prolong the text, aiding its presentation and reception. This is Genette's paratext, a spatial category structured by an assortment of discursive functions and practices and their positioning relative to other texts. He organizes these spatial categories into subcategories: *peritext* and *epitext*. The *peritext* is the inner part of the paratext. It consists of titles, prefaces, and notes.[4] The *epitext* is the outer part of the paratext consisting of interviews, conversations, and correspondences.[5] These spatial categories amount to this textual equation: *peritext* + *epitext* = *paratext*.[6]

The distinctions derived through the above textual equation, however, are blurred in the context of newspapers. Nicola Kaminski, Nora Ramtke, and Carsten Zelle, for instance, propose in their introduction to the volume *Zeitschriftenliteratur/Fortsetzungsliteratur* that Genette's dichotomous distinctions between *peritext* and *epitext* are impractical when it comes to the literary ecosystem of nineteenth-century periodicals.[7] This is particularly true in the case of periodicals where editors doubled as authors of columns, poems, and editorials—presenting a categorical conundrum to Genette's structuralist distinctions. As Joshua Ratner posits in his study of the paratext and authorship, "Genette's definition of what is and is not a paratext is explicitly limited to those parts of a text 'characterized by an authorial intention and assumption of responsibility', which presents some problems for its application to the nineteenth-century literary marketplace."[8] For example, in newspapers, what Genette labels the publisher's *peritext* (material constructions typically outside of the author's control) could have been composed and/or shaped by the author, especially when the author is also the editor. The same can be said about the authorial *peritext*, which in nineteenth-century newspapers was often composed and/or shaped by the editor/publisher. Thus, as Tobias Hermans posits in his study of editorial footnotes as paratext and reader agency, "the hierarchy of textual elements in periodicals is not fixed. Every single reading act delineates text from paratext for itself."[9]

Empirically, we can think of the paratext, in the case of newspapers, as a heterogenous assemblage of aesthetic practices and discourses with a varying degree of convergent effects, meanings, and values. Accordingly, the paratext enables a poem to become a part of the newspaper and to be offered as such to the public. According to Genette, the paratext is also

> an "undefined zone" between the inside and the outside, a zone without any hard and fast boundary on either the inward side (turned toward the text) or the outward side (turned toward the world's discourse about the text), an edge, or, as Philippe Lejeune put it, "a fringe of the printed text which in reality controls one's whole reading of the text."[10]

In the world of newspaper poems, this multidirectional fringe or zone is both transactional and transitional: it is transactional because poems were transacted in public exchange from newspaper to newspaper and from reader to reader, and also transitional because they functioned as transitions between other items on the page, whether they be news, editorials, advertisements, or other poems.

Determining the effect paratexts have on texts is not in itself new. There has been extensive theorization and historization on the function of the paratext vis-à-vis fictional prose (Anthony Grafton and Shari Benstock) and to a lesser extent on periodical poetry.[11] As Hermans posits:

> The dominant, Goffmanesque metaphor of the "frame narrative" illustrates the fascination narratologists hold for the liminal and transitional. True enough, most narrative models are concerned with the structure of narration, not the material environment of the narrative text itself and its placement on the page.[12]

In the last twenty years, studies of the paratext have ranged from authorship (Joshua Ratner), material and immaterial forms (Rebecca Soares), fictional genres (Malcah Effron), supplements, and book publishers (Lucas Dietrich). In Joshua Ratner's study of the paratext and authorship, he considers the paratextual elements authors have control over, including prefaces, dedications, and footnotes. These paratextual elements show authors' attempts to make direct connections with their readers. "The paratexts that authors write," Ratner argues, "reveal how much they depend on and write within a literary ecosystem in which publishers, periodical reviewers, and booksellers play mutually dependent roles in shaping readers' opinions and purchasing habits."[13] Malcah Effron studies correlations between the boundaries of the page and the boundaries of genre through an examination of the footnote in fiction in relation to genre. The footnote in fiction, he argues, lays bare its own artifice, creating what he calls a reality effect that "reproduces and generates metafiction."[14] Taking a thing-theory approach, Rebecca Soares expands traditional notions of materiality by turning to what she deems the immateriality of nineteenth-century Victorian poetry. She posits that nineteenth-century technological advances like the transatlantic cable in 1858 and popular religious practices like spiritualism present scholars a unique opportunity to study the gaps between immaterial and material culture. Such cultural phenomena relied on the principle of invisible forces that shaped everyday life. For Soares, poetic form functions similarly to spiritualism. Both are abstract, joining the real and the unreal, the tangible and intangible. She proposes that "poetic form requires a seemingly paradoxical combination of that which is formal, structured, and 'material' and that which is inherently abstract."[15]

There has also been significant scholarship on the paratext in US periodicals and their publishers that importantly challenges the inherent whiteness of paratextual studies. Scholars have argued, for instance, that the paratext is an especially fraught space for African American literature.[16] Critics of African American literature have at times been reluctant to focus on these bibliographic materials at the risk of further diminishing the text to its context. As Beth A. McCoy argues in her 2006 *PMLA* article, for example, the paratext that emerges from African American literature can be a producer of anti-Blackness, as it often functions as "a zone transacting ever-changing modes of white domination and of resistance to that domination."[17] More recently, scholars of African American literature have turned to the paratext as a space to contextualize the anti-racist goals of nineteenth-century African American writers. In her analysis of advertisements as paratext in William Wells Brown's *Clotel: The President's Daughter* (1853), Mary T. Ganster argues that Brown strategically uses advertisements and newspaper articles to both "authenticate his claims and draw attention to reified history's representational inadequacies."[18] For Brown, the paratext "acts as a transitional hinge, guiding the reader from the biographical preface and statement of [his] antislavery goals."[19] In his study of Charles W. Chesnutt's interactions with his book publisher, Houghton, Mifflin and Company, Lucas Dietrich posits that a critical focus on the paratext reveals the framework of literature as it was presented to readers. Dietrich argues that "because the paratext is an especially fraught space for African American literature, these framing materials can point to important tensions and disconnections in what Robert Darnton calls the 'communications circuit' between author, publisher, and reader."[20] Reclaiming the paratext in minoritarian studies, scholars like Dietrich and Ganster show us how the paratext reveals the framework of literature as it was presented to readers, pointing to key tensions between authors, publishers, and readers.

Scholars of book history, print culture, and periodical studies have taught us, as Kathryn Ledbetter claims, that the "bibliographic codes inherent in such varied texts invite multiple interpretations, and all these texts mediate the periodical with its reader."[21] Yet there is a dearth of long-form scholarship on the paratext centralizing the newspaper poem. Drawing from the available scholarship on the paratext and poetry studies, *Paratextuality in Anglophone and Hispanophone Poems in the US Press, 1855–1901* analyzes periodical poems as both textual and paratextual nodes. Although Genette's focus is the book form, the scholars above have made it clear that the paratext applies to newspapers as well. Newspapers are an assortment of titles, news, ads, illustrations, and poems, amendable by the way readers enter and exit the fringe or undefined zone of the page. As Georg Stanitzek observes, Genette "is not willing to risk the category of the text as book (or the work) itself."[22] *Paratextuality in Anglophone and Hispanophone Poems in the US Press, 1855–1901* is willing to make this sacrifice in order to expand the paratext beyond fixed forms. Like Stanitzek, this book champions a more transmedial epistemology of paratextuality, without sacrificing the basic pragmatic tenets Genette outlines.

Employing Genette's concept, I propose a theory and methodology of "poetics of paratextuality"—a theory that I argue shaped the production of newspaper poetry, and a methodology derived from the archive that lets us analyze the anatomy of the page, the links between and among poems and reprint poems, as framing elements that could generate poetic value and taste. A poetics of paratextuality grounds newspaper poems in their cultural, historical, and discursive moment to investigate crucial textual transitions and transactions on the page, that is, what words, themes, concepts, and impressions transitioned from one text to another, and what aesthetic practices and customs were transacted among editors, publishers, poets, and readers. A poetics of paratextuality also helps us to better understand newspaper (re)print culture: why and how certain poems were (re)printed and edited for new paratextual spaces and publics. Reading through a poetics of paratextuality is to account for the affective fusion of paratextual ornaments, their place of publication, and their intended public as one calls into question how newspaper poems fit or fail to fit on the page.

By centralizing newspaper networks and systems of circulation over bylines and titles, *Paratextuality in Anglophone and Hispanophone Poems in the US Press, 1855–1901* complicates the author- and book-reader relationship we too often use to approach nineteenth-century poetry. Traditionally, book forms tend to privilege authors over networks, which frequently prompt hierarchical distinctions between the text and the paratext. Stanitzek posits that this is precisely the problem with Genette's paratext, which "concerns the significance of the book as a key item of cultural and intellectual processes."[23] In order to realize the hermeneutic potential of the paratext, *Paratextuality in Anglophone and Hispanophone Poems in the US Press, 1855–1901* looks beyond the book form and turns to newspapers. A newspaper's paratext merits our attention because, as Genette argues, the paratext is "at the service . . . of a better reception of the text and a more pertinent reading [of it]."[24] Thus, a newspaper's paratext expands our own reception and reading practices, offering points of interaction and transaction between and among periodicals, books, printers, publishers, booksellers, and their audiences—extending beyond geographies and languages.

Hispanophone Poems

It is one of this book's arguments that the Spanish-language press was and still is the US press. This is particularly true after the US–Mexico War in 1848 when the US forcefully purchased Northern Mexico, land that makes up all or parts of present-day Arizona, California, Colorado, Nevada, New Mexico,

Utah, and Wyoming, where English was not the lingua franca. Thus, any comprehensive study of nineteenth-century US newspaper poetry must contend with the presence of the Spanish-language press. Of course, this argument is not intended to reduce the presence and significance of other non-Anglophone newspapers, including Cherokee, German, Italian, Chinese, and French papers that circulated in this period. These newspapers too deserve separate and in-depth study. I am specifically interested in the Spanish-language press for two reasons: (1) for its colonial and imperial significance to the US, and (2) its traditional categorization as regional newspapers.

The Spanish-language newspapers in Chapters 2 and 5 are geopoliticized respectively in the Southwest and the Caribbean, showcasing important networks and tensions between colonial and imperial powers. Many of the Spanish-language newspapers in this book reveal how the cultural politics of newspapers become embedded in the paratextual frameworks of the poems. *El Clamor Público*'s anti-imperialist news (Chapter 2), for instance, becomes textually entangled in the reprint poems Ramírez published. Similarly, Gertrudis Gómez de Avellaneda's poems and reputation are filtered through the partisanship of the Puerto Rican and New York newspapers that published her. A poetics of paratextuality reveals how the varying degrees of political investment (revolutionary, colonial, imperial, and anti-imperial) of these newspapers become intertextual, that is, they are tethered to the material conditions of the poems and the value ascribed to them.

Furthermore, the paratext of these poems complicates traditional notions of regional Hispanophone newspapers. From an Anglophone US perspective, the Spanish-language press is often cordoned off as regional with an audience of Spanish readers contained in the US and its borderlands. Although many Hispanophone newspapers in the US catered to regional Spanish-speaking communities with access to their newspapers (with some exceptions), some periodicals garnered national and international readers. In editorials and ads that addressed "Hispano Americanos," *El Clamor Público* spoke to readers across state lines and the US–Mexico border. Likewise, Spanish-organ, Caribbean newspapers like *El Boletín mercantil de Puerto Rico* and *La correspondencia de Puerto Rico*, because of their colonial investments, drew in readers, many of whom were colonial stakeholders, from Spain, the US, and South America. Moreover, the content of these newspapers was anything but regional as they regularly featured international news, editorials, and poems from all over the Spanish-speaking world. Paratextual readings of poems printed in Spanish-language newspapers reveal this broader national and international network, complicating the cultural borders often ascribed to regional newspapers and poetry. The Spanish-language chapters show that like its Anglophone counterpart, the Hispanophone press in the US resonated with readers beyond its original place of publication, often crossing international lines in scope and significance.

While the major difference between the Anglophone and Hispanophone press is language, both relied on networks of writers, readers, and editors to sustain production and circulation. Spanish- and English-language US-based newspapers were conterminous with the national news cycle. In newspapers, Hispanophone readers in the Southwest—many of whom were new treaty citizens struggling to keep their lands after the US–Mexico War—and Northeast Anglophone readers alike, encountered presidential speeches, legal decisions on homesteading laws, information about railroad bonds and construction, and international news about Latin America alongside a nexus of newspaper poetry. Many exiles from the Hispanophone Caribbean established their own newspapers in the city of New York, often using the same printers as their Anglophone counterparts. In this exile press, Cuban and Puerto Rican readers read news and literature about independence, abolitionism, and war.

Scholars working in nineteenth-century Hispanophone materials, including Rodrigo Lazo, Jesse Alemán, Kirsten Silva Gruesz, Raúl Coronado, Lorgia García Peña, Marissa K. López, and John Alba Cutler, have begun piecing together histories of the cultural productions of Latinx people using valuable but incomplete archives. *Paratextuality in Anglophone and Hispanophone Poems in the US Press, 1855–1901* enhances the fragmented nineteenth-century US Hispanophone archive via its Anglophone counterpart, and vice versa. Each archive brings something new to the conversation, a fragment of the collective that adds to our understanding of cultural production, circulation, and editorialization in the period. English- and Spanish-language nineteenth-century newspapers can help us to better appreciate this complex conterminous relationship, a relationship that existed on the page and between various publics in New York, California, and the Caribbean. Both English- and Spanish-language newspaper poems existed within the expanding empire of the US, crossing audiences, sharing printing houses, geographic locations, and the physical page. The readers of these papers were part of parallel publics which often overlapped and clashed. By treating English- and Spanish-language newspaper poems and their reprinting culture as a related act of cultural production, *Paratextuality in Anglophone and Hispanophone Poems in the US Press, 1855–1901* allows for a confluence of linguistic play, integration, and tension akin to the nineteenth-century press.

Reputation of Newspaper Poems and Modernist Erasures

It is not an overstatement to say that the history of nineteenth-century US poetry is inseparable from the history of newspapers. Yet newspaper poems in the US press have never been the topic of a book-length work of scholarship. The stereotype of what counts as "good poetry" and "bad poetry" is in part to blame. Nineteenth-century newspaper poems have suffered rebukes by some of the most read critics in American letters. Influential nineteenth- and twentieth-century critics and editors, including Margaret Fuller, Horace Greeley, Edmund

Clarence Stedman, and Frank Luther Mott, long regarded newspaper poems as not real poetry and/or as mere fillers. These claims had lasting effects on the alleged aesthetic and scholarly value of the newspaper poem. Fuller, who was the literary editor for the *New York Tribune* between 1844 and 1846, openly expressed her views on newspaper writing. She believed that newspapers were reinventing the country, giving publics unprecedented access to print that connected readers to "the ideal presence of human nature."[25] "Newspaper writing," she posits, "is next door to conversation, and should be conducted on the same principles," allowing for readers and writers to "address America rather than Americans."[26] The newspaper's ability to connect readers to their country made this print venue "the natural receptacle for the lyrics of the day."[27] At the same time, however, Fuller expressed objections to the quality of poetry published in newspapers, "whose light leaves fly so rapidly and profusely over the land."[28] She claims, "That so few good ones deck the poet's corner, is because of the indifference or unfitness of editors, as to choosing and refusing, makes this place, at present, undesirable to the poet. It might be otherwise."[29] Fuller blames unqualified editors who curate and publish poems with ignorance toward good poetry for this depreciated state of newspaper poetry. These bad newspaper poems, she continues, "are written for the press, in the spirit of imitation or vanity, the paltriest offspring of the human brain, for the heart disclaims, as the ear is shut against them."[30]

Fuller was not alone in condemning newspaper poetry for its imitation and lack of quality. The editor of the *New York Tribune*, Horace Greeley, expressed similar views on newspaper verse in a letter to Robert E. Bonner of the *New York Ledger* regarding a volume of poetry Bonner intended to publish. Greeley congratulated Bonner for featuring poems not "contained in Mr. [Charles A.] Dana's *Household Book of Poetry*" (1858) while at the same time discouraging the *Ledger*'s editor from publishing lesser and unknown poets alongside worthy talent.[31] Greeley writes, "take care not to neutralize or nullify your chivalrous championship by burying them under a cartload of rhymed rubbish."[32] For Greeley, the mere textual proximity to this lesser brand of poetry nullified Bonner's efforts to publish good poetry.

Such stereotypes about the newspaper poem were generative in how twentieth-century critics, looking to the past for literary value, understood nineteenth-century poetry. In *A History of American Magazines*, the American historian Frank Luther Mott writes that critics in the mid-nineteenth century discounted American poetry, particularly the overly sentimental verse that appeared in periodicals. He quotes the *Western Review*, stating that "the poetasters feel a 'certain craniological maggotry', and thinking it the spur of the muses, down they sit, and the materials committed to memory from reading the verses of others are cut down, remolded, and reappear in new form."[33] Mott and others argue that this "deluge of indifferent poetry," as the *Union Magazine* called newspaper poems, served as a filler for editors burdened with random amounts of space at the ends of articles and stories.[34]

At the turn of the nineteenth century, American poets and critics reflected on cultural shifts brought about by industrialization, urbanization, and the First World War. Many poets rebelled against Victorian norms, values, and aesthetic conventions and dismissed outdated cultural items that referenced them. As a result, for many modern readers of the twentieth century, the nineteenth-century newspaper poem and many of the poets of this bygone era became the reprehensible overly genteel representation of the non-modern. Scholars of nineteenth-century poetry have argued for decades that the history of American poetry is often cast as a drive toward modernism. Consequently, as this book shows, the history of the newspaper poem has been consigned to the periphery of literary significance. As Nina Baym forcefully argued in the 1980s, "a radical break between the nineteenth and twentieth centuries in poetic taste" engendered a refusal to critically engage with the greater number of nineteenth-century poems, specifically those by lesser-known women and people of color.[35] Since then, scholars working in historical poetics, like Meredith McGill, Virginia Jackson, Paula Bernat Bennett, Elizabeth Renker, Kirsten Silva Gruesz, Shira Wolosky, Jennifer Putzi, Yopie Prins and others, have thrown into sharp relief the (proto-)modernist discontinuity of nineteenth-century poetics and how it has shaped, and continues to shape, how critics and readers conceptualize the literary and aesthetic value and taste of pre-1900 poems.

By the nineteenth century's end, Shira Wolosky posits, there is an evident "redrawing of poetic lines as a boundary against the active world, with the poem now emerging as a self-enclosed aesthetic object separate from public social life."[36] This self-enclosed aesthetic object became the modernist barometer for canon formation. For many years, the break and redrawing of poetic taste resulted in the abridgment of nineteenth-century American poetics to the study of Walt Whitman and Emily Dickinson, whom critics distinguished from other poets owing to the semblance of modernity in their work. "This selective account of poetic inheritance," Meredith McGill argues, "has produced the unusual circumstance of a canon that needs to be opened to not only culturally marginal but also culturally dominant poets and poetic forms."[37]

Recently, scholarship has begun to open the canon by overturning longstanding assessments of nineteenth-century poetics that privilege (proto-)modernist conceptions of aesthetics and culture and render American periodical poems as negligible ephemera. In Paula Bernat Bennett's study of women newspaper poets in the nineteenth century, she argues that

> resituating nineteenth-century American women's newspaper and periodical poetry within the tradition of social dialogue and debate from which it sprang and to which it belongs, will clarify this poetry's function as a form

of public speech addressed to concrete, empirically identifiable others. Doing so, this reconfiguration will establish the vital role that women's poetry, taken collectively, played within the intersubjective framework of the public sphere.[38]

Drawing examples from periodicals published between 1800 and 1900, Bennett examines nineteenth-century American women's poetry in terms of what the German social philosopher Jürgen Habermas calls "everyday communicative practice."[39] That is, Bennett treats this poetry as an instance of speech whose expressive and mimetic power is organized explicitly or implicitly for argumentative ends to achieve the practical discursive goal of persuasion.

Similarly, the work of Wolosky takes up the question of poems as forms of public rhetoric. In her social-formalist readings of nineteenth-century poets, Wolosky argues:

> Poetry directly participated in and addressed the pressing issues facing the evolving nation through its responses, circulation, and creative reflections on the rhetoric of national life. Poetic language and composition draw on, but also illuminate and redirect the rhetorics of social cultural life.[40]

In Wolosky's work, we see how the complex deployment of poetic discourses and compositional practices emphasizes the rhetorics of nineteenth-century social cultural life. An examination of poetry's transformative relationship to the rhetorics that contextualize it calcifies how nineteenth-century "poetry gains both historical grounding and aesthetic coherence and force."[41] Still, in this turn toward historical poetics, Wolosky cautions, "[t]he challenge remains on how to pursue social-formalist readings without reducing poetry to the first or excluding history in the second."[42]

Critics have responded to this challenge with studies of the social (Michael C. Cohen), poetic genre and literary category (Elizabeth Renker), imitations and copy (Jennifer Putzi), as well as aesthetic unoriginality (Claudia Stokes). In Michael C. Cohen's study of the social lives of poems, he explores the multiplicity of imaginative relationships forged between poems and those who made use of them from the post-Revolutionary era to the turn of the twentieth century. He argues that poetry occupied a complex position in the social life of nineteenth-century America:

> While some readers found in poems a resource for aesthetic pleasure and the enjoyment of linguistic complexity, many others turned to poems for spiritual and psychic wellbeing, adapted popular musical settings of poems to spread scandal and satire, or used poems as a medium for asserting personal and family memories as well as local and national affiliations.[43]

In her study of realist poems, Elizabeth Renker revisits modernist truisms of nineteenth-century poetry popularized in Jorge Santayana's influential University of California, Berkeley address in August 1911. Renker argues, "The triumph of the twilight tale of gentility erased postbellum voices into a flattened account of 'poetry' as a monolithic terrain."[44] Jennifer Putzi also interrogates this monolithic wasteland of nineteenth-century poetics in her study of the composition, publication, and circulation of antebellum US women's poetry. Putzi challenges modernist cultural stereotypes of nineteenth-century poetry by proposing a theory and methodology of relationality that centralizes texts over individuals and poems over poets. "Imitation, community, and collaboration," she posits, "are central to a relational poetics—in poems themselves, in the avenues women poets take to gain access to print, and in the ways their poems function within a variety of print cultural contexts."[45] Claudia Stokes too moves us away from author- and poet-based studies. In her work on unoriginality as an aesthetic practice that shaped literary style, Stokes directs critical engagement to the cultural value of imitation and copy in nineteenth-century American poetry. She argues that nineteenth-century readers believed that "originality was by no means an intrinsic literary virtue."[46] Many readers were taught to perceive originality "with suspicion: originality connoted irregularity, sensationalism, and vulgarity, and its execution could impugn an author's taste and education."[47]

Following the methodological turn toward historical poetics in nineteenth-century literary studies, and the charge by scholars to redirect our attention away from the original, modern, and canonical, and toward the unoriginal, imitated, and forgotten, *Paratextuality in Anglophone and Hispanophone Poems in the US Press, 1855–1901* focuses on the textual spaces between poems that are seldom a part of this critical conversation. This book fills a gap in the scholarship of nineteenth-century poetry because, until now, the paratext has not been critically engaged with as an aesthetic design and practice. The paratext reveals more clearly and immediately that nineteenth-century newspaper poems were not self-enclosed aesthetic objects separate from public life. Many of these verses were not simply read but also memorized and quoted, reworked and imitated, collected, scrapbooked, anthologized, edited, and exchanged within and outside of complex paratextual spaces in tune with the readerly needs of consumers. The complex social lives of newspaper poems, their connections and disconnections to genres, poets, editors, and periodicals, raise important and difficult questions about how readers engaged with newspaper poems, and, particularly, how they understood poetic speakers.

Speakers in Newspaper Poems

Modernist reading practices have made it routine for readers of poetry to always distinguish the poet from the speaker. As Virginia Jackson powerfully argues in *Dickenson's Misery: A Theory of Lyric Reading*, this is a creation of contemporary reading practices applied to the past based on modern theories of the lyric. The modern lyric, Jackson explains, bears little resemblance to nineteenth-century poetic genres like the ode, elegy, song, dedication, and occasional poem, genres that dominated the US press.[48] Similarly, Jonathan Culler's study of the collapse of narrative fiction and poetry argues that contemporary readings of poetry are based on "the fictional representation of a speaker character, whose novelistic situation the reader is asked to reconstruct by asking, what would lead someone to speak thus and to feel thus?"[49] To close read the speaker consequently becomes a project of interpreting "what sort of person is speaking, in what circumstances and with what attitude or, ideally, drama of attitudes."[50] These reading practices, Culler argues, are based on novelistic reading habits that privilege narrative form over everything. It is for these reasons that the speakers in *Paratextuality in Anglophone and Hispanophone Poems in the US Press, 1855–1901* are not always the modernist collective, the universal "we" in Walt Whitman's *Leaves of Grass* that is regularly ascribed to the poem. The poetic speaker in this book is multifaceted. At times, the speaker is the woman poet negotiating the cultural space of the poetess figure (Chapters 1 and 5). At times, the speaker is a byline-less Spanish-speaker in the throes of love (Chapter 2). At other moments, the speaker is a bankrupt businessman or a disease-ravaged city. In all these cases, the poem's paratext is an episteme for historical and cultural traction that helps us to read the poetic voice beyond the strictures of the modern lyric subject.

Paratextuality in Anglophone and Hispanophone Poems in the US Press, 1855–1901 also raises questions about the potential readers of these poems: Who were they, and how do we know this? "Our inability to know how nineteenth-century American readers encountered poems," Putzi reminds us, "prevents any thorough recovery of this work."[51] This book begins to conceptualize nineteenth-century readers, commencing the important recovery of these verses, by thinking about audience as types of publics.

Newspaper Poem's Potential Audience

In *Paratextuality in Anglophone and Hispanophone Poems in the US Press, 1855–1901*, a newspaper's audience is a public, that is, a social group that the paper addresses. Michael Warner reminds us that a public creates social entities and that those social entities can revise what it means to be a public.[52] Such a reciprocal exchange also determines what is "private" and how the private can turn into a public. Warner argues that the terms "private" and "public" "often seem to be defined against each other, with normative preference for one term."[53] For instance, the etymology of "private" is "*privatus*, deprived," the cancelation of public value. Warner correspondingly provides common relational oppositions for private and public that are helpful for thinking about newspaper poems. Those relevant to my study are "Public: open to everyone" / "Private: restricted to some" and "Public: circulated in print or electronic media" / "Private: circulated orally or in manuscript."[54] These relational oppositions determine a rather obvious point: newspaper poems are public. Yet, traditional studies of nineteenth-century poetry (analyses that centralize an author, genre, or manuscript) tend to give preference to the private. Conversely, I read newspaper poems as an open and media-based genre with an emphasis on the public. I do not aim to distinguish the private and public in strict definitive terms because these categories are not always mutually exclusive. The work of Ellen Gruber Garvey, for example, shows us how public snippets easily became private when "people in positions of relative powerlessness used their scrapbooks to make a place for themselves in their communities by finding, sifting, analyzing and recirculating writing that mattered to them."[55] Scrapbookers were like editors curating the pages of their newspapers, shaping the public into the private, as they created value for themselves and their own communities out of an abundance of print material.[56]

Certain newspaper poems resonated with the needs and interests of nineteenth-century publics. These culturally resonant poems acquired more than ephemerality in the pages of newspapers. These poems acquired and generated various forms of poetic value and cultural taste that depended upon the poems' ability to create, sustain, and appeal to publics through wide circulation. In a sense, these poems and bylines created a tautological feedback loop where value and taste generated reprints, and reprints generated value and taste. At the center of this feedback loop are the public's undocumented demands and desires for ontological fulfillment. Chapters 3 and 4 begin to uncover some of these demands and desires through quantitative studies: tracing and analyzing the number of poem reprints and their publication location, and, most importantly, interpreting editors' and typesetters' (non-)intentional contextualization of these poems as a way of making and remaking meaning.

Reprint poems circulated within complex print and distribution networks for a variety of publics that ascribed value to circulation. In many cases, the more a poem circulated, the greater its value was to readers. Operating alongside, yet distinct from, original poems, reprint poems were often remixed and recontextualized for new paratextual spaces. As these poems circulated throughout the country, some verses were, at times, altered. Inadvertent errors committed by typesetters and/or editors changed poem titles, epigraphs, lines, stanzas, and/or words. At other times, these changes were intentional, altering the poem's physical form so that it could fit into the empty space between columns. Some changes were made to a poem's content for readerly effect with regard to other items on the page, such as news, ads, and other poems. The paratextual connections newspaper poems had to, say, news items about financial panics (Chapter 3) and cholera epidemics (Chapter 4) were often determined, if not forced, by this editorializing process. How newspapers editorialized a poem and the effects this process generated were different for nearly every poem publication, meaning that the same poem could appear twice in the same newspaper a week apart and have a completely different paratextual connection. Whether it was a typesetting error or an intentional edit, such irregularities in newspaper poetry were frequent.

Networks and Printscapes

Circulation as movement between space, whether textual or geographical, is an important and complex component of *Paratextuality in Anglophone and Hispanophone Poems in the US Press, 1855–1901*. "Networks" and "printscapes" are useful metaphors for elucidating this complex spatial movement. The meaning-making possibilities of newspaper poems and reprints depend on a unique nexus of networks and printscapes. Networks, as arrangements of interconnected publics, poets, and newspapers, can help us to imagine the dissemination of nineteenth-century newspaper poems. Kelley Kreitz posits that "networks are metaphors that invite spatial thinking"; however, Kreitz continues, "[i]t is difficult to write about networks without articulating some kind of space in which they operate."[57] Reprint networks, in particular, ask us to think about space and distance in creative ways. For example, many nationwide networks in this book extended thousands of miles from Brooklyn to San Francisco, as well as internationally from Latin America and Spain to Southern California. These various sites of publication and republication allow us to measure distance and time between readers who were neighbors, or who lived across towns, cities, and states, as well as in different nations and continents. While some publics were connected via their locality, family relations, workplace, church, and/or place of business, others were only linked via an imagined community of readers sustained by the newspapers available to them.

We should also think about space and distance within the parameters of the "printscape." Mark Noonan reminds us:

> the term "printscape" functions as a useful framing device that attends to the fluid borders of the printed page, which traverse both geographical and imaginative space and are propelled by a variety of actors, historical, and technological forces continually on the move.[58]

Examining how poems are contextualized within printscapes invites us to read in material and textual ways. Like newspaper readers today, many nineteenth-century readers read across the printscape, engaging columns from top to bottom, and left to right. The printscape calls attention to how page and place suffuse poems with possibilities of meaning that, as we will see, inform poetic taste and value. In this book, the page is a roadmap that guides readers in and out of meaning. The physical contours of the page covey as much meaning as the form and content of poems. This analytical approach puts into practice close reading that is both material and textual.

Through close readings, historical and paratextual inquiries, and quantitative and data analyses, *Paratextuality in Anglophone and Hispanophone Poems in the US Press, 1855–1901* offers ways of interpreting the meaning-making potential of not just the ephemeral but also the peripheries of nineteenth-century poetics and culture. I look at editors in New York and California, specific popular poems circulating broadly across the United States, and poets whose wide circulation and popularity made them celebrities. Many of the methods we use to study nineteenth-century newspaper poems are still embedded in the value of the bound book, comprehensive archive, and/or the significance of a canonized poet, leaving out, for the most part, the role of ephemerality, distribution, and the public. But what happens when we disrupt these methodologies and centralize, to an extent, the hundreds of thousands of unknowns of the periodical world: the unknown poets and unknown versions of reprint poems that circulated in English and in Spanish? How do we bring these voices, forms, and artifacts into the fold of nineteenth-century poetics? In other words, how do we responsibly place tasteless verses and little-valued poets at the center of a field and genre routinely associated with the book form and the poet figure? These are some of the guiding questions in *Paratextuality in Anglophone and Hispanophone Poems in the US Press, 1855–1901*. This book does not propose definitive answers to these questions, in part because the archive of nineteenth-century newspaper poems is too large, too complex, and too fragmented to conceptualize in five chapters. What the following chapters do offer is a disruption to some of these academic associations by replacing the book and poet with the paratext and its boundless associative properties (editors, circulation, pandemics, panics, and colonization).

Chapter Map

Paratextuality in Anglophone and Hispanophone Poems in the US Press, 1855–1901 begins in 1855, but it does not start with the publication of Whitman's proto-modernist *Leaves of Grass* as is common in studies of nineteenth-century poetry. Instead, this book shifts our gaze from Whitman to the nascency of a common national (popular) culture of poems that developed in newspapers and their paratexts. Each chapter highlights a different framework for paratextuality, a different context in which its workings can be demonstrated. I make this case in archival detail in five chapters that delineate the complex social and cultural functions played by newspaper poems and reprints in the everyday lives of Anglophone and Hispanophone publics. Chapter 1 examines how the newspaper poem is a celebrity-making genre that fed the celebrity status of poets like Lydia H. Sigourney and Alice Cary, two of the most popular "poetesses" of the mid-nineteenth century. Through paratextual readings, I argue that while

Robert E. Bonner, editor of the *New York Ledger* (1855–98), used Sigourney's and Cary's celebrity status to aid the cultural legitimacy of his paper, these two poets negotiated that status by giving expression to anti-patriarchal poetics and complex forms of women's agency that refute the gendered codes of the cult of true womanhood.

Chapter 2 turns to another editor who founded his newspaper in the same year as Bonner, Francisco P. Ramírez, to show a different editorial relationship with newspaper poets. I recover transamerican Spanish-language poems in Ramírez's *El Clamor Público* (1855–59), the first Spanish-language weekly owned and operated by a Californio after the US–Mexico War. In this chapter, a poetics of paratextuality signifies Ramírez's own editorial practice of altering reprint poems culled from periodicals, books, and anthologies from across the Hispanophone world and reprinted in Southern California. These unauthorized, location-specific alterations created new transitions and transactions between the poets, genres, and regions gestured to in and outside of the printscape. I am interested in what Ramírez's poetics of paratextuality can teach us about *El Clamor Público*'s reprint culture and its specific relationship to authorship and genre. How did Ramírez's printscape and public influence his selection of the poems, poets, and genres he reprinted and edited? I answer this question by critically engaging with Ramírez's reprint practices, isolating *El Clamor Público*'s poems, mapping their potential citational provenance and/or place of publication, and comparing original publications with their reproduction in *El Clamor Público*. I propose that *El Clamor Público* is an important example of the print culture norm of editing reprint poems to centralize the reading public's interests and experiences. Since Hispanophone texts do not neatly fit into Anglophone literary classifications, *El Clamor Público* is incongruous with forms of US literary history which, as Rodrigo Lazo argues, are "driven by the canonical desires of U.S. American literature and the fetishization of major writers" (as Chapter 1 exemplifies).[59] The *New York Ledger* and *El Clamor Público* are foundational for my book on Anglophone and Hispanophone poems and their paratext. They frame the US geography of newspapers from coast to coast and in terms of two of the most printed languages in the US, especially after the US–Mexico War. These two chapters show varying degrees of interrelation between editors, poets, and the page, which will develop in the rest of the book.

Chapters 3 and 4 move away from editors to focus on the phenomenon of the reprint poem in circulation. These chapters show a robust and uncharted archive of reprint poems that responded to two major hemispheric crises, the Panic of 1857 and the New York cholera epidemic of 1866. These networks of circulation, which were in part facilitated by the growing nineteenth-century economy and the railroad, are the feature of Chapter 3 on newspaper panic poems. In this chapter, the culture of the reprint poem meets the historical phenomenon of the Panic of 1857. I explore the unknown correlation between the economy of 1857 and the inflationary social value of three reprint poems: "The Lay of the Directors," "Lines by Buster" (both anonymously published), and "Hard Times" by Alfred "Alf" F. Burnett. Here, a poetics of paratextuality helps us to better understand why these poems stand out among the trove of mid-century newspaper poems published during the Panic of 1857, how they participated in social and political debates, and gained a renewed sense of significance in the public through robust circulation. Through paratextual readings that focus the rhetoric and discourse of the Panic, I argue that these "panic poems" gained social value through robust reprinting and circulation. Through reprinting, these poems acquired specific forms of value that were not primarily aesthetic or poetic but "social." The poems' use of railroad and bank slang made them particularly valuable to the media market of the time and to the publics that encountered them. Appealing to merchants, abolitionists, railroad operatives, "young ladies," and other social groups, these poems drew from the socially relevant discourse of the Panic of 1857—the same language that appeared in news, ads, and editorials to form and sustain disparate yet intertwined reading publics. In their reprint afterlives, the poems in this chapter contributed to discursive networks of cultural production, disseminating (dis)information that was current, intertextual, paratextual, and poetic.

Still focusing on mass reprint culture and circulation, Chapter 4 explores another high-impact episodic event, the New York cholera epidemic of 1866. As disease plagued the streets of the city, many newspaper poems were occasioned by cholera and its calamitous impact on society. Readers encountered these poems in their preferred newspapers and next to their daily dose of newsprint. Thus, like many of the poems in this book, cholera poems are inherently paratextual. These poems reimagined and sometimes contributed to contemporaneous debates about sanitary reform, contagion, immigration, and preventative measures through verse that drew from the discourse of epidemiology, shaping, in many cases, how reading publics understood and managed the disease. In this chapter, I recover three popular cholera poems widely reprinted in New York during the 1866 epidemic: "The Voice of the Pestilence," "King Cholera," and "The Health Bill: A Talk Between Two Repubs at Albany." Previous chapters have centralized the poem's peritext (paratext published alongside and/or next to poems). Chapter 4 expands the paratext to include the epitext (paratext published outside of the proximity of poems in other contemporaneous newspapers, books, and magazines). By analyzing the poems' relationship to their epitext of news, ads, editorial, and verse, the cholera poems in this chapter acquire historical contextualization and aesthetic significance that goes beyond the parameters of the page.

The final chapter turns away from the mainland US toward Puerto Rico to conceptualize a poetics of paratextuality at the margins of the US before and after the Spanish–American War. Not yet ceded to US (this did not happen until after the Spanish–American War in 1898), the island of Puerto Rico provides a window into the colonial machinations of Spain in proximity to the expanding US empire. The subject of this chapter is the Cuban-born transamerican poet Gertrudis Gómez de Avellaneda (1814–73) and her appearance in the periodical press.

Avellaneda's presence in the periodical press reveals a triptych image of colonial, anticolonial, and decolonial interests that linked the Hispanophone Caribbean to Spain and the United States long before the US's involvement in Cuba's and Puerto Rico's wars for independence. As a celebrity poetess with nationally recognized affiliations in Cuba, Spain, Puerto Rico, and the US, Avellaneda's poems and reputation were bound up in a dialectical push and pull of colonial, anticolonial, and decolonial desires. By comparing the varied representations of Avellaneda in the city of New York's exile press with those in leading Spanish political organs in Puerto Rico, such as *El Boletín mercantil de Puerto Rico* and *La correspondencia de Puerto Rico*, I reveal how Avellaneda's poems and reputation were reimaged via certain manipulative editorial practices, including public censorship and partial political reportage. As the single author study in this book, this chapter provides an important context for newspaper poets born outside of the mainland, whose cultural image and reputation were routinely shaped by the paratext.

Regional, National, and International Networks

The five chapters in this book reveal distinctions, similarities, and overlaps between and among the regional, national, and international trends in content, authorship, readership when it comes to newspaper poems and their networks. The first two chapters show us how trends in authorship, content, and readership varied between two newspapers that were founded in the same year and country and featured a significant number of poems. The *Ledger* published original celebrity poems by Sigourney and Cary which for the most part catered to a national audience that, as Michael Denning and other scholars have argued, was working class, Anglophone, and made up of women and children. *El Clamor Público*, on the other hand, was more regionally concentrated in the US Southwest and catered to a Hispanophone, mainly Californio, audience. Although *El Clamor Público* was regional, Ramírez importantly culled reprint poems from an international Spanish-language archive, not once publishing a poem by an Anglo-American poet.

Chapters 3 and 4 demonstrate how regional trends more clearly coincided with national trends, as both chapters deal with newspaper poems occasioned by national crises. In these chapters, authorship is secondary to content and readership because the content (the Panic and cholera) was already in the minds of readers as it circulated in the news. Both chapters reveal how trending discourses regarding episodic newsworthy events became the language of poetry. Chapter 4 on newspaper poems occasioned by the Panic of 1857 and their reprints shows how regional contexts relate to national trends in content, authorship, and readership at multiple levels at once. For example, when panic poems appeared in abolitionist newspapers like the Ohio *Anti-Slavery Bugle* or the Boston *Liberator*, they were imbued with the surrounding discourse of manumission and racial justice. This chapter also provides a unique instance when the regional differs from the national and how this difference shapes the reading of a poem. For example, the Southern states did not suffer the same losses as Northern states during the Panic of 1857, yet, like Northern states, they published poems about the financial depression. In this chapter, I show how this crucial context is important for how readers interpreted and found value in panic poems in the South as well as the North. Lastly, this chapter importantly studies how the regional context relates to national trends in content, authorship, and readership across time. One of the three poems, "Hard Times," was initially published during the Panic of 1837. Yet newspapers across the US reprinted it broadly during the Panic of 1857 because of its social urgency and content, reviving the poem's social value for a new generation of readers.

The focus of Chapter 4 on newspaper poems occasioned by the New York cholera epidemic of 1866 shows how regional contexts relate to national trends in content, and how these trends generated a poetic genre of disease. Chapter 5 provides an opportunity to study international trends in authorship, readership, and content via a study of Gertrudis Gómez de Avellaneda, whose poems were reprinted in New York and Puerto Rico (then a Spanish colony). Here, regional contexts are important for how readers interpreted Avellaneda's poems, for while in the New York press she is positioned as a feminist, abolitionist, and Cuba Libre poet who opposed Spanish sovereignty, Puerto Rico's colonial press portrayed her as a Spanish loyalist.

Paratextuality in Anglophone and Hispanophone Poems in the US Press, 1855–1901 invites scholars working in the fields of American literature and culture of the long nineteenth century—including the Latinx nineteenth century, print culture, and transamerican and historical poetics—to centralize the newspaper poem and its paratext as a mode of recovery and redefinition of nineteenth-century poetry, publics, and periodicals. The histories, productions, and reproductions of these varied materials require scholars to engage with the randomness, the unknowns, and the contradictions that regularly appear on the page. The limits of this book's methodologies are significant to how we study newspaper poems. So much of what we do as scholars of nineteenth-century newspaper poetry is based on imagining, reconstructing, and conceptualizing the reader's experience, a task that, at best, provides a snapshot of a limited number of readers, leaving out the majority. This study does not feign a comprehensive understanding of the reading public's experience. The close readings and historical analyses provide what I call the meaning-making potential of newspaper poems and reprints, possible readings out of many, that are specifically informed by the newspaper's form: its columns, pages, and font, as well as the newspaper's content, date of publication, illustrations, serials, ads, and news. This analysis engages with multi-generic printscapes where meaning is not isolated on a particular column, item, or genre, but is rather disseminated across the dynamics of the printscape.

The omissions of this book should make it clear that the traditional nineteenth-century canon was never in my sights. I offer no significant interpretations of nineteenth-century canonized poets or their poems. Nor, for that matter, do I engage with generic literary history outside of the newspaper poem and the reprint. However, I hope to demonstrate that although I have read unconventionally, I have read widely. While doing justice to the accumulated archival richness of the period, I hope to centralize publics and public archives that interrogate the ideological constraints of the project of canonical literary history, which privileges the author, book, and anthology.

The years that bracket this study, 1855 to 1901, delineate both the rise and fall of the newspaper poem. By the late nineteenth century, the prestigious monthly magazines of the Northeast, the custodians of the genteel tradition which Nancy Glazener calls "the *Atlantic* group," began to include more and more poetry.[60] Magazines like *Graham's Magazine* (1851–58), *Godey's Lady's Book* (1830–78), *The Atlantic Monthly* (1857–present), and *The Century Magazine* (1881–1930) appealed to the interests of a popular culture audience absorbed in entertainment genres like realist serial fiction and the occasional celebrity poem. Newspapers dropped their literary offerings, as yellow journalism, with its sensationalist style, seemed to provide entertainment and news all at once. By the turn of the nineteenth century, the designated home of the periodical poem was the magazine. In 1912, the American editor, scholar, and literary critic Harriet Monroe founded *Poetry Magazine*, which went on to become a hotbed for modernist poetry and poetics, solidifying the place and prestige of periodical poetry.

Before the collapse of newspaper poems, story papers—weeklies closely related to newspapers and literary magazines—regularly published poems. Story papers resembled the form of many newspapers, varying in size from tabloid sheets (8.5 x 11.5 inches) and broadsheets (14 x 18 inches) to mammoth sheets (22 x 32 inches). They often featured illustrations, serials, poems, and advice columns with little to no news. As Glazener reminds us, story papers bear an important connection to the *Atlantic* group, "precisely because the *Atlantic*'s legitimacy was premised on the illegitimacy of story papers and dime novels, an opposition that structured the *Atlantic* group's scheme of fictional classification."[61] The question of legitimacy was in the mind of the story paper editor Robert E. Bonner, who, as the first chapter shows, depended on the cultural capital of writers, particular women poets, to counter negative stereotypes of his *New York Ledger*.

Notes

1. The five boroughs of New York were consolidated within one municipal government under a new city charter in 1898, forming the modern New York City we know today. To account for this historical event, this book will refer to New York City as the city of New York before 1898.
2. Gérard Genette, *Paratexts: Thresholds of Interpretation* (Cambridge: Cambridge University Press, 1987), 2.
3. Gérard Genette and Marie Maclean, "Introduction to the Paratext," *New Literary History* 22, no. 2 (1991): 261.
4. Genette and Maclean, "Introduction to the Paratext," 263.
5. Genette and Maclean, "Introduction to the Paratext," 264.
6. Genette and Maclean, "Introduction to the Paratext," 264.
7. Nicola Kaminski, Nora Ramtke, and Carsten Zelle, "Zeitschriftenliteratur/Fortsetzungsliteratur: Problemaufriß." *Zeitschriftenliteratur/Fortsetzungsliteratur*, ed. Nicola Kaminski, Nora Ramtke, and Carsten Zelle (Hanover: Wehrhahn, 2014), 33–38.
8. Joshua Ratner, "Paratexts," *Early American Studies: An Interdisciplinary Journal* 16, no. 4 (2018): 734.
9. Tobias Hermans, "Poetics of the Periodical Paratext: Editorial Footnotes and Reader Agency in Robert Schumann's *Davidsbund* Writings," *Colloquia Germanica* 49, no. 2/3 (2016): 159.
10. Genette, *Paratexts*, 2.
11. See Anthony Grafton, *The Footnote: A Curious History* (Cambridge, MA: Harvard University Press, 1997) and Shari Benstock, "At the Margin of Discourse: Footnotes in the Fictional Text," *PMLA* 98, no. 2 (1983): 204–25.
12. Hermans, "Poetics of the Periodical Paratext," 158.
13. Ratner, "Paratexts," 733.
14. Malcah Effron, "On the Borders of the Page, on the Borders of Genre: Artificial Paratexts in Golden Age Detective Fiction," *Narrative* 18, no. 2 (2010): 200.
15. Rebecca D. Soares, "Material Spirits and Immaterial Forms: The Immaterial Materiality of Elizabeth Barrett Browning's Abolitionist Poetry," *Victorian Poetry* 53, no. 4 (2015): 355.
16. Lucas Dietrich, "Charles W. Chesnutt, Houghton Mifflin, and the Racial Paratext," *MELUS* 41, no. 4 (2016): 166.
17. Beth A. McCoy, "Race and the (Para)Textual Condition," *PMLA* 121, no. 1 (2006): 156.
18. Mary T. Ganster, "Fact, Fiction, and the Industry of Violence: Newspapers and Advertisements in 'Clotel,'" *African American Review* 48, no. 4 (2015): 431.
19. Ganster, "Fact, Fiction," 431.
20. Dietrich, "Charles W. Chesnutt," 166.
21. Kathryn Ledbetter, "Bonnets and Rebellions: Imperialism in 'The Lady's Newspaper,'" *Victorian Periodicals Review* 37, no. 3 (2004): 252.
22. Georg Stanitzek, "Texts and Paratexts in Media," *Critical Inquiry* 32, no. 1 (2005): 35.
23. Stanitzek, "Texts and Paratexts," 29.
24. Genette and Maclean, "Introduction to the Paratext," 262.

25. Margaret Fuller, *Art, Literature, and the Drama* (Boston: Brown, Taggard, and Chase, 1860), 316.
26. Fuller, *Art, Literature, and the Drama*, 316.
27. Fuller, *Art, Literature, and the Drama*, 315.
28. Fuller, *Art, Literature, and the Drama*, 315.
29. Fuller, *Art, Literature, and the Drama*, 316.
30. Fuller, *Art, Literature, and the Drama*, 306.
31. James Parton, *The Life of Horace Greeley, Editor of the New-York Tribune* (New York: Derby and Miller, 1868), 555.
32. Parton, *Life of Horace Greeley*, 555.
33. Frank Luther Mott, *A History of American Magazines, 1741–1850* (Cambridge, MA: Harvard University Press, 1966), 414.
34. Mott, *History of American Magazines*, 414.
35. Nina Baym, "Rewriting the Scribbling Women," *Legacy* 36, no. 1 (2019): 146.
36. Shira Wolosky, *Poetry and Public Discourse in Nineteenth-Century America* (New York: Palgrave, 2010), xi.
37. Meredith McGill, *The Traffic in Poems: Nineteenth-Century Poetry and Transatlantic Exchange* (New Brunswick: Rutgers University Press, 2008), 4.
38. Paula Bernat Bennett, *Poets in the Public Sphere: The Emancipatory Project of American Women's Poetry, 1800–1900* (Princeton: Princeton University Press, 2003), 5.
39. Bennett, *Poets in the Public Sphere*, 5.
40. Wolosky, *Poetry and Public Discourse*, x.
41. Wolosky, *Poetry and Public Discourse*, x.
42. Wolosky, *Poetry and Public Discourse*, ix.
43. Michael C. Cohen, *The Social Lives of Poems in Nineteenth-Century America* (Philadelphia: University of Pennsylvania Press, 2015), 10.
44. Elizabeth Renker, *Realist Poetics in American Culture, 1866–1900* (Oxford: Oxford University Press, 2018), 8.
45. Jennifer Putzi, *Fair Copy: Relational Poetics and Antebellum American Women's Poetry* (Philadelphia: University of Pennsylvania Press, 2021), 1.
46. Claudia Stokes, *Old Style: Unoriginality and Its Uses in Nineteenth-Century U.S. Literature* (Philadelphia: University of Pennsylvania Press, 2021), 1.
47. Stokes, *Old Style*, 1.
48. Virginia Jackson, *Dickinson's Misery: A Theory of Lyric Reading* (Princeton: Princeton University Press, 2005).
49. Jonathan Culler, "Why Lyric?," *PMLA* 123, no. 1 (2008): 201.
50. Culler, "Why Lyric?," 201.
51. Putzi, *Fair Copy*, 13.
52. Michael Warner, *Publics and Counterpublics* (Brooklyn: Zone Books, 2002), 11.
53. Warner, *Publics and Counterpublics*, 28.
54. Warner, *Publics and Counterpublics*, 29.
55. Ellen Gruber Garvey, *Writing with Scissors: American Scrapbooks from the Civil War to the Harlem Renaissance* (Oxford: Oxford University Press, 2012), 2–3.
56. Garvey, *Writing with Scissors*, 3.

57. Kelley Kreitz, "Network," *American Periodicals: A Journal of History & Criticism* 30, no. 1 (2020): 6.
58. Mark Noonan, "Printscape," *American Periodicals: A Journal of History & Criticism* 30, no. 1 (2020): 9.
59. Rodrigo Lazo, "Introduction: Historical Latinidades and Archival Encounters," *The Latino Nineteenth Century*, ed. Rodrigo Lazo and Jesse Alemán (New York: New York University Press, 2016), 7.
60. Nancy Glazener, *Reading for Realism: The History of a U.S. Literary Institution, 1850–1910* (Durham, NC: Duke University Press, 1997), 5. Glazener defines the *Atlantic* group as "[a] set of late nineteenth-century magazines that regularly classified and discussed various kinds of fiction" (5).
61. Glazener, *Reading for Realism*, 9.

I

POETESS AS PARATEXT: THE CONTEXTUALIZING INFLUENCE OF LYDIA H. SIGOURNEY AND ALICE CARY IN THE *NEW YORK LEDGER*

In January 1870, the editor of the *Christian Standard*, Isaac Errett (1820–88), wrote in the *Christian Quarterly* that the popular press developed a "lower type of literary and sensational journals, filled with tales of horror and narratives of crime . . . [which] familiari[zed] the reader with the grossness, slang, and semi-barbaric grotesqueness of manners of the lower orders of our city population."[1] Errett singled out Robert Edwin Bonner's (1824–99) the *New York Ledger* as not belonging to this "lower type of literary . . . journal," claiming that "[t]he *Ledger* is not positively bad. It is negatively good. It is free from immoralities, and refuses to cater to vile tastes."[2] How Bonner's *Ledger* escaped the reproaches of stodgy editors like Errett is matter of ingenious marketing.

Resembling the broadsheets of newspapers yet publishing poets and serialists often featured in literary monthlies, the *Ledger* occupied an interstitial place in the print market world between popular culture and genteel society. Unlike the selective scope of intellectual monthlies—including *Munsey's*, *Ladies' Home Journal*, and *Cosmopolitan* that assumed that their readers were educated and part of the middle class—the *Ledger* catered to a vast and classless public that Bonner simply called "the family." This seemingly cult-of-domesticity moniker underscored the family as audience.[3] With its undiscerning scope, the *Ledger* was more like the serious newspapers of the time, casting a wide net to readers of all social classes. Because socioeconomic factors did not categorically define the family, the *Ledger*'s emphasis on this public was an important strategy for reaching an audience of diverse classes and societies.

The *Ledger*'s branding as a family paper implied that it was suitable for men, women, and children alike. One frequently printed *Ledger* advertisement, for example, proclaimed:

> We aim to make a paper that every father and mother can leave on the family table with perfect freedom. The *Ledger* will be unexceptionable in character and moral tone. Diligent and scrupulous judgement will be exercised in providing matter that will be both entertaining and instructing—that will elevate the mind and purify the heart.[4]

Bonner purchased hundreds of similar ads throughout the periodical press. These ads effectively garnered the interest of readers of news, serials, poetry, and advice columns, helping the *Ledger* achieve tremendous success for not just a weekly story paper, but for any periodical of its time. By the 1860s, Bonner's *Ledger* circulated nationally and claimed a readership of over 400,000. Literary celebrities from both sides of the Atlantic published in the *Ledger*, including William Cullen Bryant, Henry Ward Beecher, Henry Wadsworth Longfellow, Charles Dickens, and many others.[5]

Ledger scholarship tends to focus on the work and status of celebrity serialists and columnists like Sylvanus Cobb Jr., E. D. E. N. Southworth, Emerson Bennett, and Fanny Fern who turned Bonner's paper into a leading disseminator of original and entertaining sensational fiction and advice columns.[6] We know less, however, about the women poets that graced the pages of the *Ledger* and the significance and function of their writing. In Joyce W. Warren's study of Fanny Fern, the *Ledger*'s highest paid woman columnist, Warren argues that Bonner was determined to "print material that would be interesting and provocative but would be suitable for the whole family."[7] Just because Bonner's paper was "good," Warren continues, did not mean "it was innocuous, only that it was not vile."[8] To legitimize the family-appropriate image of his story paper, Bonner's perpetual task during his thirty-two-year tenure was to strike a balance between innocuous and morally questionable content. He did this with an editorial eye on the paratext that accompanies his serial publications. Through a poetics of paratextuality, this chapter argues that Bonner's balance between vile and innocuous content—which is literarily an equilibrium between "entertaining and instructing" material—could not have been possible without the regular publication of celebrity poetesses, Lydia Huntley Sigourney (1791–1865) and Alice Cary (1820–71), who helped him to establish the *Ledger*'s cultural legitimacy among the dominating monthly magazines of the time. For Bonner, the paratext was a space to quell social angst about his paper. His intentional positioning of these two poetesses in proximity to his most sensational serials activated thematic parallels and clashes between his publications that were meant to create a semblance of balance between instructing and entertaining material. Thus, in a story paper that capitalized on forms of sensationalism, Sigourney's and Cary's poems play up the story paper's instructing content and, ultimately, position the poetess figure as an arbiter of morality, femininity, aesthetics, and empowerment of women.

Rather than assume that Bonner's fascination with poetry explains his interest in Sigourney's and Cary's work, I want to suggest that his publication of their poems was based on their capacity to captivate readers by personifying the poetess figure. Bonner recognized and sought to appropriate Sigourney's and Cary's celebrity status, or, as Bonnie Carr O'Neill defines it, their "heightened publicity experienced by relatively few people in society."[9] Through the paratext, Bonner staged Sigourney's and Cary's celebrity status to promote the cultural image of his story paper as an instructing family paper. Furthermore, I want to also distinguish the *Ledger*'s revenue-induced agenda from Cary's and Sigourney's aesthetic and cultural choices in their poems. As major players in the production of the *Ledger*'s poetry, Sigourney and Cary gave expression to complex forms of women's agency that refute gendered codes of the cult of domesticity which often deemed women unfit for the public sphere.

Sigourney and Cary contributed to the *Ledger*'s rich variety of genres, which ran the gamut from Romantic poetry to sensational serials. Their poems appear alongside some of the most popular serialists of the time, including Sylvanus Cobb Jr., E. D. E. N. Southworth, and Emerson Bennett. Bonner's strategic placement of Sigourney's and Cary's poems reveals a poetics of paratextuality, that is, a systematic account of the poems, prose, and illustrations that animate the genteel Victorian soubriquet "poetess." Páraic Finnerty defines "the poetess" as the popular term used for a "denigrated figure [i.e. poet] associated with excessive feeling and interiority."[10] Culturally, the poetess was not simply a woman poet, but a persona characterized by gendered norms that promoted the values of the cult of domesticity. In her study of Sigourney's aesthetic "plentitude," Paula Bernat Bennett redefines the "poetess" as "one who writes 'Woman's (generic) pain, making it synonymous' with her verse."[11] In this sense, Bennett converts the poetess into a sentimentalist persona rather than simply a woman who writes feminine poetry. Sigourney, who according to Bennett avoided the sobriquet "poetess," identified as "a schoolmistress and a literary woman."[12] Although not all nineteenth-century US women poets called themselves poetesses, readers, editors, poets, and book publishers certainly interpellated them in this category. For instance, describing Sigourney's visit to London, the English literary socialite Jane Welsh Carlyle deprecatingly called Sigourney a "figure of an over-the-water-Poetess—beplastered with rouge and pomatum—bare-necked at an age which had left *certainty* far behind."[13] In another example, when the American book publisher James Cephas Derby writes about first meeting Alice Cary, he does not fail to mention how "Alice was alluded to on the occasion as 'Our poetess from the West,' or our 'Western poetess.'"[14] From popular poets like Sigourney and Cary to lesser-known poets like Ethel Lyn Beers and Emma Alice Brown, poetess figures found a place in the pages of Bonner's paper.

Bonner's capitalization of celebrity poetesses' reputations is, of course, not unique to the *Ledger*'s editor. In her study of the poetess figure in Frances Sargent Osgood's popular romance poetry, Eliza Richards explores Edgar Allan Poe's attempt to control "Osgood's poetic dissemination and assume her intimate relation with print under his signature."[15] Osgood, who promoted the poetry of romance as effectively as Sigourney sold the elegy, was known for her tantalizing, coquettish poetic voice that male readers often conflated with her own. Poe regularly published Osgood's poems in *Graham's Magazine*, initiating what Mary De Jong calls an uneven "literary alliance," in which Poe stood to benefit from publishing Osgood's work and promoting her reputation.[16] Richards argues that through these publications, Poe "staged a public literary romance [with Osgood] because he valued her capacity to captivate readers by personifying a poetic muse."[17] In an 1845 review of Osgood's *Poems* for the *Broadway Journal*, Poe boasts about Osgood's reputation: "we have no poetess among us who has been so universally *popular* as Mrs. Osgood."[18] The review's paratext, which included both Poe's and Osgood's writing and signatures in close proximity, enabled "an analogy with lovers conversing intimately in a salon setting."[19] This paratextual exchange between these poets, Richards posits, stirred readers to assume that the poets were each other's love interest. Animating the printed page itself as a scintillating printscape for popular gossip, Poe, as Richards explains, becomes both the "editor and suitor."[20] Bonner's preparation of Sigourney's and Cary's poems and their paratexts may not be as sexy as Poe's and Osgood's textual arrangements suggest. However, Bonner's paratext was based on the same principle of appropriation of the poetess's poetic abilities. Like Poe, Bonner too asks readers to speculate about the logics influencing his editorial decisions. Bonner understood that his paper would be read paratextually and used this knowledge of reading practices to encourage readers to ponder his choice and positioning of poems, and to contemplate whether readers were discovering thematic (dis)connections between texts on the page or projecting their own whims upon an impartial arrangement.

The paratext reveals the complex relationship between celebrity poetesses and the marketplace. In Joe Moran's study of celebrity writers, he argues:

> The encroachment of market values on to the literary production, while clearly having a major impact on literary celebrity, has not occurred in a vacuum—it forms part of a complicated process in which various legitimating bodies compete for cultural authority and/or commercial success, and regulate the formation of a literary star system and the shifting hierarchy of stars.[21]

In the *Ledger*, these legitimating bodies are the paratext (i.e. sensational serials, ads, and illustrations that brush against the fringe of the poem) that elaborate mid-nineteenth century market values and the commodification of culture. Since anything from a publisher's preface to a cover image or even an author's byline constitutes the paratext, Gérard Genette posits that all context is paratextual. If this is true, then the paratext extends to cultural attributes associated with the text, including a poet's sobriquet and reputation. While Sigourney and Cary likely did not have a say about where to position their poems on the page, they did have a choice to publish their poems with a byline in Bonner's story paper. We cannot overlook such agentive choices by women writers in a period when an ideology of separate spheres deemed publishing, at best, inappropriate. Reading their signed poems alongside their paratext is a way of giving contextualizing agency to their subjectivities as women and writers. In return, their poems allow us to negotiate the traffic in texts on the page, revealing the complex relationship between poetesses and the marketplace. To make sense of the paratexts that frame Sigourney's and Cary's poems in the *Ledger*, we must first take a look at the role of poetry in Bonner's story paper.

Poetry in the *Ledger*

For the *Ledger* to succeed, Bonner had to factor in the discrepancy between the public's disapproval and its approval of his paper's content. While publishing sensational serials often deemed vile and morally inept, the *Ledger* benefited from cultural stereotypes about the gentility and prestige often ascribed to nineteenth-century verse. In the cultural imaginary of nineteenth-century publics and editors, poetry had an elevated status. As Linda K. Hughes posits, "[o]ne reason that editors from early to late in the century valued poetry . . . was that its inclusion could enhance the cultural value and prestige of the periodical itself."[22] Fittingly, it made sense that Bonner supposed that printing poems would enhance the *Ledger*'s literary prestige.

Cultural prestige and familiarity were a matter of convention informed by the public's consensus on what a poem was and what it should do. Meredith McGill claims that nineteenth-century poets and readers often resisted poetic innovation, thus reinforcing the poem's formal and cultural conventions.[23] Kirsten Silva Gruesz points out that "poetry reigned both as the prestige genre of high-cultural literary production and as one of the most familiar forms of expression in popular life."[24] Bonner made tactical use of poetry's formal and cultural conventions and genteel status to serve his family-paper brand. In the eyes of nineteenth-century publics, who were invested in conventions of gentility while also consuming sensational entertainment genres, periodical poems in the *Ledger* provided a sense of gentility, manners, and moral guidance which, next to sensational serials, eased the feeling of perversion socially tagged on to these "lower types of literary and sensational journals."[25]

Beginning in 1855, each issue of the *Ledger* printed two poems, typically on the first column of the front and back pages. Bonner soon added another poem to the third page of the *Ledger*'s eight pages. By the end of the decade, Bonner printed poems on nearly every page of the *Ledger*. Alongside these poems, readers encountered three to four serials by different authors as well as editorials ranging from various topics including "Wit and Humor," "Notices to Correspondents," "Woman's Sacrifices," and "How to Make Money," to name a fraction of them. In addition to Lydia Sigourney and Alice Cary, Bonner published many poets whose fame ranged from unknown to well-known, including Flora Thorne, C. D. Stuart, Findley Johnson, George D. Prentice, August Herbert, Emma Alice Brown, Sarah Morgan Bryan Piatt (under Sally Bryan), William Ross Wallace, Mary Clemmer Ames, Phoebe Cary, Ethel Lynn, Nathan D. Urner, Willie E. Pabor, Josephine Pollard, and many others. Bonner grew accustomed to publishing unknown writers in the same issues and printscapes as public luminaries, giving readers the opportunity to determine for themselves the value of each writer with impartiality.

Horace Greeley, who saw Bonner as a champion of periodical poetry, expressed concern about the neutralization of worthy poetry when it appeared next to bad poems. In February 1859, Greeley wrote to Bonner congratulating him for his undertaking of publishing poems not included in Charles A. Dana's popular anthology *Household Book of Poetry*. Greeley described Bonner's selection of poems as a "pantheon ... of genuine poems of moderate length which cannot be found in [Dana's] collection."[26] He advised, "only take care not to neutralize or nullify your chivalrous championship by burying them under a carload of rhymed rubbish."[27] By rhymed rubbish, Greeley was likely referring to the poems Bonner published in the *Ledger*'s debut year in 1855. Many of these earlier poems have pseudonymous bylines like "Woodland Millie," while a great number of others were left anonymous. The poets who first appeared in the early years of the *Ledger* were seldom printed again, including "Mrs. M. J. Robertson" and "John George Watt."[28]

The *Ledger*'s rhymed-rubbish beginnings did not stop it from becoming a leading disseminator of nineteenth-century poetry. Analyzing the *Ledger*'s poems within their paratexts of sensational serials and illustrations reveals the importance verse bore on the story paper's cultural legitimacy as a periodical "Devoted to Choice Literature, Romance, The News, and Commerce," as the paper's nameplate states. Studying poems in the *Ledger* means examining what they tell us about Bonner's role as an editor, his editorial process, as well as his opinions on poetry and women writers. Was Bonner, as Margaret Fuller says of many newspaper editors of the time, "indifferen[t] or unfit ... [for] choosing and refusing" poetry? The short answer is no. Bonner was famously involved in the publication of his paper's poems. This is evident in the letters he exchanged with poets and the ads that he took out in periodicals. For instance, Bonner was aware of the lineup of poets he was to publish and often shared bylines in his correspondence and advertisements. On September 24, 1860, in a letter to the celebrated Romantic poet and editor of the New York *Evening Post* William Cullen Bryant, regarding the publication of "Italy," Bonner wrote, "I am glad that you sent me this poem, this morning, as in the same number . . . I shall have original poems from Willis, Saxe, Alice Cary, Mrs. Sigourney."[29] The fact that Bonner shared bylines with other poets implies that he was aware of the cultural capital of these poetic signatures, assuring his contributors that they would be accompanied by other notables and not simply, as Greeley calls it, rhymed rubbish. In September of 1856, Bonner began featuring a "Special Contributors" list on page 4 of the *Ledger* where he regularly included the names of celebrity poets. He called these notables an "unequaled arrayed of distinguished authors," playing up the *Ledger*'s own prestige as the eminent periodical that made these "Special Contributors" available to the public.

More than Bonner's letters, ads, and lists of "Special Contributors," it is the price that he paid certain poets that displays his views on poetry. Bonner was a savvy businessperson who understood the marketing power of a celebrity byline. He typically paid $10 per poem and had some regular contributors on the payroll. For instance, Amelia E. Barr, a regular *Ledger* contributor, wrote in her autobiography, "I did not dream at that date of a time when Robert Bonner would pay me ten dollars every week for a poem, and that for a period of nearly fifteen years."[30] Bonner's bankroll was nearly unrestricted for celebrity poets. A few years before John Greenleaf Whittier died, Bonner paid him $1,000 for "Captain's Well."[31] He paid Bryant $3,000 for two short poems.[32] In March 1874, Bonner published Henry Wadsworth Longfellow's "The Hanging of the Crane," paying the sum of $3,000.[33] In 1872, Bonner offered Alfred, Lord Tennyson £1,000 for any three-stanza poem. Tennyson submitted an 1830s poem which he altered and retitled "England and America in 1782."[34]

Sigourney was the earliest celebrity poet to publish in the *Ledger*, appearing in Bonner's paper as early as 1853, only a couple of years after Bonner had purchased the *Merchant's Ledger* from D. Anson Pratt and changed the paper's name to the *New York Ledger* in 1851.[35] At sixty-two years old, Sigourney's reputation as the poetess of morality and Christian virtue was already deeply rooted in the US's reading public when Bonner first published her. Cary began to appear regularly in the *Ledger* in 1856. Both poets were featured in nearly every issue until the time of their respective deaths in 1865 and 1871. Throughout their tenure at the *Ledger*, these poets were the quintessential example of the celebrity poetess, supplying *Ledger* readers with a moral and aesthetic firmness. On the one hand, Sigourney's *Ledger* poems, particularly her scriptural verses, represent a domestic vision of true womanhood to the *Ledger*, a vision that often thematically interacts with the story paper's serials and illustrations. On the other hand, Cary's verses capture the opposition between nature and civilization, furnishing Bonner's paper with a pastoralism otherwise left out of the predominantly sensational columns of serials and illustrations that represent the age of industrialization in urban settings. Appearing above, beneath, and next to the *Ledger*'s most popular serial installments, Sigourney's and Cary's poems simultaneously interrupt and advance the narratives and illustrations of serials and vice versa, aiding Bonner's efforts in achieving a balance between what Errett calls the "not positively bad [and] negatively good" of the *Ledger*'s offerings.[36] Although both of these poets played major roles in the *Ledger*'s financial and cultural success, their *Ledger* poems are almost entirely unknown to scholars of print culture and poetry.[37]

"Sweet Singer of Hartford"

Bonner first encountered Sigourney's poems soon after arriving in Hartford, Connecticut from Northern Ireland in 1839. He was fifteen years old when he started as an apprentice setting poems and reprints for the *Hartford Courant*.[38] By this time, Sigourney's celebrity reputation as the "Hemans of America" and the "Sweet Singer of Hartford" was well established. As Jennifer Putzi reminds us:

> The practice of referring to Sigourney as the "American Hemans" began back in the 1820s, long before the British poet's death. When used generously, the label was meant to point favorably to similarities between the two poets' subject matter, particularly their attention to domestic and religious topics.[39]

Furthermore, I would add, the "Hemans of America" sobriquet conveyed to many readers Sigourney's celebrity status and success as a public writer, placing her poems in a class that was culturally commensurate with Felicia Hemans's poetry. To financially support her family, Sigourney often capitalized on her association to Hemans and the consequent public demands for her poetry.

Since Ann Douglass's groundbreaking study of sentimental values and mass culture in *The Feminization of American Culture*, where Douglass recovers Sigourney as not just a poetess of consolation but a poet "preaching with full ministerial confidence to a more general audience," Sigourney's work as a poet has been excavated and reevaluated for its popular status and wide-ranging readership.[40] Recovery work by Glenn Hendler, Nina Baym, Jane Tompkins, Paul Lauter, Paula Bernat Bennett, and Jennifer Putzi demonstrates that sentimental poetry was not always apolitical or empty of social concerns. Recent studies of Sigourney's work have steered away from the poet's commitment to standards of gendered etiquette and manners and have focused on what Putzi calls Sigourney's creative "negotiation of the print-cultural contexts within which she worked."[41] Mary Louise Kete studies how Sigourney's sentimental poems construct "imagined communities," a nationality and political union made possible by the homogenizing interiority of Sigourney's work.[42] Similarly, Eliza Richards argues that Sigourney's poetry serves a "republican project."[43] Richards states that "poetry binds individuals together with ties as strong as the pain it converts to solace . . . Offering her services to the cause [of consolation and social healing], Sigourney claimed that poetry converted private suffering into communal bonds."[44] Bryan Sinche analyzes Sigourney's sentimental outlook, charting the limits of sentimentalism as a literary mode and an imaginative force. He argues that Sigourney's poems exhibit "a remediative force," and that her poems attempt to heal social problems with faith and sympathy.[45] In 2018, Sigourney scholarship culminated in the first critical anthology of her work, *Lydia Sigourney: Critical Essays and Cultural Views*. The editors, Mary Louise Kete and Elizabeth Petrino, showcase Sigourney's extensive output and career through chapters that range across varied aspects of Sigourney's poetics, reception, circulation, and legacy. The essays that make up the volume challenge us to reconsider Sigourney through multiple perspectives: "her achievements as a professional author, and educational theorist, political activist, an entrepreneur, and cultural icon."[46]

Sigourney's poetry in part confirmed the existence of an American literary tradition on par with the English poetic tradition.[47] Through the first half of the nineteenth century, Sigourney, according to Gary Kelly, was "the most popular American woman poet on both sides of the Atlantic."[48] Sigourney's fame was unprecedented for an American poetess: "Her name alone," Cheryl Walker posits, "was worth money."[49] This celebrity status was in part owed to Sigourney's immense productivity. She wrote a lot. Her oeuvre would go on to include more than 46 distinct volumes and 2,000 articles in 300 journals, more than a dozen books of poetry, and two conduct books, *Letters to Young Ladies* (1833) and *Letters to my Pupil* (1851).[50] As Sinche argues, she was read because of the affecting accessibility of her work to all readers: "Indeed, the fact that her work was widely thought to be lovely and affecting without being 'intense' or 'odd' is what made her so very popular throughout her lengthy career."[51] Such affecting accessibility helped Sigourney garner both fiscal and cultural capital throughout her lifetime. Along with Sarah Joseph Hale, the renowned editor of *Godey's Magazine*, Sigourney was awarded an honorary "Mistress of Arts" by Franklin Female College in 1853.[52] In the late 1850s, Butler University students in Indiana founded a society after her: the Sigourney Society.[53] Although the subject of Sigourney's celebrity status is important for understanding her career and output, Putzi encourages Sigourney scholars to look beyond the poet's fame and reputation and to focus on the print culture that contextualizes her work. Such a focus "reveals that [Sigourney's] sense of poetic authorship was shaped by the opportunities for publication and circulation available to her."[54]

Sigourney found writing for newspapers particularly challenging because of their overwhelming demand. In her posthumously published autobiography, *Letters of Life* (1867), Sigourney recalled her writing for these periodicals:

> On this sea of miscellany I was allured to embark, and, having set sail, there was no return. I think now with amazement, and almost incredulity, of the number of articles I was induced by the urgency of editors to furnish. Before I ceased to keep a regular catalogue, they had amounted to more than two thousand. Some of these were afterwards comprehended in selections, though enough for several volumes must still be floating about, like sea-weed among the noteless billows.[55]

The oceanic imagery in Sigourney's description of her productivity softens the reality of her labor and the consequent obscurity of its future. Many of these periodical poems are, to extend her conceit, lost at sea. Part of the labor, as she explains, is the speed at which she had to write and how this haste presented obstacles to her domestic duties:

> Promptitude was the life-blood of these contributions. Hungering presses must be fed, and not wait. How to obtain time to appease editorial appetites, and not neglect my housekeeping tactics, was a study. I found the employment of knitting congenial to the contemplation and treatment of the slight themes that were desired, and, while completing fifteen or sometimes twenty pairs of stockings yearly for our large family, or for the poor, stopped the needles to arrest the wings of a flying thought or a flowing stanza. Still, I always corrected, and rewrote more than once, these extemporaneous effusions, not considering it decorous to throw crude matter at the head of the public.[56]

For Sigourney, knitting was like writing newspaper poems. Requiring the regular steady movement of the hand, they were both made to order, one for her family and the other for "hungering presses." Sigourney's ability to multitask—fast-rate writing for periodicals and fulfilling domestic duties—showcases her incredible resilience and dedication as a woman writer. Yet while she produced in great quantity, Sigourney expressed regret about the quality of her work.[57] "This habit of writing *currente calamo*," Sigourney claimed, "is fatal to literary ambition. It prevents that labor of thought by which intellectual eminence is acquired."[58] The mechanical and assembly-line pace of newspaper writing may have left Sigourney aesthetically unfulfilled. However, many editors were satisfied with her contributions as they equated her byline with morally conscious writing ideal for readers.

Sigourney's fame and productivity came with its challenges. She was a full-time writer and woman in the nineteenth century, which meant that she had to carefully maneuver in the realms of the public and private spheres. Throughout the nineteenth century, readers commonly linked a woman's byline with her sexualized body. Nineteenth-century readers often did not distinguish sentimental utterances from the woman poet, collapsing poems into persons. This readerly personification made it difficult for women writers like Sigourney, whose poetess sobriquet already tethered them to the female subject, to expand their poetic voice beyond their bodies. Sigourney's husband, for instance, allied her public writing to sexual indiscretion. Her husband's chastisements, Richards posits, "may have helped to inspire Mrs. Sigourney's maintenance of a relentlessly impersonal poetic self-presentation, [but] they did not keep her from reaching an agreement with editors who offered to pay more for signed contributions."[59] While signed poems were financially more valuable, the signature also deepened their identification with the female objectified body. Sigourney countered the gendered collapse of "female public expression with prostitution" by specializing in elegies and biblical poems, many of which she wrote for the *Ledger*.[60]

Sigourney's Hermeneutic Poems

Sigourney wrote biblically inspired verses for the *Ledger* that I call hermeneutic poems. These poems begin with a biblical epigraph and promote Christian ideals and values through interpretations of scripture. In *Letters of Life*, Sigourney claimed that her biblical poems stemmed from an indulgence to imitate "the style of the historical parts of the Old Testament" as well as her lifelong interest in Christian prayer and orisons.[61] At various moments in her autobiography, Sigourney contemplated the weight of this "work on the subject of Prayer," describing it as "heavy, inasmuch as I never could bear to read it myself."[62] As if physically turning to these materials, she noted, "When last I saw [the scriptural writing,] there seemed some danger of its being suffocated under a pile of incumbent manuscripts."[63] Sigourney materializes the text in her description of the pile, giving it a material form, paratext, and interiority. Even though "the pile of incumbent manuscripts" and "work on the subject of Prayer" are in proximity to each other, literal paratexts to one another, Sigourney distinguishes them. The suffocating pile appears to belong to the public sphere while the scriptural writing belongs to the private, that is, the interior, buried beneath the weight of the manuscripts. Sigourney's hermeneutic poems in the *Ledger*, however, cannot be easily categorized within the strict contours of the separate spheres, especially once the poems are printed and circulated. These poems are both "work on the subject of Prayer" and a part of the *currente calamo* publications that she throws at "the head of the public."[64] The unification of these two types of writing helps us to understand the speaker in Sigourney's hermeneutic poems as an extension of Sigourney herself, a writer of scriptural literature who also published in great quantity for the public. This textual merger salvages her poetic voice from what Virginia Jackson calls the proto-modernist universal lyric subject.[65] Among the very pile of incumbent manuscripts that Sigourney claims suffocated her scriptural writing, it would have been likely to uncover a hermeneutic poem or two for Bonner's *Ledger*.

Between December 1856 and January 1857, Bonner published a particularly important series of Sigourney's hermeneutic poems that aided the *Ledger*'s Protestant and family-appropriate image. With regard to these poems, I want to focus on two types of paratexts: the first is Sigourney's biblical epigraphs, which open the poem and are then referred to in the stanzas. The epigraph and poem are intertextually liked in these publications, informing each other's individual and collective meaning and significance. The second type is the *Ledger*'s paratext of sensational tales and illustrations, which frame and contextualize Sigourney's poems. Within this paratextual printscape, Sigourney's religiously instructive poems provided readers with scriptural lessons about usury, hubris, death, and munificence. When read alongside their paratext, Sigourney's hermeneutic poems guide the reader's attention, influence how texts are read, and transfer such information as to give the text its first contours.

Often jeremiadic in style, Sigourney's hermeneutic poems provided readers with a type of redemption and reprieve from the gore and sensationalism of the *Ledger*'s serials. For example, in Sigourney's "Leave Time and Place to God," published on January 3, 1857, the speaker contemplates life and death. Comprising three irregularly metered stanzas, "Leave Time and Place to God" explores the certainty and omnipresence of death and the limits of human knowledge. Sigourney's speaker questions the particulars of death, that is, the "*when* and *where*," time and place of mortality (22).[66] The answers to these questions, according to the speaker, are better left for God. The poem begins with an epigraph from the Book of Job, often cited as an example of hubris, followed by a series of interpretative questions about death in each stanza. The first stanza begins:

> "*Then I saw, I shall die in my nest.*"
> Die in thy nest?
> How know'st thou? Who hath given
> Promise like this? Did the stern archer make
> Such reservation? Will he keep the pledge?
> His office is to smite, and not to hold
> Parley with any one of woman born (1–6)[67]

For the "woman born" speaker, mortality is an epistemological quandary, limited by what we think we know. This unknowing informs the speaker's series of rhetorical questions: How can one know the particulars of death, who has "promised," made the "reservation," and "pledged" the answer that confirms when and where one dies? Invoking the image of a smiting Calvinist God in the final two lines, the speaker claims that God's occupation is not to answer these questions but to simply give us our inevitable ending. The second stanza shows that this mortal ending that comes to everyone is omnipresent:

> Die in thy nest?
> From thy more distant course
> O'er vale or ocean, or a stranger clime,
> Or even from briefest range among the flowers,
> Who told thee thou should'st return again? (7–11)

In this stanza, readers are poetically transplanted from the busy streets of the city of New York, where the *Ledger* is published, to alternative climes. The poem's shifting setting moves the public through "vale or ocean, or a stranger clime," and "range" as the speaker asks, "who told thee thou should'st return [home] again?" (9–11). The question refers to the addressee's homecoming but also to the poem's formal structure, which is a return to the same question, "thy nest?" (7).

The reverberation of "thy nest?" throughout the poem is not just a geographical and formal motif but also a philosophical signifier for theorizing change and transformation of place. In the third and final stanza, the speaker posits "—Thy nest? / Some have come home and found no nest—" (12–13). Upon returning, one finds that the nest is altered by the natural changes and the passage of time, "wreck'd by winds, tree broken, birdlings gone" (14). Death leaves our "Forest uprooted" and "Forgotten," making home a memory and feeling (15).[68] Sigourney's poem concludes, "leave *when* and *where* to God—and be content" (21). The speaker positions a deterministic view of life and death as she relinquishes control over her destiny and claims that one must "be content" with not knowing the "Time and Place," as the poem's title suggests, of our mortality.

The determinism in Sigourney's "Leave Time and Place to God" extends to the poem's paratext. Below Sigourney's poem appears the thirteenth chapter of Caroline Ingraham's serial *Sarah Percival; or the Bride of 'The House of Gold'*. The paratextual placement of the serial and poem creates both an intertextual exchange between the content and themes in the texts as well as a cultural exchange between two writers that varied in cultural publicity and significance. For readers unfamiliar with Ingraham's byline, Sigourney's signature elevated the relatively unknown serialist to a relative state of prominence. Bonner understood how his readers would have encountered Ingraham's byline alongside one of the most famous poets in the mid-nineteenth century. With no differentiation between Ingraham and Sigourney, Bonner's paratext gave *Ledger* readers the opportunity to determine for themselves the value of Ingraham's *Sarah Percival*.

Before getting into a paratextual reading of *Sarah Percival* and "Leave Time and Place to God," it would be helpful to first summarize Ingraham's serial.

Sarah Percival is an intricately plotted story of love, deception, marriage, death, and travel involving the entangled fates of the Percival family. The serial's twenty chapters include seven installments that ran in the *Ledger* from December 13, 1856 until January 24, 1857. In the first installment, readers learn about Sarah Percival, a beautiful eighteen-year-old orphan, who lives in a sleepy town outside the city of New York with her cruel aunt and cousin, Kate and Mrs. Percival, respectively. Sarah, the narrator claims, is a product of an "unfortunate marriage" between a wealthy English woman, Mrs. Hamilton, and Frank Percival. In the second installment, readers gather that Mrs. Hamilton was tricked into believing that Frank was having an affair. As a result, Mrs. Hamilton abandons Frank and Sarah. Frank ultimately dies, leaving Sarah to the care of his older brother and family. After the death of Sarah's benefactor, she decides to move to the city of New York to become a seamstress. Soon after arriving in the city, Sarah meets a sailor named Ross Neville, who helps her find a carriage to her residence. They fall in love at first sight. Sarah has little hope of ever seeing Ross again. In the city, Sarah learns about her mother's identity from her landlady, Janet, and decides to search for her mother. However, the wicked Mrs. Percival hires a spying lawyer to prevent mother and daughter from finding each other.

In the third installment, the story shifts to the perspective of Kate and Mrs. Percival who are vacationing in Paris, France. There, they meet Clarence Hamilton, the stepson of Mrs. Hamilton, Sarah's mother. Clarence, also called Colonel Hamilton and Guy, is aware that his stepmother is searching for her estranged daughter who will inherit a large fortune from her. When he learns from his servant that a "Miss Percival" is in Paris, Clarence assumes that she is Sarah Percival and pursues her to obtain the large inheritance which he feels rightfully belongs to him. Aware of the inheritance, Kate and Mrs. Percival, respectively, pretend to be Sarah and Sarah's stepmother. Kate, masquerading as Sarah, marries Mr. Hamilton who soon introduces her to Mrs. Hamilton.

In the fourth installment, readers learn that the real Sarah Percival is traveling in Venice, Italy, working for an elderly woman named Mrs. Rosenheim, who describes herself as a widow "at heart, if not in reality." As Sarah ponders the whereabouts of the man she met in New York, Ross Neville, a trio of Americans appear below her window. Coincidentally, Neville is one of them. Soon after, they declare their love for each other and become engaged.

In the fifth installment, Clarence Hamilton arrives in Venice with his new wife and family on the day of Sarah and Ross's marriage ceremony. Clarence stumbles onto the ceremony and finds it strange that the bride has the same name as his wife. Once Kate and Mrs. Percival learn that Sarah is in Venice, they become apprehensive about Clarence finding out about their treachery.

In the sixth installment, Mrs. Percival hires her Italian servant Pietro to kidnap Sarah and remove her from Venice. Pietro tries to kidnap Sarah and Janet, but a bystander, who turns out to be Mrs. Rosenheim's long-lost husband, rescues them. Pietro confesses everything to Clarence Hamilton. Clarence, Ross, and the real Sarah Percival confront Kate and Mrs. Percival in front of Mrs. Hamilton. Mother and daughter are reunited.

In the final installment, titled "The Death Bed," overwhelmed with guilt and frustration, Kate poisons herself in an attempt to win back her husband, Clarence. She dies in Clarence's arms, and Sarah and Neville live happily ever after.

Like Sigourney's poem, Ingraham's serial presents a persona leaving her "nest," traveling "O'er vale or ocean, or a stranger clime," from her hometown to the city of New York and to Venice ("Leave Time," 10). In the installment where Sigourney's poem appears, the narrator returns to the serial's "real heroine," Sarah Percival, who experiences "some change in her destiny" now that she is on her own in the city.[69] Due to her fiscal precarity and social standing, Sarah has little control over her own destiny. She is an orphan, disconnected from her birth mother and her love interest.

Sigourney's poetic interpretation of *"Then I saw, I shall die in my nest"* as epistemological hubris seems to foreshadow Sarah Percival's prospects abroad. Like the speaker in Sigourney's poem who contemplates a returned unknowingness, Sarah longs to know the whereabouts of Ross Neville, the love interest she met in the city of New York: "Her heart and her thoughts were far away. The incidents of her first night in the city of New York came up before her, and she smiled tenderly, as she thought of the gallant young man who had so kindly assisted her. Where was he now?"[70] On this *Ledger* page, sentimental longing intertextually links the poem and serial, allowing for Sigourney's speaker and Sarah to feign control over a deterministic telos. However, the faraway thoughts of longing for answers (time of death or the whereabouts of a lover) carve an epistemological distance between the characters and the answers they seek.

Ideas of home and homecoming take clearer shape in later parts of the serial installment. In a meditative spell, while pondering the whereabouts of her New York lover, Sarah sings a ballad "which had been the favorite of her childhood and was now dearer than ever":[71]

> How could I but list, but linger
> To the song, and hear the singer,
> Sweetly wooing heaven to bring her
> Jamie from the stormy sea.
> And when once her lips did name me—
> Forth I sprang—my heart o'ercame me—
> "Grieve no more, sweet—I am Jamie,
> Home returned to love and thee!"[72]

The lines Sarah sings are from the final stanza of Bernard Covert's song "Jamie's On the Stormy Sea," a popular ballad about a lovestruck "lonely maiden" who sings for the return of Jamie who is at sea. Published in 1847, Covert's ballad was performed and reprinted in periodicals across the Anglophone world. The final lines in Covert's ballad are intertextually tethered to Sigourney's speaker's words of grief and home. Sigourney's speaker grieves for herself as she contemplates mortality while Covert's speaker and Sarah, who sings this ballad, grieve for lost love. The source of the speakers' grief is shaped by an ambiguous return home, which both Sigourney's and Covert's poems explicitly allude to: "Some have come home and found no nest" ("Leave Time," 12) and "Home returned to love and thee!" ("Jamie's On the Stormy Sea," 40). Later in the installment when Ross reappears in Sarah's life, the narrator once again intertextually links Covert's ballad to the serial by proclaiming that "[Sarah's] 'Jamie' had returned." Ross's and Sarah's fates are tied from here on. Like the speaker in Sigourney's poem who relinquishes control over her destiny and claims that one must "be content" with not knowing the "Time and Place," Sarah allows her fate to play out without intervention. After all, her reunion with Ross (and later with her mother) is merely accidental and determined by a series of coincidences. While Sigourney's "Leave Time" thematically complements Ingraham's serial, displaying a poetics of paratextuality that features intertextual connections of lost love, home and homecoming, and hubris, many of Sigourney's hermeneutic poems thematically contrast their paratext.

In another of Sigourney's hermeneutic poems, "Fair Traffic," published in the *Ledger* on January 24, 1857, the speaker displays moral credibility by defining and modeling Christian charity. The title of the poem refers to the trade of Christian love. Like in "Leave Time," the stanzas of "Fair Traffic" are intertextually linked with the poem's epigraph, "Owe no man anything, except to love one another" from the sixth book in the New Testament, the Epistle to the Romans.[73] The stanzas that follow are an exegesis of this line, which Sigourney's speaker interprets as a case against usury. The first stanza reads:

> "*Owe no man anything, except to love one another.*" St. Paul.
> "Owe no man anything." Why should we wish
> To keep what is not ours? What right have we
> Unto the usufruct of others' toil,
> Unrecompenced? 'Twere better to forego
> All Luxury—all circumstance of wealth,
> Palatial mansion, or patrician robe,
> Than have the secret curses of the poor,
> And with the fraud-spot on the soul, go forth,
> Unto the clear Eye of the Perfect Judge. (1–9)[74]

The speaker juxtaposes the epigraph "'*Owe no man anything*'" with rhetorical questions directed at the reader: "Why should we wish / To keep what is not ours? What right have we / Unto the usufruct of others' toil?" (1–3). Usufruct is a specific legal concept commonly used in the discourse of lawsuits in the early to mid-nineteenth century. It means that one can use land (that one does not own) so long as one does not destroy the land. In the poem, however, "usufruct" suggests the opposite, that no one has a right to what others have earned via their own "toil." "'Twere better," she continues, "to forego / All luxury" and avoid material possessions "Than have the secret curses of the poor" (4–5, 7). In other words, the speaker suggests that those who want luxury are haunted by their desires, the "wish / to keep what is not ours" (1–2). Sigourney continues her hermeneutic exercise in the second and final stanza, where the speaker repeats the biblical epigraph that opens the poem:

> "Owe no man anything, except love."
> The debt of holy love hath no remorse:
> It bringeth blessedness. For God is love,
> And he who dwells in love, doth dwell with Him!
> —Take freely of the fountain that our Lord
> Open'd on earth,—"peace and good-will to man."
> Love's debt is never fully paid, till Heaven
> Unlocks the exchequer of unrusting gold;
> But he who loveth all whom God hath made
> Hath foretaste of the bliss that ne'er shall end. (10–19)

"Love," the speaker asserts, is God. Thus, one can indulge in the "debt of holy love," for this type of divine debt has "no remorse" (11).[75] The reading of "Love" as a type of abridgment for Christian duties parallels Sigourney's speaker's interpretation of "love" as a type of debtless resource. The use of economic language reminds readers that love is a sort of limitless currency that one can "Take freely" and that "Love's debt" is paid only after death (14, 16). But if readers begin loving while on earth, they will "foretaste" what waits for them in heaven (19). The inherent didacticism of "Fair Traffic" would have been particularly effective for pious fans of Sigourney's writing, in part because the poem provides them with a sense of moral guidance based on Christian love and the rejection of worldly or secular desires.

The speaker's sentiments about love and the message of "'peace and good-will to man'" (15) are lost on the rest of the *Ledger* page. These themes clash with the poem's surrounding paratextual context, specifically when read alongside Emerson Bennett's serial, *The Refugees: An Indian Tale of 1812*. Bennett's *The Refugees* is a historical serial that follows the frontier lives of the Stanforths, a Connecticut family that relocates to Ohio a year before the War of

1812.⁷⁶ When the war breaks out, local Native Americans attack and pillage the Stanforths' remote farm. The Stanforths abandon their home and farm and soon meet with the dangers of the wilderness. The protagonist, Eden Stanforth, a soldier in the US army, tries to get his family out of harm's way with the help of a scout he meets in the forest, Pete Bracy. The first three chapters recount their travels in the forest, encounters with Native Americans, and the Stanforths' cunning efforts to stay alive.

Bonner advertised Bennett's serial in newspapers across the country, which created an enormous amount of hype around the story's publication in the *Ledger*. Many readers waited with bated breath for each installment of Bennett's *The Refugees*. One newspaper described a scene of readers lining up for the *Ledger* to eagerly read Bennett's story:

> Passing down the avenue this morning our attention was attracted by a large crowd pressing around our friend Shillington's store. All seemed intent on passing in one door and out the other . . . We followed in with the crowed to learn the cause of so much anxiety, when "Ledger, sir? New York Ledger, sir?" Greeted our ears. It seems the New York Ledger for January 10 had just arrived, and our literary friends were intent on reading the admirable tale by Emerson Bennett.[77]

Bonner's story paper was not the first periodical to publish Bennett's serial. *The Refugees* was first published in the *Detroit Daily Advertiser* in 1856. The *Ledger*'s first installment of *The Refugees* ran concurrently with the debut issue of *Harper's Weekly* on January 3, 1857, which also ran the serial. What made the *Ledger*'s version of Bennett's often reprinted serial stand out among competing publications was the detailed etchings by the British engraver Alfred Bobbett.[78] Figure 1.1, for example, shows the *Ledger*'s January 24 installment of *The Refugees*, featuring Bobbett's etching entitled "Pete, The Scout, Triumphant" to the left of Sigourney's "Fair Traffic."

Bobbett's image depicts a bearded white man in rags, holding a knife in one hand and the scalp of a Native American in the other. This man is Pete Bracy, who stands "triumphant" above the corpse of the Native American. The chapter that corresponds with the illustration graphically describes the fight between a nameless Native American and Pete, who is ultimately victorious. After violently stabbing the Native American in the chest and scalping him (as the illustration shows), Pete soliloquizes the following in his rural Ohio dialect:

> Thar . . . what d'ye think o'that ther now, fur a specimen o'the way we white fellers use up sich—nasty, greasy varmints as you—hey? You war a—fool to come agin sich a old hoss as Pete Bracy, and 'spect to take your infarnal scalp back agin! and ef my advice's good fur anything, I

Figure 1.1 "Pete, The Scout, Triumphant," *The New York Ledger*, January 24, 1857. Public domain.

reckon you'd better take it, and when you git into t'other world, just keep yourself on your own stomping ground, and not go for to mix yourself up with your betters! You war too young a cur fur such a old dog as me; and you ought to been shut up in a lodge, with squaw fixings on to ye, you had, you—greasy scoundrel! Cut me, did ye? drawed blood of a white gintleman, hey? Wall, then, 'spose I just takes that thar scalp of yourn fur a sticking plaster![79]

Pete Bracy's racist monologue is part of nineteenth-century fearmongering representations of Native Americans that ranged from savage to benign. In her study of literary representations of Native Americans, Gretchen Bataille posits that "[i]n late-nineteenth-century literature, the captivity narratives had given way to dime novels and books with lurid covers and titles . . . tales that warned readers of menacing Indian males."[80] Bracy dehumanizes the unnamed Native American, calling him "vermin" for attacking a white man. He then goes on to imagine a segregated afterlife, "t'other world," where white people and Native Americans are separated. He tells the dead Indigenous person to "keep yourself on your own stomping ground [in heaven], and not go for to mix yourself up with your betters!" Thus, for Pete Bracy, scalping the Indigenous person is a type of racist vengeance not just for attacking a "white gintleman" but for threatening whiteness in general. The thematic clash between Sigourney's poem, Pete's monologue, and Bobbett's illustration, in part, suggests that the "Fair Traffic" of "holy love" articulated in Sigourney's poem does not extend into the wilderness and to non-white peoples. More importantly, this paratextual clash also tells us something about the cultural role of Sigourney's byline on the *Ledger*'s page.

One could argue that the placement on the page of "Fair Traffic" could merely be a matter of editorial convenience on Bonner's part (i.e. just enough textual space for a short poem). Perhaps it is also mere coincidence that both the Stanforth family in Bennett's story and Sigourney (commonly known as the "Sweet Singer of Hartford") are from the state of Connecticut. However, readers familiar with Sigourney's Native American writings and activism, as Bonner surely was, having read and set her poems to type for the *Hartford Courant* as early as 1839, would have experienced a jarring juxtaposition between the triumph of love and Christian charity in Sigourney's poem and the "triumphant" murder in Bobbett's illustration. Many critics—including Mary Hershberger, Karen L. Kilcup, Tiya Miles, and Angela Calcaterra—have pointed to Sigourney's commitment to Native American literature and activism. In *Traits of the Aborigines of America* (1822), for example, Sigourney converts Indigenous tales into blank verse urging Native Americans to convert to Christianity. In her foundational study of nineteenth-century women's literature and environmental activism, *Fallen Forests*, Karen L. Kilcup reminds us that Sigourney publicly "supported Indian assimilation, including religious conversion."[81] *Traits of the Aborigines of America*,

POETESS AS PARATEXT

Angela Calcaterra argues, was widely read and circulated among members of the Cherokee and Choctaw Nations.[82] Popular poems like "Indian Names" (1834) and "Indian Girl's Burial" (1838) directly addressed Jacksonian America and the consequent Trial of Tears, which forcefully displaced approximately 100,000 Native Americans between 1830 and 1850. Beyond her literary output, Sigourney was famously a part of a white, middle-class, woman-led nineteenth-century movement that opposed the removal of Indigenous peoples from their lands. Mary Hershberger writes that Sigourney helped to organize "the first national women's petition campaign and flooded Congress with antiremoval petitions, making a bold claim for women's place in national political discourse."[83] Sigourney's personal investment in Indigenous rights and literature stemmed from her proximity to Cherokees and Christian Missionaries in Hartford, Connecticut. As Tiya Miles posits, "only Sigourney had had previous, extensive contact with Cherokees, and Missionaries; only Sigourney had a personal letter from a Cherokee woman protesting removal ten years prior."[84] So, why does Bonner place one of the leading popular figures in Native American rights and anti-removal next to an image of anti-Indigenous persecution and removal? For an editor concerned with the family-appropriate image and messaging of his story paper, this jarring juxtaposition in the *Ledger*'s printscape absolved readers from the moral corruption of *The Refugees*, providing moral equilibrium on the page that allowed readers to enjoy Bennett's popular and sensational tale with impunity.

Thematic clashes like the one above grew to be a trend in the *Ledger*. On February 21, 1857, a month after Sigourney's "Fair Traffic," Bonner printed another hermeneutic poem, "The Best Investment," encouraging Protestant ideals like generosity and munificence. "The Best Investment" begins with a biblical epigraph: "'He Hath dispersed abroad, / He hath given to the poor: / His righteousness endureth forever'" (Psalms 112:9).[85] Throughout the body of the poem, the speaker provides examples of munificence:

> Give to the poor thy bread,
> Clothe the uncover'd form,
> Throw shelter o'er the homeless head,
> That shrinks before the storm:
> So shall the prayers that grateful rise
> Win blessings for thee from the skies. (1–6)

In the opening stanza, the speaker insinuates that munificence on earth will be repaid in Heaven. In other words, God rewards earthly generosity with "blessings" (6). Sigourney's speaker goes on to encourage readers to "Disperse thine alms abroad . . . / And thus shall gain accrue to thee, / When Heaven's dread books shall opened be" (19, 23–24). The poem's message of "righteousness" and munificence clashes with its violent and graphic paratextual context, as Figure 1.2 shows.

Figure 1.2 "The Scout and the Indian Sentinel," *The New York Ledger*, February 21, 1857. Public domain.

"The Best Investment" appears above an installment of Bennett's *The Refugees* and next to Bobbett's illustration "The Scout and the Indian Sentinel," which, once again, features a violent scene of Pete the scout and a Native American. Bobbett's illustration corresponds to a section in Bennett's installment where Pete attempts to retrieve a boat a Native American stole from him and Eden in an earlier part of the story. Bennett's description of Pete's murderous strike is long and detailed. The narrator states:

> As the back of the Indian was not toward the scout, it required less caution of position to steal upon him unaware; and gradually straightening himself up to his full height, and clinching his tomahawk with his right hand and his knife with left, Peter glided forward, with a step that Tarquin might have envied, till he stood within a foot of his foe; when, raising his tomahawk with a cool deliberation, till he had poised it far back and taken a fair aim, he brought it forward and down with all his might. It struck the head of the savage with a dull sound, and buried itself in his brain. For a moment he stood as if nothing had hurt him; and then, without a word, a groan, or a sigh, he sunk down heavily, a bleeding corpse. The moment his enemy had fallen, Peter made sure of him, by plunging his knife into his heart; then whipping it out.[86]

The narrator's description of Pete's murder of the Native American reads like a sensational news report of crime scene. Details like the "dull sound" of the tomahawk and Pete's craniectomy are indulgent and gratuitous scenes of gore and murder that amplify the serial's own sensationalism. Bennett's narrator does not condemn Pete's acts of violence, however. Instead, the narrator portrays Pete as fearless, that is, "a man as totally devoid of that emotion, passion, or sensation known as fear."[87] Although the narrator does not denounce Pete, Sigourney's byline, as the defender of Indigenous rights, might have prompted readers to question Pete's fearlessness. The poem literally looms over the serial, reminding readers of the not-so-distant history of Indian removal, provoking them to make up their own minds about who the villains and heroes of Bennett's story are.

The paratextual juxtapositions between Sigourney's hermeneutic poems and Bennett's *The Refugee* lend agency to Sigourney's byline, subverting notions of the poetess as an idle observer. In her paratextual study of middle-class women readers' desires in the *Lady's Newspaper*, Kathryn Ledbetter reads thematic clashes between articles about bonnets and news about violence "as a textual displacement, an irregular, anti-thematic juxtaposition and collision of the traditional feminine domestic sphere with the masculine imperialist world."[88] In the *Ledger*'s printscape, textual displacements between Sigourney's poems and Bennett's serial enable the poetess as an agentive force in reframing how readers engage with the story. These poems play up readers' Christian-inspired morality, calling into question the serial's sensationalization of Indigenous murder and removal.

The thematic transactions and transitions between Sigourney's hermeneutic poems and their paratext allow us better to understand how Bonner's strategic placement of her poems created discursive connections with Ingraham's and Bennett's serials. In the case of Ingraham's *Sarah Percival*, Sigourney's signature elevates Ingraham's relatively unknown byline to that of a notable writer. At the same time, the nearness of Sigourney's "Leave Time" to Ingraham's serial enables readers to make intertextual connections between themes of lost love, hubris, and home that could only exist in the *Ledger*'s printscape. Bennett's story and Bobbett's illustrations portray the gruesome murders of Native Americans while Sigourney's "Fair Traffic" and "The Best Investment" uphold the virtues of munificence and charity, a jarring juxtaposition that asks readers to consider the rights and humanity of Indigenous people.

Less than a year after their publication in the *Ledger*, Sigourney collected a number of her hermeneutic poems for a popular book entitled *The Daily Counsellor* (1858). The collection was a kind of private scripture, modelled on psalms—in which she provided a meditation on scriptural verse—one for each day of the year. In the preface to her collection, Sigourney describes the poems as "simple parodies or amplifications of the sacred precept selected for daily use throughout the year."[89] These poems, she claims, invite all age categories: they "have no exclusive reference to any peculiar period of life. They seek alike the friendship of youth, maturity, and age."[90] Sigourney intended for these poems to be for "systematic and devotional use" and, citing Luther, claimed that a single verse of hermeneutic poetry "is sufficient for the spiritual meditation of a day."[91] These poems were a way for Christian readers to connect to spirit by the act of reading, "committing to memory the same passage of Divine truth, which its lyrical echoes repeat."[92] As seen in the examples above, these lyrical echoes take the form of biblical epigraphs in the *Ledger* that are the source of Sigourney's "Divine truth." These "Divine truth[s]" are echoed throughout the poems' stanzas via repetition and in the poems' paratexts as they complement and collide with serials and illustrations. The original publication of Sigourney's hermeneutic poems in the *Ledger* helps us see how Bonner turns the paratext into a worthy catalyst for poetic inspiration and spiritual reflection.

As we saw above, a poetics of paratextuality displays how Sigourney's Christian didacticism could have complemented and interrupted the moral attitude of neighboring serials and illustrations. The following section proposes more flexible paratextual readings centralizing the cross-genre pastoral writing of Alice Cary, another "poetess" that Bonner frequently published in an effort to cater to a family audience. A cross-genre (or hybrid genre) is a variety of compositions that fuse themes and elements from two or more different genres. To better understand the collaborative essence of Cary's cross-genre columns,

I focus on two types of paratexts: Bonner's paratext of serials and advice columns as well as Cary's own usage of poetic citations as paratext. Cary's *Ledger* columns present intertextual cross-genre forms that display textual transactions and transitions between prose and poetry, exhibiting important links between pastoralism and working-class women that resist gendered cultural and aesthetic structures.

Alice Cary's Cross-Genre Pastoralism

A poetics of paratextuality allows us to study the function of Alice Cary's columns as part of the opposition between nature and civilization in the *Ledger*. Often thematically complementing and interrupting the serials of Emerson Bennett, Sylvanus Cobb Jr., and Caroline Ingraham that appeared in the *Ledger* (as we saw with Sigourney's poems), Cary's columns offered urban readers self-nurture in suburban environments as an antidote to the malaise of city life. These columns provided readers with a space for reflection and a reprieve from sensationalist serials and the city of New York. On the surface, Cary's columns fulfilled conventional genteel and Romantic roles in the *Ledger* that gave readers the impression of serenity, purity, and tranquility—the typeface of the pastoral. Below the surface, however, her cross-genre columns were feminist rebukes of patriarchal cultural norms, including feminine youth and working-class life.

Alice Cary and her sisters, Phoebe and Elmina, were born and raised in the rural village of Mount Pleasant, Ohio. Cary's parents, Robert and Elizabeth Cary, were pious Universalist farmers with liberal and reformist political views. Like many young writers of their generation, Alice and Phoebe moved to the city of New York to escape the tedium of rural life and to pursue a career in writing. They arrived in the big city in 1850 and, soon after, the Philadelphia publisher Moss and Brother printed their first joint volume of poems, *The Poems of Alice and Phoebe Cary*. In New York, their literary labor often went unrewarded. Horace Greeley, who shared a long friendship of religion and faith with the sisters, recalled on their arrival in the city:

> I do not know at whose suggestion they resolved to migrate to this city, and attempt to live here by literary labor; it surely was not mine. If my judgement was ever invoked, I am sure I must have responded that the hazard seemed to me too great.[93]

The city presented dire prospects, but the Cary sisters were not defeated. Although they struggled financially the entire time they lived in New York, they made a living writing for many weeklies and monthly magazines, including *New York Weekly*, *New York Independent*, *Packard's Monthly*, *Atlantic Monthly*, and the *Ledger*, which, Greeley proclaimed, paid more than "*all* the magazines and weeklies issued from this city."[94] Within a short time after 1856,

Alice and Phoebe purchased a house on 53 East 20th Street, which they owned until the time of their deaths in 1871.[95] In this house, they held weekly social and literary gatherings where they hosted the likes of Greeley, Elizabeth Cady Stanton, P. T. Barnum, and other celebrities of the day.

By the time Alice started writing for Bonner's *Ledger* in 1856, she had established herself as an esteemed poet and novelist. Alice embraced the city of New York. She admired its tall buildings and crowded streets. Yet her affection for childhood pastoral scenes stayed with her throughout her life. Five years after Cary's death, Mary Clemmer Ames, a journalist, poet, and close friend of Alice, writes in *A Memorial of Alice and Phoebe Cary* (1876) that "[e]ach sister, within the blinds of a city house, used to shut her eyes and listen till she thought she heard the rustle of the cherry-tree on the old roof, and smelled again the sweet-brier under the window."[96] Alice's cross-genre *Ledger* writing captures memories of her pastoral past, which for many of the *Ledger*'s readers were figurative reprieves from the hustle and bustle of city life.

In her study of nineteenth-century portrayals of domestic men, Maura D'Amore argues that mid-century readers of periodicals sought escape from the world of "urban apartments, offices, and garrets" in writings about suburbanized and pastoralized domestic landscapes.[97] While few nineteenth-century city-dwellers could afford literal retreats from the confines of the metropolis, many sought figurative getaways from the city through the pastoral and suburban settings in periodical literature. Readers of Bonner's *Ledger* regularly encountered Cary's pastoral writing as potential metaphorical Romantic escapes from the cityscape. But Cary's writing did more than deliver pastoral reprieves to readers. Her *Ledger* columns also resisted the patriarchal aestheticization of the pastoral and the rural. The pastoral for Cary is anti-patriarchal. It is a space for women to denounce social standards of beauty and youth. It is pure and beautiful not because it is young and youthful but because it is full of experience and knowledge, traits that she associates with feminine aesthetics. Ultimately, Cary's cross-genre pastoral writing in the *Ledger* delivers readers outside of the city into a pastoral setting that definitively rejects patriarchal forms of Romanticism.

Turning to the pages of the *Ledger* means accounting for the ostensible chasm between nature writing and the urban streets of the city of New York, the *Ledger*'s place of publication. In the years of the Industrial Revolution, societal notions of agrarianism ("the garden") collided with the ideals of the industrial age ("the machine"), a collision evident in the poetry of the time.[98] In Leo Marx's scenario, Cary's pastoral writing is "the garden" situated within the industrial machinery of the *Ledger*, that is, the predominantly sensationalist columns of serials that represent the age of industrialization in urban settings. In the mid-nineteenth century, the popularity of pastoral Romanticism was a reaction to the rapid speed of industrialization and urbanization. As Mark Coeckelbergh argues in his study of Romanticism and technology, mid-century pastoral Romanticism may not have been totally opposed to industrialization "but had an ambiguous relationship to it: the machine is something that disrupts the pastoral idyll, but it is also a sublime sign of the mastery over nature."[99] As a byproduct of a growing industrialist economy, the city reminded citizens of the failures of urbanization: poverty, disease, and the city's criminal underbelly. This vision of the urban world was at odds with the stereotypical serenity and simplicity of the rural. James S. Duncan and David R. Lambert claim:

> Most urban Americans during the second quarter of the nineteenth century held a romantic view of the rural as people living in harmony with each other and the land. Such images were fostered by a continuing literary tradition of pastoral romanticism.[100]

With the binary classification of the city and the country, as well as the consequent popularity of literary pastoral Romanticism as an escape, the celebration of nature in poetry and prose came into its own in mid-nineteenth-century periodicals.

Characterized by scholars as a latter-day Romantic, Cary is not a nature poet in the tradition of Walt Whitman, Ralph Waldo Emerson, and Henry David Thoreau. In her study of nineteenth-century women's environmental writing, Kilcup claims that, in fact, most women writers were unlike the transcendentalists:

> Unlike male writers . . . who regarded nature as a means to individual self-development . . . who understood [nature] as an object for contemplating the sublime, women in this period more often perceived "nature" and "the environment" within a complex framework of embodied and social experiences.[101]

Cary's pastoral writing is less legible today as nature writing than Thoreau's and Emerson's in part because, unlike these esteemed transcendentalists, a great number of Cary's nature writings appeared in periodicals alongside a trove of paratextual items. Furthermore, Cary is not solely concerned with communicating individual self-development (a trope of canonical transcendentalist thought) but rather a collective improvement of women. She achieves this in the *Ledger* through cross-genre columns that feature intertextual pastoral and rural scenes where women refute and negotiate the values of patriarchal society.

On December 27, 1856, Bonner printed an advice column by Cary titled "Looking Back" which halfway through features a poem by Cary herself. "Looking Back" explores the perceived pleasures of youth as resistance to the stigma of aging. The column's meditative tone is paratextually framed by two items. The first is the third installment of Caroline Ingraham's serial *Sarah Percival*, depicting a scene where Kate Percival, under the guise of Sarah Percival, meets

Mrs. Hamilton (Sarah's mother) for the first time. Mrs. Hamilton, intuitively suspicious of Kate, reflects on her long-lost child: "I am thinking of my child who is as a stranger to me."[102] The second paratextual frame is a short item titled "Life" that advises readers on the importance of "reflecting on the duration of life."[103] The author of this column counsels, "Observe, as we advance in life . . . how our interest ceases in all the objects before us."[104] Seemingly in conversation with both paratextual items which concern a reflection on the passing of time, Cary's column encourages her readers to look toward their present existence and not the past:

> The spring with her blossoms is not brighter than the summer with her leafs [sic] and pleasant shadows, and the autumn is welcome as either, as in sober gladness she comes with red-cheeked apples and field of ripe corn— the sound of dropping nuts, and the gleam of gold spread along the broad aisles of the woods, and heaped in ridges where the rabbit may make her house, and the winds play hide and seek. Even the winter with his clouds, his stormy strength, and all the curious masonry of his snows, is, in his time, beautiful; and we grow to love him, as much for his icicles and his bare boughs as for his genial fires. All pleasure does not die with youth. We have then, to be sure, a crop of flowers which will not be repeated for us; but the full harvest—the sober certainty of waking bliss—comes with riper years . . . it is never too late for the best things of life.[105]

Cary's anthropomorphized setting of "red-cheeked apples and field of ripe corn" and "stormy strength and . . . curious masonry" transfers the reader from the cityscape—the *Ledger*'s natural habitat—to a bountiful pastoralism. Here, the reader encounters an alternative, restorative Nature that does not idealize youth but rather "the sober certainty of waking bliss" that comes with age. As a Romantic episteme, youth is often characterized as an idealized form of innocence, a beckoning nostalgic imaginary of a more perfect past. In the adjacent *Sarah Percival* column, we see this type of Romantic youth in Mrs. Hamilton's idealized memory of Sarah Percival:

> Her child whom she had forsaken. Her child whom she had, as it were, never, seen. Her child who had never been really loved till now. Her child from whose eyes the father's soul had looked out in infancy, and would look out now, to pierce her faltering heart with a thousand wounds.[106]

Guilt-driven as her memory of Sarah appears, Mrs. Hamilton's nostalgic imaginary is emblematic of a simpler time when she was a good mother and wife. Cary's *Ledger* column, in part, discredits this stereotype of patriarchal Romanticism, shifting one of its central epistemes from youth to the mindful clarity that "comes with riper years."[107] This epistemic shift is not simply an attack on aesthetic convention. It is also a rebuke of cultural standards of beauty and knowledge that acutely impact women and girls. Delinking youth from beauty, or rather linking beauty to maturity, as Cary does above, destabilizes nineteenth-century patriarchal standards of beauty that base it on youth or youthful physical traits. A paratextual reading of Cary's column provides feminist alternatives for youth in Ingraham's serial that are liberating and not strictly patriarchal. As a character haunted by her past, a past intimately tied to her identity as a mother and wife, Mrs. Hamilton's fate is linked to the patriarchal understanding of youth. It is, after all, the male gaze tied to her husband, the father of her child, that "pierces her faltering heart with a thousand wounds."[108]

Cary's cross-genre columns also offer readers genre-based escapes that move them from prose to poetry. Poetry, Cary claims, gives "expression to my own feeling in reference to growing old."[109] Fittingly, "Looking Back" concludes with a title-less poem, which in Lydia Maria Child's anthology *Looking Toward Sunset* (1865) appears under the title "To One Who Wished Me Six-Teen Years Old."[110] The poem is a dramatic monologue between an aging woman speaker and a young man who complains about the woman's maturity. Midway through the poem, the speaker admits:

> Nay, done with youth are my desires—
> Life has no pain I fear to meet;
> Experience with its awful fires
> Melts knowledge to a welding heat. (17–20)

The stanza shows that the speaker's desires have changed. She denounces her youthful desires and instead longs for a type of a posteriori knowledge that breaks away from gendered stereotypes about feminine youthful beauty. Although "experience" burns with its "awful fires," this epistemic blaze also "Melts knowledge to a welding heat," granting the speaker the ability to fuse and forge how she sees herself (20). In the following stanza, the speaker pleads with her "gentle friend" to quit grieving over her age: "that I am at the time of day, / When white hairs come, and heart-beats send / No blushes through the cheeks astray" (25, 26–28). Here, the speaker's maturity and experience guard her against youthful naivety. In the final stanza and conclusion of the column, the "gentle friend" more clearly becomes a stand-in for the forces of patriarchal Romanticism, which the speaker outwardly rejects:

> For could you mold my destiny
> As clay, within your loving hand,
> I'd leave my youth's sweet company.
> And suffer back to where I stand. (29–32)

The speaker imagines her interlocutor's hand molding her fate and chooses to "leave [her] youth's sweet company," a euphemism for the abandonment of patriarchal Romantic ideals of male dominance (31). The last phrase in the poem, "I stand," is a proclamation of the speaker's subjectivity, her will to mold her own destiny out of the clutches of masculinist dominance (32). At the same time, this "I" is also a declaration of Cary's own voice. She was an unmarried thirty-six-year-old when "Looking Back" was published in the *Ledger*. Thus, the poem that gives "expression to [her] feeling in reference to growing old" speaks to Cary's personal experience with the patriarchal pressures of marriage and child-rearing associated with a youthful female body.[111]

Through transitions and transactions between prose and poetry, Cary's cross-genre *Ledger* columns are not only about questions of youth and beauty. They also deal with agrarian labor and work ethic that intertextually gesture to other publications, poems, and poets. This type of poetics of paratextuality leaps beyond the *Ledger*'s page, showing us the type of work that Cary herself does in assembling and sometimes disassembling her cross-genre writing. On January 10, 1857, Bonner published Cary's column "Work," a treatise about the privileges and satisfactions of work life which weaves Romantic imagery and language into a hybrid column of prose and poetry. Cary's "Work" was clearly inspired by a previous publication of the same title for the *National Magazine* in November 1854, which is heavily edited at the sentence and paragraph levels for the *Ledger*.[112] The changes between the two publications are so vast that they constitute a new version in Bonner's story paper. For example, the version printed in the *Ledger* is only one column in length while the *National Magazine*'s version takes up six and a half columns. The version printed in the *Ledger* recycles and rearranges quotes from Elizabeth Barrett Browning and Samuel T. Coleridge found in the *National Magazine*'s version, which I get to below. Cary even reuses her own poems, including "Homesick" and "Nobility."[113] For example, the first and fourth lines of the epigraph to "Work" are from her poem "Homesick," depicting an inviting Romantic image of georgic felicity:

> The gold-headed wheat-field a-slanting,
> The vine and the tree,
> The sweet-smelling earth at the planting—
> How pleasant they be. (1–4)[114]

"Homesick" was first published in a short-lived, Cincinnati-based magazine called *The Parlor Magazine* (1853–55) that Cary edited while living in Cincinnati between 1853 and 1855.[115] The recycled lines allowed her to regenerate, as if were, the rest of the poem for both the *National Magazine* and the *Ledger*.

Determining whether it was Bonner or Cary who edited "Work," locating their editorial roles, is conceptually elusive. As Jim Casey and Sarah H. Salter remind us in their introduction to *American Periodicals*' forum on "Locating the Practices of Editors in Multi-Ethnic Periodicals," "[i]t is frequently difficult to attribute the editing of a given text, issue, or publication to any single individual."[116] We have no correspondence between Cary and Bonner discussing this publication. They were "close friends" living in the same city, which allowed ample opportunity for them to discuss editorial choices in person.[117] Instead of ascribing the edits to one, it is perhaps more helpful to imagine the ways Cary and Bonner collaborated in the publication of "Work." Bonner and Cary were both experienced in editing and rewriting columns. Cary edited *The Parlor Magazine* (as noted) and wrote cross-genre columns that employ techniques of textually abridging and editing, while Bonner, as editor, had to regularly solicit, curate, and fit columns on the page. Cary and Bonner's collaborative editorship of "Work" is encoded not just in the shape the column had to take to fit in the page but also in the text's content.

Although both the *National Magazine*'s and the *Ledger*'s versions of "Work" are a pastoral meditation on farm labor and the labor of writing, the *Ledger*'s version emphasizes correlations between labor and poets. For example, the epigraph's "sweet-smelling" and "pleasant" Romantic imagery shifts to a philosophical meditation in the prose portion of the *Ledger* column: "'We have a brave world to sin and suffer in', says some one of the poets; and it seems to me we have also a brave world to labor and to rest in; and it seems to me further, that labor is our best rest."[118] The words "of the poets" are added to the *Ledger*'s publication ascribing the quoted lines to "the poets" and not simply to "some one," as done in the *National Magazine*. In Cary's chiasmatic structure, "Sin and suffer[ing]" run parallel to "labor and rest."[119] This parallelism, along with the column's pastoral epigraph, encourages readers to generate connections between unlike concepts, compelling us, for example, to think broadly about the behaviors that we rehearse in nature or in "a brave world."[120] Furthermore, Cary complicates the dialectical relationship between "labor" and "rest" by redefining their connotations and rewards. She cites Elizabeth Barrett Browning to make this point clearer: "'Work', says Mrs. Browning, 'is better than what we work to get', and I wish from my heart the people of this generation could be made to believe it."[121] Browning's quotation provides another connection, this time between "work" and what "we work to get."[122] Ultimately, for Cary, true fulfillment comes from knowing that "we have originated some good" in nature; and labor, regardless of what kind, is a way of achieving that.[123] Labor, Cary emphasizes, is not just any type of rest. It is "our best rest" from its antithesis: idleness.[124]

Idleness, for Cary, is a type of anti-nature. It is a stance against the natural movement of the environment and a disruption of society because idleness unsettles the roles people play in their ecosystems. Later in the column, Cary warns readers against idleness. Our basic natures, she says, "oblige us to do."[125] Doing is a primordial obligation, the inherent characteristic that connects people

55

to one another. Those who disdain work will learn that "we may fold our hands, if we choose, but avenging aches and pains will come upon us, and ultimately the idleness will become the hardest work."[126] Idleness is importantly intertextual in Cary's column, that is, it is a concept that she explores via citational links between "some one of the poets."[127] Midway through the column, Cary integrates an excerpt from Samuel Taylor Coleridge's poem "Work Without Hope" (1827):

> All Nature seems at work—slugs leave their lair,
> The bees are stirring—birds are on the wing—
> And Winter slumbering in the open air
> Wears on his face a dream of Spring!
> And I the while, the sole unbusy thing
> Nor honey make, nor pair, nor build, nor sing. (1–6)[128]

Coleridge's poem invokes Cary's own feelings about the imprudence of idleness and the immanence of labor. Like the bees and winter in Coleridge's poem, the organic principles of labor (in the context of both Romantic poetry and pastoral imagery) have the potential to be immanent. Coleridge's concept of work is collaborative purposeful action, a manifestation of the jobs nature assigns to all. Through Coleridge, Cary summons a speaker who fails to contribute to the divinity of nature, lamenting an "unbusy" existence while "All Nature seems at work" (5, 1). Cary's work too is dynamic and divine. However, in the context of her pastoral Romanticism, work is not merely a Romantic abstraction. Cary is talking about real work and its relationship to workers as well as her own work as a writer. Work is an experience that connects the harmony of nature to the best that people can do: "labor is our best rest" and "work is better than what we work to get."[129] Thus, work for Cary, is a teleological becoming of purposeful action that reflects in the laborer the movements of nature.

The lyric subjects in Coleridge's poem and Cary's column are contained by the same epistemological bonds of the natural world, the fact that all things live, work, and die without exception. Toward the end of her *Ledger* column, Cary claims that "death will work in us, for work is going on in the leaf that rots, the same as in the rose that blooms."[130] In this zeugmatic line, work is something that is "going on in" the process of life and death. Thus, work is not simply a part of nature for Cary. It is nature at work. Laborers, Cary tells us, should be inspired by the immanence of what they do, and find pleasure in their work, that is, in their own nature and not simply in the product of their labor. In "Work," Cary's transitions and transactions between prose and poetry are an attempt do more with texts. This doing too is work that Cary manifested onto the page. It is collaborative labor between her voice and Bonner's as well as those of Coleridge and Browning that polyvocally articulates the universal immanence of something most of *Ledger*'s working-class readers did, which is to work.

Cary's cross-genre poems in the *Ledger* bend the conventions of periodical genres. In "Looking Back" and "Work," poetry and prose work together rhetorically and aesthetically to convey not just messages but cultural expressions of youth and the pastoral, respectively. Cary's writing is complex, exhibiting socially and economically minded concerns that reflect and articulate changes in mid-century America. The Romantic pastoralism of her columns, the implied public, and personae of Cary's speakers do not deprive her work of political import and social consciousness. Kilcup argues that the reluctance of critics to consider the work of periodical poets like Cary in the tradition of women's nature or environmental writing "may emerge from the characterization of [these poets'] work[s] as entirely sentimental and the denigration of sentimental attitudes toward nature and pastoralism."[131] Cary's poems are not simply Romantic abstractions of genteel culture. The natural discourse and settings in Cary's pastoral writing function as tools for resisting culturally gendered and classist conventions like nineteenth-century double standards, female objectification, and labor. While Cary's brand of pastoralism in the *Ledger* may have depicted scenes of felicity in nature, her pastoralism also encapsulates a feminist aesthetic that, most importantly, is pro-woman and pro-working class.

Cary may not have perceived divinity in nature as Emerson does in "Two Rivers," Whitman in "Give Me the Splendid Silent Sun," or Thoreau in *Walden*. As a spiritual individualist, Cary incorporates pastoral and nature imagery in writing about beauty standards, labor, and the female body in her cross-genre column in the *Ledger*. Instead of corroborating legible forms of patriarchal Romanticism as Whitman does in "Song of Myself" through a masculinized poetics of war and violence, Cary's generic hybridization of poetry and prose is a synthesis of nature and the city that carves out space for the social experience and consciousness of working-class women.

Conclusion

This chapter leads to several preliminary conclusions about how Sigourney's and Cary's *Ledger* contributions shaped the cultural image of Robert Bonner's *New York Ledger*. Often viewed as poetesses during and after their lifetimes, mostly for being women and less for finessing cultural stereotypes about women writers, Sigourney and Cary evince how pervasive and integral the poetess persona was to the paratextual gaps in Bonner's story paper. The poetess personae that Sigourney and Cary complicated in their *Ledger* writing allowed Bonner to market his story paper as "instructive" and "good" for the entire family. Sigourney's hermeneutic poems, in particular, represent a domestic vision of true womanhood in the *Ledger*, a vision that often thematically interacts with the story paper's serials and illustrations. Sigourney's periodical verses endowed the *Ledger*'s readers with biblical teachings regarding usury, hubris, death, and munificence which thematically complemented and clashed with the *Ledger*'s popular sensationalist serials about love, hate, crime, and murder.

Although Cary was also deemed a poetess, her *Ledger* writing was different from Sigourney's. Giving her own shape to the genre of the periodical column by crossing genres, Cary's *Ledger* writing complicates how we think about paratextuality entirely. While her writing is, of course, in paratextual dialogue with other items on the page, Cary is also hyper aware of the genres, poets, and poems that she integrates in her own writing. Cary's cross-genre columns are multi-generic, intertextual, and polyvocal in form and content. They capture the opposition between nature and civilization, furnishing Bonner's paper with a pastoralism otherwise left out of the predominantly sensational columns of serials and illustrations that represent the age of industrialization in urban settings.

Writing into existence speakers that embody characteristics of the poetess persona, Sigourney's and Cary's writings are poetic oases in the *Ledger*'s desert of sensational serials and illustrations. Their poems are textual gaps as well as bridges between the narrative flow of serials that shaped the *Ledger*'s public image as a family paper. Both poets helped the *Ledger* garner major success. They did this while at same time maneuvering through the public sphere via writing that both resisted and at times promoted the tenets of true womanhood. Sigourney and Cary played by the cultural rules, as it were, of the cult of true womanhood while at the same time bending and defying some of its cultural virtues of piety and submission, which often deemed women unsuitable for the public sphere.

We should continue distinguishing the poetess persona from the women writers who wrote them into existence to understand how successful these writers were in maneuvering through cultural and social expectations of the publishing world. At the same time, we should not erase or diminish their personal bodies and subjectivities. We must acknowledge that they were individuals who understood the risks of publishing under their signatures but did so anyway because they had something valuable to say about themselves and society.

While Bonner contracted and paid celebrity poets to garner readers, other editors, as we will see in the following chapter, grew accustomed to publishing unauthorized reprints. In the same year that Bonner commenced the publication of his popular story paper in New York, 2,500 miles away, a seventeen-year-old frontier editor in Los Angeles began collecting Spanish-language poems to assemble alongside a bilingual paratext of local news, ads, and editorials. In this printscape, a poetics of paratextuality is a visible form of editorializing where reprint poems are changed into new poems for new publics.

Notes

1. Isaac Errett, "The Newspaper and Periodical Press," *The Christian Quarterly* 2 (January 1870): 67.
2. Errett, "Newspaper and Periodical Press," 67.

3. Matthew Schneirov, *The Dream of a New Social Order: Popular Magazines in America 1893–1914* (New York: Columbia University Press, 1994), 97.
4. This ad appeared in the *Muskogee Phoenix* in Muskogee, Oklahoma on November 22, 1888; *The Wichita Weekly Express* from Wichita in Kansas on November 24, 1888; *The Cerrillos Rustler* in New Mexico on November 30, 1888; and *The Princeton Bric-A Brac* (1890).
5. In 1859, Bonner published Charles Dickens's "Hunted Down," the first American publication Dickens wrote exclusively for an American periodical; from 1858 to 1861, William Cullen Bryant published a series of poems in the *Ledger*, including "The Swallow" (February 1858), "The Cloud on the Way" (February 1860), and "The Constellations" (August 1861). William Cullen Bryant, *Poems by William Cullen Bryant: Collected and Arranged by the Author* (New York: D. Appleton and Company, 1854), xxv. Erin A. Smith claims that in 1868, Bonner paid Henry Ward Beecher $30,000 in advance for *Norwood*. Erin A. Smith, "Religion and Popular Print Culture," *The Oxford History of Popular Print Culture, Volume Six: US Popular Print Culture 1860–1920*, ed. Christine Bold (New York: Oxford University Press, 2012), 285; Henry Wadsworth Longfellow's "The Hanging Crane" appeared in the *Ledger* on February 1874. Henry Wadsworth Longfellow, *The Letters of Henry Wadsworth Longfellow, Volume V: 1866–1874* (Cambridge, MA: Harvard University Press, 1982), 714.
6. In Christopher Looby's paratextual analysis of Southworth's *Hidden Hand*, published in the *Ledger* in 1859 (a decisive moment for the question of slavery in the US), he argues that "serialization offered her particular strategic opportunities in addressing her readers, and she was adept at exploiting the immediate paratextual environment of the *New York Ledger* to her distinct advantage . . . As a writer she carefully exploited the material circumstances of seriality and used them according to her authorial purposes; she also cooperated tacitly—and also (I will argue) deliberately—with the conventions and editorial qualities of the *New York Ledger*." Christopher Looby, "Southworth and Seriality," *Nineteenth-Century Literature* 59, no. 2 (2004): 183.
7. Joyce W. Warren, *Fanny Fern: An Independent Woman* (New Brunswick: Rutgers University Press, 1992), 58.
8. Warren, *Fanny Fern*, 58.
9. Bonnie Carr O'Neill, *Literary Celebrity and Public Life in the Nineteenth-Century United States* (Athens: University of Georgia Press, 2017), 3.
10. Páraic Finnerty, "Women's Transatlantic Poetic Network," *A History of Nineteenth-Century American Women's Poetry*, ed. Jennifer Putzi and Alexandra Socarides (Cambridge: Cambridge University Press, 2017), 176.
11. Paula Bernat Bennett, "Was Sigourney a Poetess? The Aesthetics of Victorian Plenitude in Lydia Sigourney's Poetry," *Comparative American Studies: An International Journal* 5, no. 3 (2007): 271, quoting Yopie Prins, *The Victorian Sappho* (Princeton: Princeton University Press, 1999), 226.
12. Bennett, "Was Sigourney a Poetess?," 269.
13. Jane Welsh Carlyle, *Jane Welsh Carlyle: Letters to Her Family, 1839–1863* (Garden City: Double, Page & Company, 1924), 78.
14. James Cephas Derby, *Fifty Years Authors, Books and Publishers* (New York: G. W. Carleton & Co., Publishers, 1884), 253.

15. Eliza Richards, *Gender and the Poetics of Reception in Poe's Circle* (Cambridge: Cambridge University Press, 2004), 65.
16. Mary De Jong, "Lines From a Partly Published Drama: The Romance of Frances Sargent Osgood and Edgar Allan Poe," *Patrons and Protégées: Gender, Friendship, and Writing in Nineteenth-Century America* (New Brunswick: Rutgers University Press, 1988), 35.
17. Richards, *Gender*, 94.
18. Edgar Allan Poe, "Review of *Poems*, by Frances S. Osgood," *Broadway Journal* 2, no. 23 (December 13, 1845).
19. Richards, *Gender*, 94.
20. Richards, *Gender*, 94.
21. Joe Moran, *Star Authors: Literary Celebrity in America* (London: Pluto Press, 2000), 4.
22. Linda Hughes, "What the 'Wellesley Index' Left Out: Why Poetry Matters to Periodical Studies," *Victorian Periodicals Review* 40, no. 2 (2007): 94.
23. McGill, *Traffic in Poems*, 5.
24. Kirsten Silva Gruesz, *Ambassadors of Culture: The Transamerican Origins of Latino Writing* (Princeton: Princeton University Press, 2002), 21.
25. Errett, "Newspaper and Periodical Press," 67.
26. Parton, *Life of Horace Greeley*, 555.
27. Parton, *Life of Horace Greeley*, 555.
28. Woodland Millie, "The Voice of my Heat-Harp," *The New York Ledger*, February 9, 1856; Mrs. M. J. Robertson, "The Serenade," *The New York Ledger*, February 9, 1856.
29. William Cullen Bryant, *The Letters of William Cullen Bryant Volume IV, 1858–1864* (New York: Fordham University Press, 2019), 174.
30. Amelia E. Barr, *All the Days of My Life: An Autobiography* (New York: D. Appleton and Company, 1913), 194.
31. Will T. Hale, "Authors and the Mighty Dollar," *Christian Advocate*, July 20, 1913.
32. Junius Henri Browne, *The Great Metropolis: A Mirror of New York* (Hartford: American Publishing Company, 1869), 402.
33. Henry Wadsworth Longfellow, *The Poetical Works of Henry Wadsworth Longfellow: Volume III* (Boston: Houghton, Mifflin and Company, 1886), 179.
34. Barbara R. Clark, "Tennyson Across the Atlantic," *Tennyson Research Bulletin* 5, no. 1 (1987): 2.
35. James Playsted Woods, *The Story of Advertising* (New York: The Ronald Press Company, 1958), 161.
36. Errett, "Newspaper and Periodical Press," 67.
37. The poems in this chapter are not included in Gary Kelly's important anthology, *Lydia Sigourney: Selected Poetry and Prose* (Ontario: Broadview Editions, 2008).
38. "September Birthdays," *Journal of Education*, August 26, 1897.
39. Putzi, *Fair Copy*, 23.
40. Ann Douglass, *The Feminization of American Culture* (New York: Straus and Giroux, 1977), 203.
41. Putzi, *Fair Copy*, 34.
42. Mary Louise Kete, *Sentimental Collaborations: Mourning and Middle-Class Identity in Nineteenth-Century America* (Durham, NC: Duke University Press, 2000), 122.

43. Richards, *Gender*, 67.
44. Richards, *Gender*, 68.
45. Bryan Sinche, "Lydia Sigourney's Sailors and the Limits of Sentiment," *Legacy: A Journal of American Women Writers* 29, no. 1 (2012): 63.
46. Mary Louise Kete and Elizabeth Petrino, *Lydia Sigourney: Critical Essays and Cultural Views* (Boston: University of Massachusetts Press, 2018), 6.
47. Jane Donawerth, "Hannah More, Lydia Sigourney, and the Creation of a Women's Tradition of Rhetoric," *Rhetoric, the Polis, and the Global Village*, ed. C. Jan Swearingen (Mahwah, NJ: Lawrence Erlbaum Associates, Publishers, 1999), 155.
48. Gary Kelly, Introduction to *Lydia Sigourney: Selected Poetry and Prose*, 11.
49. Cheryl Walker, *American Women Poets of the Nineteenth Century* (New Brunswick: Rutgers University Press, 1992), 1.
50. Walker, *American Women Poets*, 1; Lydia Sigourney, *Letters to Young Ladies* (Hartford: P. Canfield, 1833); Lydia Sigourney, *Letters to my Pupil* (New York: Robert Carter & Brothers, 1851). Printed more than twenty-five times, *Letters to Young Ladies* commanded a strong following among middle-class white women. In the preface to this book, Sigourney identifies her audience as "the youth of my own sex" (7). She claims that women "exercise influence in society" (7) and thus must practice proper etiquette and cultural customs. Each chapter of *Letters to Young Ladies* is titled after a gendered topic such as "Domestic Employments," "Health and Dress," "Friendships," "Self-Government," and "Utility." Sigourney, who was an enthusiastic advocate of the formation of reading societies for women, also offers advice on epistolary writing, memorization, paraphrase, and note-taking. Published in 1851, Sigourney's second conduct book *Letters to my Pupil* details nineteenth-century women's etiquette and emphasizes the significance of speech, pronunciation, and conversation for young ladies. She claims that proper elocution, even for women who do not practice public speaking, is utterly necessary. For Sigourney, one of the most important qualities of oral discourse is the use of what she calls "Fitly-Spoken Words." She says, "it is expected of a well-trained lady, that she should oversee both agreeably and usefully; and you, my young friends, will desire in this, as in other accomplishments, to give pleasure, in order to do good" (44). Women's social intercourse, she says, should give pleasure, be instructive, and be comforting. Women, Sigourney continues, should also be good listeners and "learn . . . when to be silent, as well as how to speak" (44). Such conduct books were instrumental for many young ladies entering nineteenth-century society.
51. Sinche, "Sigourney's Sailors," 62.
52. Walker, *American Women Poets*, 1.
53. Wendy Dasler Johnson, *Antebellum American Women's Poetry: A Rhetoric of Sentiment* (Carbondale: Southern Illinois University Press, 2016), 180. It is important to note that Sigourney was an advocate of feminine manners. The notions of political and social change implicated in her poetry were often rooted in accommodationist feminism, which in essence promoted an ideology of separate spheres. According to Jane Donawerth, Sigourney followed the examples of Hannah More in constructing gendered rhetorical theory, which may be seen in Sigourney's early books on conduct and manners. Donawerth, "Hannah More, Lydia Sigourney."
54. Putzi, *Fair Copy*, 57.

55. Lydia H. Sigourney, *Letters of Life* (New York: D. Appleton and Company, 1867), 366.
56. Sigourney, *Letters of Life*, 366.
57. Walker, *American Women Poets*, 1.
58. Sigourney, *Letters of Life*, 366.
59. Richards, *Gender*, 66.
60. Richards, *Gender*, 66.
61. Sigourney, *Letters of Life*, 180.
62. Sigourney, *Letters of Life*, 179.
63. Sigourney, *Letters of Life*, 180.
64. Sigourney, *Letters of Life*, 366.
65. Jackson, *Dickinson's Misery*, 42.
66. Lydia H. Sigourney, "Leave Time and Place to God," *The New York Ledger*, January 3, 1857.
67. Sigourney, "Leave Time and Place to God."
68. Sigourney's poetic interpretation of Job in this poem correlates with other contemporaneous readings that warned against hubris. For example, in 1852, the year before his death, the English preacher and writer Reverend William Jay (1769–1853) writes that Job's words imply that "[e]ven in his greatest prosperity, Job thought of dying: whatever changes he hoped to escape in life, he expected an hour of dissolution, and knew, if his possessions were continued, he should be called to leave them." Like Sigourney, Jay instructs his readers on how to interpret death and dying. He claims that there are people who "put far off the evil day and live as if he flattered himself with an immortality upon the earth. But the believer keeps mortality upon earth." For both Jay and Sigourney, faith in Christ is a type of ontological certainty in mortality. Both encourage their readers to be like Job, that is, to never forget the looming inevitability of death. Both advise readers to keep death nearby as a way of repudiating hubris. William Jay, *The Works of the Rev. William Jay, of Argyle Chapel, Bath: Comprising Matter not Heretofore Presented to the American Public in Three Volumes*, Vol. 3 (New York: Harper & Brothers Publishers, 1852), 120.
69. Caroline Ingraham, "Sarah Percival; or the Bride of 'The House of Gold,'" *The New York Ledger*, January 3, 1857.
70. Ingraham, "Sarah Percival," *The New York Ledger*, January 2, 1857.
71. Ingraham, "Sarah Percival," *The New York Ledger*, January 3, 1857.
72. Ingraham, "Sarah Percival," *The New York Ledger*, January 3, 1857. In the original poem, line 37 appears slightly different as "And while yet her lips did name me."
73. Lydia H. Sigourney, "Fair Traffic," *The New York Ledger*, January 24, 1857.
74. Sigourney, "Fair Traffic."
75. Charles Ferme, *A Logical Analysis of the Epistle of Paul to the Romans, by Charles Ferme, Translated from the Latin By William Skae, A.M.; and A Commentary on the Same Epistle, by Andrew Melville in the Original Latin*, ed. William Lindsay Alexander, D.D. (Edinburgh: Woodrow Society, 1801), 299.
76. Bennett's "The Refugees" is a historical serial, but this does not mean that it was historically precise. Gretchen Bataille argues that "[i]n many cases, costumes and settings were more important than historical accuracy in the artistic depictions." Gretchen M. Bataille, *Native American Representations: First Encounters, Distorted Images, and Literary Appropriations* (Lincoln: University of Nebraska Press, 2001), 3.

77. "Passing Down the Avenue," *Evening Star*, January 1, 1857.
78. The serial was also reprinted in *The Burlington Free Press* (December 26, 1856); *Wisconsin State Journal* (December 26, 1856); *The Lancaster Examiner* (December 31, 1856); and *The Buffalo Daily Republic* (January 14, 1857). Clarence A. Andrews, *Michigan in Literature* (Detroit: Wayne State University Press, 1992), 36.
79. Emerson Bennett, "The Refugees: An Indian Tale of 1812," *The New York Ledger*, January 24, 1857.
80. Bataille, *Native American Representations*, 3.
81. Karen L. Kilcup, *Fallen Forests: Emotion, Embodiment, and Ethics in American Women's Environmental Writing, 1781–1924* (Athens: University of Georgia Press, 2013), 24.
82. Angela Calcaterra, *Literary Indians: Aesthetics and Encounter in American Literature to 1920* (Chapel Hill: University of North Carolina Press, 2018), 89–90.
83. Mary Hershberger, "Mobilizing Women's Abolition: The Struggle Against Indian Removal in the 1830s," *Journal of American History* 86, no. 1 (1999): 1.
84. Tiya Miles, "'Circular Reasoning': Recentering Cherokee Women in the Antiremoval Campaigns," *American Quarterly* 61, no. 2 (2009): 235.
85. Lydia Sigourney, "The Best Investment," *The New York Ledger*, February 21, 1857.
86. Bennett, "The Refugees: An Indian Tale of 1812," *The New York Ledger*, February 21, 1857.
87. Bennett, "The Refugees: An Indian Tale of 1812," *The New York Ledger*, February 21, 1857.
88. Ledbetter, "Bonnets and Rebellions," 252.
89. Lydia H. Sigourney, *The Daily Counsellor* (Hartford: Brown and Gross, Publishers, 1858) iii.
90. Sigourney, *Daily Counsellor*, iii.
91. Sigourney, *Daily Counsellor*, iii.
92. Sigourney, *Letters of Life*, 179, 364.
93. Mary Clemmer, *The Poetical Works of Alice and Phoebe Cary: With a Memorial of Their Lives* (Boston: Houghton, Mifflin and Company, 1876), 13.
94. Clemmer, *Poetical Works of Alice and Phoebe Cary*, 13.
95. In 1871, Alice died from tuberculosis. Five months later, Phoebe died of hepatitis.
96. Clemmer, *Poetical Works of Alice and Phoebe Cary*, 1.
97. Maura D'Amore, *Suburban Plots: Men at Home in Nineteenth-Century American Print Culture* (Amherst: University of Massachusetts Press, 2014), 3.
98. Leo Marx, *The Machine in the Garden: Technology and the Pastoral Ideal in America* (Oxford: Oxford University Press, 1964), 4.
99. Mark Coeckelbergh, *New Romantic Cyborgs: Romanticism, Information Technology, and the End of the Machine* (Cambridge, MA: MIT Press, 2017), 88.
100. James S. Duncan and David R. Lambert, "Landscape, Aesthetics, and Power," *American Space/American Place: Geographies of the Contemporary United States*, ed. John A. Agnew and Jonathan M. Smith (New York: Routledge, 2002), 266.
101. Kilcup, *Fallen Forests*, 2.
102. Ingraham, "Sarah Percival," *The New York Ledger*, December 27, 1856.
103. "Life," *The New York Ledger*, December 27, 1856.

104. "Life."
105. Alice Cary, "Looking Back," *The New York Ledger*, December 27, 1856.
106. Ingraham, "Sarah Percival," *The New York Ledger*, December 27, 1856.
107. Cary, "Looking Back."
108. Ingraham, "Sarah Percival," *The New York Ledger*, December 27, 1856.
109. Cary, "Looking Back."
110. Lydia Maria Child, *Looking Toward Sunset* (Boston: Ticknor and Fields, 1865), 322.
111. Cary, "Looking Back."
112. Alice Cary, "Work," *The National Magazine*, November 1854.
113. "Nobility" is not titled in the *Ledger* and the *National Magazine*. Mary Clemmer Ames later collects the poem with the title "Nobility" in *The Last Poems of Alice and Phoebe Cary* (1874).
114. Alice Cary, "Work," *The New York Ledger*, January 10, 1857.
115. Cary published the poem in an effort to boost the magazine's sales. She resigned from her position as editor and returned to New York in 1855. *Magazine of Western History*, Vol. VIII (Cleveland, OH, 1888), 303.
116. Jim Casey and Sarah H. Salter, "Challenges and Opportunities in Editorship Studies," *American Periodicals* 30, no. 2 (2020): 102.
117. William Henry Venable, *Beginnings of Literary Culture in the Ohio Valley: Historical and Biographical Sketches* (Cincinnati: Robert Clarke & Co., 1891), 496.
118. Cary, "Work," *The New York Ledger*.
119. Cary, "Work," *The New York Ledger*.
120. Cary, "Work," *The New York Ledger*.
121. Cary, "Work," *The New York Ledger*.
122. Cary, "Work," *The New York Ledger*.
123. Cary, "Work," *The New York Ledger*.
124. Cary, "Work," *The New York Ledger*.
125. Cary, "Work," *The New York Ledger*.
126. Cary, "Work," *The New York Ledger*.
127. Cary, "Work," *The New York Ledger*.
128. Cary, "Work," *The New York Ledger*.
129. Cary, "Work," *The New York Ledger*.
130. Cary, "Work," *The New York Ledger*.
131. Kilcup, *Fallen Forests*, 372.

2

REPRINT POEMS IN FRANCISCO P. RAMÍREZ'S *EL CLAMOR PÚBLICO*

The four-page, Los Angeles-based newspaper *El Clamor Público* was the first Spanish-language weekly owned and operated by a Californio (i.e. a Hispanophone resident of California during the Spanish and Mexican era between 1769 and 1848) in Southern California after the US–Mexico War (1846–48). Although other contemporaneous California-based periodicals, like *The Star of Los Angeles*, featured Spanish-language pages, *El Clamor Público* was the only Hispanophone newspaper in circulation free from Anglo-American and French control and exclusively bound to the Spanish-speaking community.[1] In 1855, seven years after the signing of the Treaty of Guadalupe Hidalgo, the paper's seventeen-year-old editor, Francisco P. Ramírez, almost singlehandedly began editing, printing, and marketing his new venture. He solicited subscribers for *El Clamor Público* at the rate of $5 per year. As editor, Ramírez wrote and edited news and editorials on the pressing issues of the day including California's land grants, the Gold Rush, the filibustering of Nicaragua, and the Know-Nothing Party. However, one of the most important (yet under-studied) things he did as editor was to engage in the editorial practice of altering reprint poems.

In this chapter, a poetics of paratextuality signifies Ramírez's own editorial practice of altering reprint poems culled from periodicals, books, and anthologies from across the Hispanophone world and reprinted in Southern California. These location-specific alterations created new transitions and transactions between the poets, genres, and regions gestured in and outside of the newspaper's printscape. By isolating *El Clamor Público*'s poems, digitally mapping their potential citational provenance and/or place of publication, and comparing reproductions with originals, I show how Ramírez's reprint practices shaped authorship and genre in his paper. Ramírez deliberately edited titles, bylines, geographical references, and cultural signifiers to Spain and Latin America. As a result, he unbound many reprint poems from the nation-making artifact of the author, book, and anthology, warping and, in some cases, erasing popular poetry genres like satire and the dedication. I propose that Ramírez's reprint practices are important examples of the print culture norm of editing reprint poems to centralize the reading public's interests and experiences. Ramírez's reprint practices made his reprint poems more accessible to, and relevant for, a Californio audience, while at the same time facilitating an intellectual and cultural sense of belonging that resists the reproduction of knowledge and aesthetics from a non-Californio episteme. Along with close reading, I employ a GIS Google Map to showcase the points of provenance, hemispheric reach, and possible networks of circulation of Ramírez's reprints. Using traditional as well as digital-humanities methods to bring such a landscape into view, this chapter highlights a new, multilingual, and transnational reprint culture that contributes to our understanding of nineteenth-century US-based poetry beyond the Anglo-American paradigm.

This chapter continues to answer Kirsten Silva Gruesz's call "for a strong revision of literary-historical narratives of the U.S. national tradition" that is not simply "an additive process of restoring lost texts from the Spanish borderlands to the canon, [but rather] a nongenealogical view of Latino identity grounded in a larger web of transamerican perceptions and contacts."[2] While a fair amount of scholarship has considered Ramírez's political interventions on behalf of the Spanish-speaking communities of California, little attention has been paid to the paper's poetic offering. Scholars of Chicanx newspapers, including Luis Leal and Nicolás Kanellos, argue that Ramírez's newspaper is a significant site for the historical nascency of Chicanx literature, a development usually associated with hemispheric exchanges between the Southwest US and Mexico. Paul Bryan Gray deems the paper an important textual space for "the clash between American and Mexican cultures following the conquest of California."[3] Building on this important scholarship, I turn to *El Clamor Público*'s reprint poems, their paratexts (poem titles and bylines), and their (dis)connections to California, Europe, and the greater part of Latin America to better understand what these transamerican networks reveal about nineteenth-century Latinx editors and their reprint culture.

Ramírez's reprint practices in *El Clamor Público* elucidate from a Californio perspective the sociopolitical changes that the end of the US–Mexico War in 1848 brought to the US Southwest. As John R. Chávez reminds us, one such change was the US's forceful purchase of Northern Mexico, land which makes up all or parts of present-day Arizona, California, Colorado, Nevada, New Mexico, Utah, and Wyoming.[4] Thousands of Mexican citizens became US citizens by virtue of Article IX of the Treaty of Guadalupe Hidalgo signed at the war's end. The treaty was intended to safeguard the land and civil rights of Californios. However, the racial, cultural, and linguistic bias of Anglo-Americans and federal government officials often disenfranchised many "treaty citizens," as Rosina Lozano calls individuals that lived in this region after the war, stripping them of their patrimony.[5]

After the war, the US grew not just in size but also in its linguistic capacity. The newly acquired Southwestern territory was linguistically and culturally diverse. Within the 529,000 square miles of territory gained by the US, English was not the dominant language. Regional Indigenous languages like Apache, Navajo, O'odham, Hopi, Hualapai were spoken frequently, while the colonial prevailing language of Spanish was the lingua franca of this massive region. Spanish was the language of business, politics, and faith. As a result, Southwestern Spanish-language newspapers like *Los Angeles Star* (1851–79) and *El Clamor Público* (1855–59) flourished in the nineteenth century. These newspapers printed news, literary offerings, and advertisements in Spanish, English, and Spanglish. For many treaty citizens, the Hispanophone press sustained the parts of their cultural inheritance that Anglo-Americans could not easily take away: their political opinions, traditions, and literature. Many of these newspapers were conservators of local cultures and customs, sustaining and transferring the Spanish language in a region where English was increasingly becoming a part of the political, sociocultural fabric. These newspapers were not simply Mexican or US American. They were between two bordering nations and two bordering languages, US–Mexico and English and Spanish, respectively. This liminal space shaped in large part the news, advertisements, and, as this chapter argues, the poetry printed.

Nearly all Hispanophone newspapers during this period carried literary offerings and other cultural pieces, including poems, correspondence, recipes, and short fiction. As with the Anglo-American press in the region, poetry was a common occurrence in these papers. By the late nineteenth century, California established numerous Spanish-language newspapers that regularly published poetry. Many Spanish-language poets appeared only in newspapers. For example, regional poets like Juan B. Hijar y Jaro and J. M. Vigil were published in *El Nuevo Mundo* (San Francisco), José Rómulo Ribera and Luis A. Torres in *El Boletín Popular* (San Francisco), and Luis Tafoya in *El Nuevo Mexicano* (New Mexico). These local newspaper poets account for only a fraction of the bylines found in these papers. The works of many more poets appeared as unauthorized reprints without bylines. Many newspapers routinely filled their newspapers with these reprinted verses, often intentionally editing their content to fit the page of the periodical and reflect the interests of readers. Ramírez's *El Clamor Público*, for instance, reprinted over 200 poems during the paper's five-year run, revealing an expansive archive of unauthorized reprint poems from across the Hispanophone world.

A Precocious Seventeen-Year-Old

Who was this frontier editor who, at seventeen, single-handedly read, researched, and set to type poems from all over the Hispanophone world? Before analyzing his reprint poems, it would be helpful to understand a little about Ramírez's life. Ramírez grew up during a volatile period when Los Angeles was developing from an isolated adobe settlement on the Mexican frontier to a US city.[6] Born in Los Angeles on February 9, 1837, Ramírez was the fourth of thirteen children. He was named after his grandfather, who was a carpenter from Alta, California. In 1828, Ramírez's father, Juan M. Ramírez, settled in Los Angeles and built an adobe residence. Unlike many new settlers, Juan did not have political connections to obtain large land grants issued by the Mexican government. As a result, he did not acquire wealth in his lifetime. Two years later, in 1830, Juan married Francisco's mother, Petra Avila, who was a member of a prominent family. Shortly after, Francisco was born. To support his growing family, Juan purchased a small *conuco* (parcel of land) on which he grew grapes for commercial winemaking. His grape farm bordered a vineyard that belonged to Jean-Louis Vignes (1780–1862), a prosperous French vintner and naturalized Mexican citizen, who taught Francisco to read and write in French.

At thirteen, Francisco P. Ramírez was trilingual and could speak, read, and write in Spanish, English, and French.[7] He was only fourteen years old when, in 1851, the *Los Angeles Star* hired him as a compositor. Although the *Star* predominantly catered to English-language readers, the paper sought to reflect its cultural surroundings. For this reason, the *Star* printed the last page completely in Spanish under the title *La Estrella de Los Angeles*. *La Estrella* was edited by the "sometime lawyer, politician and poet of considerable learning, Manuel Clemente Rojo" (1823–1900).[8] Ramírez's apprenticeship at *La Estrella de Los Angeles* and Rojo's tutelage were foundational for the young compositor's development in writing and publishing poems. Rojo wrote poems in Spanish, which made them accessible to a literate Spanish-speaking public. In Luis Leal's study of bilingualism in nineteenth-century Chicano poems, "Truth-Telling Tongues," Leal claims that "[n]either Rojo nor Ramírez used English in their poems."[9] Despite being trilingual, Ramírez would transfer his monolingual Spanish poetics to editing and writing poems for *El Clamor Público*. After Clemente Rojo left *La Estrella* in 1853, James S. Waite, owner of the *Los Angeles Star*, offered Ramírez the editorship of the paper's Spanish page.

In addition to cultivating skills in writing and publishing poems in Spanish, Ramírez's time at *La Estrella* helped him to develop an understanding of reprint culture. Gray posits that "Ramírez's experience at *La Estrella* greatly increased his general knowledge since the paper reprinted many articles culled from a variety of domestic and foreign publications."[10] Dissatisfied with his position at *La Estrella*, Ramírez longed to start his own paper entirely devoted to Spanish-language readers. Encouraged by Waite and likely financially supported by

Vignes, the seventeen-year-old Ramírez realized his dreams of editing and operating a newspaper, naming it *El Clamor Público*, a name, Gray posits, that was "already in use by one of Madrid's great journals."[11]

Due to low literacy rates among Ramírez's intended audience of the disenfranchised and working class, as well as *El Clamor Público*'s ardent liberal politics, subscriptions plummeted, leading Ramírez to bankruptcy and self-imposed exile to Sonora, Mexico. In 1855, less than half of the Spanish-speaking adults in Los Angeles could read or write in Spanish.[12] Furthermore, the colonial press criticized *El Clamor Público* for its liberal ideologies, support of abolitionism, and promotion of the rights of the rural Mexican class. Ramírez frequently articulated radically liberal views on politics and race relations that both Hispanophone and Anglo-Americans found aggressive. According to Leal, "Ramírez favored freedom for [enslaved African Americans], education for women, civil rights for all men and religious tolerance."[13] At the same time, he promoted lingual assimilation, "propos[ing] that all Hispanics learn English, it being necessary in order for them to actively participate in the political and economic life of the country."[14] Despite Ramírez's efforts to edit a socioeconomically inclusive paper, *El Clamor Público*'s run was short-lived. The last issue was printed on December 31, 1859.

El Clamor Público and Reprint Culture

El Clamor Público's reprint practice of publishing poems originally from Latin America and Europe accounts for a literary border crossing of poems, which, as Anna Brickhouse puts it, "came to assume a central role in reshaping the public spheres of cultural production and political commentary in the United States and other parts of the American hemisphere."[15] In its full run, *El Clamor Público* published 230 poems in 233 issues between June 19, 1855 and December 31, 1859. Of these 230 poems, 227 are reprints. These poems were reprinted from other newspapers, magazines, and books of poetry from over fifteen countries and territories across Latin America and Europe. Ramírez likely drew from his own archives of Latin American and Spanish books and periodicals.

Like most antebellum newspapers in the US, *El Clamor Público* participated in what Meredith McGill calls a reprinting culture. As a way of tracing fluctuating meanings and localities of the literary, McGill shifts our "gaze from first and authorized editions to unauthorized reprints, from the form of the book to the intersection of the book and periodical publishing, and from a national literature to an internally divided and transatlantic literary marketplace."[16] This shift in how we understand the literary, McGill argues, reveals a "traffic in essays, tales, and poems copied from British and American periodicals and reassembled into literary weeklies and monthlies [serving] . . . as a constant reminder of the disjointed nature of American literary culture."[17]

Although McGill is primarily referring to Anglophone materials, this literary disjointedness also came to define forms of Hispanophone cultural production that were regional, national, and cosmopolitan in scope, including disparate languages, print traditions, and transamerican networks. *El Clamor Público* shows us how, in addition to copies of poems from British and American periodicals, Hispanophone editors in the US also copied poems from Latin America and Spain, a largely unaccounted-for aspect of reprint culture history. Like the Anglophone literary world, Ramírez's print culture practices fostered a poetic tradition untethered to authorship, place of publication, and, in some cases, generic conventions. His reprint culture is defined by varying approaches to editorship, including removing bylines, changing titles, and authoring a poem as someone who, as editor, also has control over the final product. However, the case of *El Clamor Público* importantly provides a variation on the Anglophone antebellum reprint culture that McGill describes because of the community Ramírez targeted.

In the early years of *El Clamor Público*, Ramírez had yet to define the community that he attempted to reach. Reprinting poems from Europe and Latin America constituted a primary means through which he set out to do that. As editor, he conceptualized a Californio aesthetic through his reprint practices and the select poets and poems he reprinted in *El Clamor Público*. Although most were not written by Californios, the paper's reprint poems were discursively vital in the formation of mid-century Californio poetry that reached readers throughout the state. According to an advertisement in the June 19, 1855 issue, Ramírez's paper was distributed to Spanish-reading subscribers throughout the state of California, including Los Angeles, Monterey, San Diego, San Jose, Santa Barbara, Santa Ynez, Rancho De Purificación, San Luis Obispo, and Stockton. Kanellos argues that initially Ramírez "directed his efforts to the people he called 'californios', 'nativos californios', 'la raza española', 'de ascendencia española', [and] 'la comunidad española.'"[18] When he used the term "Mexicanos," he was likely referring to immigrants from Mexico, not to be confused with US treaty citizens who were formerly Mexican citizens prior to the US–Mexico War. Ramírez, as Kanellos puts it, "continuously crossed borders, territorially as well as culturally and politically, in his search for community and nation."[19] He understood Californios to be a hemispheric people, a consequence of US imperialism, who needed to be united and defended against oppressors. In a trip to Mexico City in 1877, he claimed, "I am an American because the treaty of Guadalupe placed me on the other side of the line dividing the two nations, but I was born a Mexican."[20]

As time went on, Ramírez began to promote a type of pan-Hispanism that exemplified a need for Hispanic solidarity in California. He used the term "Hispanoamericano" in the broad sense to describe all Spanish-speaking people, even titling an editorial "A Nuestros Ciudadanos Hispanoamericanos" (To Our

Fellow Hispanic American Citizens).[21] Ramírez's "Hispanoamericano" was ethnically diverse, including Spaniards, Mexicans, Chileans, Peruvians, and Nicaraguans, a people that he often referred to as a "raza."[22] The expression "raza" was already in circulation in mid-century Hispanophone newspapers. Richard Griswold del Castillo posits that the generic term "La Raza" arose from the Spanish-language press, evincing "a new kind of ethnic consciousness."[23] In the decades following the US–Mexico War, a time of political and social upheaval, "La Raza emerged as the single most important symbol of ethnic pride and identification. There were many ways of using this term, depending on the context."[24] The Spanish-speaking community used "La Raza Mexicana," "La Raza Hispano-Americana," "La Raza Española," and "La Raza Latina" to convey a sense of "racial, class, and national variety" and, I would add, a sense of belonging and unity.[25] Closer to the phrase "people" than "race," *El Clamor Público*'s generic use of "la raza" encapsulates the specific demographic and location of California, conveying what Raúl Coronado calls "a literary and intellectual culture that emerges in the interstices between the United States and Spanish America."[26]

Ramírez saw himself as a defender of his readers. His stated mission was "a defensa de los intereses morales y materiales del Sur de California . . . al servicio de mis compatriotas nativos de California, generalmente de todos los hispano americanos" (to defend the moral and material interests of Southern California . . . serving my native California compatriots, generally all Hispanic Americans).[27] He wrote long and scathing rebukes about the Know-Nothing Party, which he saw as an oppressor of his community and described as "el maligno enemigo, el Know-Nothingismo, con su estupidez, intolerancia y conspiraciones" (the evil enemy, Know-Nothingism, with its stupidity, intolerance and conspiracies).[28]

Ramírez claimed his membership of this "Hispanoamericano" community with the pronouns he used: "nosotros," "nuestros," "nuestro pueblo," "nuestra raza."[29] He was one of them, and *El Clamor Público* was their public voice, as the title of the newspaper overtly suggests. Seeing himself as a member of his readership, Ramírez established with his own readers what Raúl Coronado calls "metaphysical certainty."[30] Coronado argues that nineteenth-century Spanish-language "writing and publishing [is an] important means for communities to search for new sources of metaphysical certainty," a term he employs to describe "a new mode of being, a grasping for language that would allow these individuals to practice new personhoods [and] to enact new ways of imagining community."[31] Coronado posits that nineteenth-century Latinx cultural production "operated as part of a larger and largely undifferentiated field of writing," which included revolutionary pamphlets, memoirs, histories, and poetry.[32] I add the reprint poem to Coronado's list as a distinct genre from that of the original poem. As a genre in *El Clamor Público*, reprint poems enact a specific form of metaphysical certainty, one that allowed Ramírez to incorporate and edit the poetic voices of California, Latin America, and Europe in an attempt to sustain a Hispanophone identity at the margins of an expanding US empire. It was Ramírez's metaphysical certainty, his ability to defend and see himself in his readers, that allowed him to curate poems for a broad pan-Hispanic public at the borders of the US empire.

Unlike original poems, reprint poems were often shaped by what Ryan Cordell calls "the continuous circulation of content to and from [readers'] local newspaper of choice."[33] Via the practice of selection and republication, Ramírez "appropriated the collective authority of the newspaper system, positioning their publication as one node within larger political, social, denominational, or national networks, and their content as drawn from and contributing to larger conversations across the medium."[34] Today, digital archives allow us to uncover possible sources of *El Clamor Público*'s reprints and to track their earlier publications. Digital archives reveal specific channels for the circulation of newspaper poems, giving us a clearer understanding of where *El Clamor Público*'s reprints come from and how they changed in the course of circulation. Although I was unable to track the original publication of all 227 of *El Clamor Público*'s reprints, I mapped the earliest known publication and provenance of 98 poems. I have organized these publications using My Maps, a Google platform, to provide a sense of the transnational print culture on which Ramírez drew (see Figure 2.1).[35]

The map visualizes how Ramírez's poetics of paratextuality engaged with a wide Hispanophone literary marketplace beyond his newspaper's place of publication. In many cases, copies upon copies of these poems were in circulation before they made their way into *El Clamor Público*'s pages. This means that Ramírez could have culled many of his reprints from books and periodicals published in places not included in Figure 2.1. In mapping *El Clamor Público*'s reprint poems, my point is not to say definitively that these are the precise publication locations from which Ramírez drew when he collected his poems. Rather, my aim is to narrativize the nuances of these poems beyond a shared language in order to visualize and organize potential national affinities and discordances through poetic circulation. Ramirez's reprint poems functioned as paratexts to local news in Los Angeles and international news in Latin America as well as advertisements for local Spanish-speaking businesses. Thus, as Joshua Ratner argues in his study of the paratext in early American literature, in the context of *El Clamor Público*, these poems "constantly resist[ed] (and thereby acknowledge[d]) or willingly participat[ed] in a wider [global] literary marketplace."[36] As we read examples of Ramírez's reprint poems, this visual narrative can help us picture the poems in their unfixed places of publication as they made the rounds from across the globe and were repurposed for *El Clamor Público*'s readers.

El Clamor Público

Europe
- Italy (1)
- France (2)
- England (3)
- Spain (26)
- Portugal (1)

Caribbean
- Puerto Rico (2)
- Cuba (13)

South America
- Peru (2)
- Colombia (8)
- Ecuador (2)
- Argentina (1)
- Chile (2)
- Venezuela (2)

Central America
- Mexico (28)
- Nicaragua (1)

U.S.
- U.S. (4)

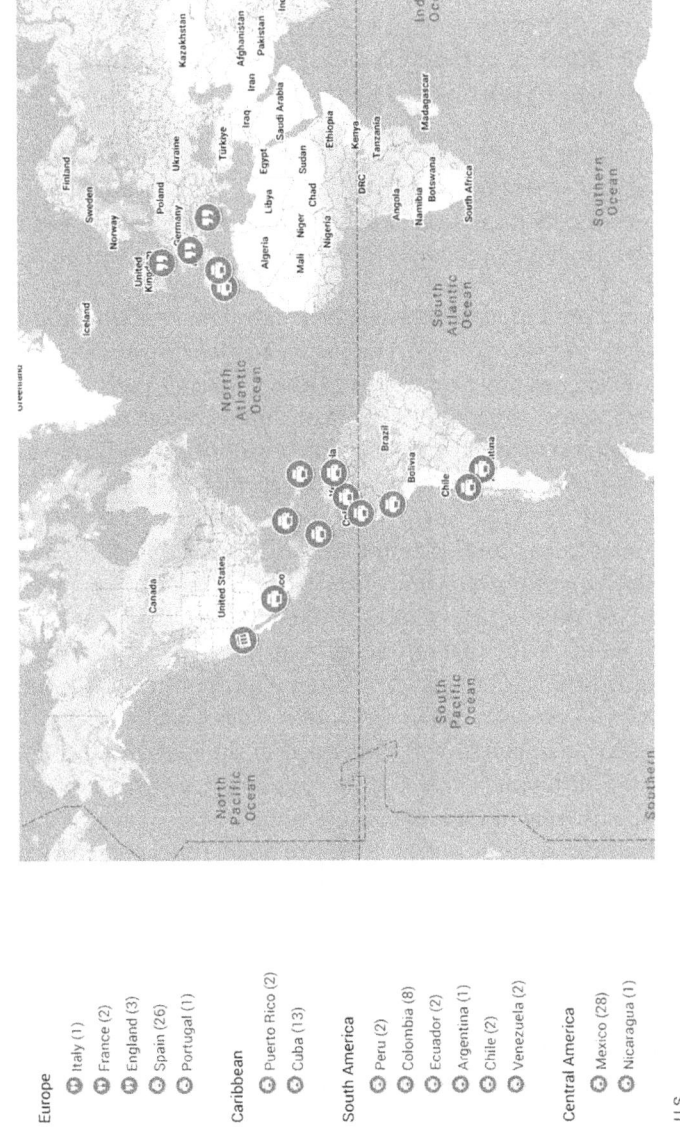

Figure 2.1 *El Clamor Público*'s poems: an interactive map. Google My Maps. Map data © 2023 Google.

Mediating a Californio Audience

Before *El Clamor Público* folded in 1859, Ramírez enacted his own reprint practices of transamerican Spanish-language poems. One of these practices was running poems without bylines. Of the 230 poems printed in *El Clamor Público*'s full run, 161 poems ran without any byline.[37] As Katherine Bode reminds us in her study of authorship and literary anonymity in the National Library of Australia's (NLA) Trove database:

> the ongoing digitization of print cultural records, and new methods for accessing and analyzing digitized documents, brings to our bibliographic attention not only thousands of new works—an issue of scale often noted with respect to digital research—but thousands of titles without authors.[38]

Literary anonymity and pseudonymity at this scale pose a bibliographic conundrum for scholars of print culture. The problem, Bode posits, is our cultural fixation on origins, "our urge to ask, as Michel Foucault put it, 'From where does [this work] come, who wrote it, when, under what circumstances, or beginning with what design?'"[39] With no single author to implicate ownership or nationality, *El Clamor Público*'s unbylined reprints are only associated with Ramírez's editorship.

Ramírez's intentional and/or unintentional exclusion of the poet's signature decentralizes the authorial figure from the poem. In his study of the social lives of poems, Michael C. Cohen claims that "circulation ... decenters authorship from authors, so that writers cannot control the proliferating representations of their work, any more than they can control who reads their books—especially when the books are not really 'theirs.'"[40] Intellectual and creative ownership was ill-defined in the mid-nineteenth century, especially in the Southwest where editors routinely reprinted news, ads, and poems to fill up columns in their newspapers.

The decentralization of the author from the poem obscures the literary, cultural, and political reputation of the poet. For example, the political views and celebrity status that are associated with Spanish writers like Juan Martínez Villergas (1817–94) are disassociated from *El Clamor Público*'s unbylined reprints, further detaching authorship, as Cohen would argue, "from publication and the singularity of the particular writer."[41] Villergas was a Spanish satirist poet, politician, and newspaper editor. He was a conservative Spanish nationalist who was the subject of heated rebukes from Latin American "liberales" (liberals), including Argentine writers Juan María Gutiérrez (1809–78) and Domingo Faustino Sarmiento (1811–88), who critiqued Villergas's stout Spanish nationalism.[42] Villergas founded short-lived satirical magazines in Spain, including *La Nube* (1842), *El Tio Camorra* (1847–48), *Jeremías* (1866–70), *Don Circunstancias* (1848–49), and *El Patifiesto* (1854).

On May 24, 1856, Ramírez reprinted Villergas's satirical poem "La Confesión" without a byline. In failing to name Villergas as author, *El Clamor Público* disassociates "La Confesión" from Villergas's reputation as a Spanish editor and as a pro-Spanish nationalist for readers familiar with his work and reputation. "La Confesión" is a ninety-seven-line satirical dramatic dialogue between a young woman named María and an unnamed priest. The poem begins *in medias res*:

Con los ojos arrasados	With tears in
en lagrimones, María,	her eyes, María,
A su confesor decia	To her confessor spoke
Sus culpas y sus pecados. (1–4)	Her guilt and her sins.[43]

Throughout María's confession, she regularly interjects the phrase, "Jesus, padre, mío, / como huele usted á Tabaco!" (Jesus, Father, / you smell of Tabaco!") (23–24). These two lines are repeated four times in the poem. They are the anaphoric joke that interrupts María's confession about her love for "un joven . . . / tan gallardo, tan buen mozo / que yo me muero de gozo / cada vez que me visita" (a youth . . . / so elegant, so handsome, / that I die with joy / every time he visits me) (37–40). After repeated interruptions, the priest becomes disconcerted and sends María off: "basta de historia: / aquí paz y después gloria, / levántate, que *ego te absuelvo*" (enough of your story: / here peace and then glory, / lift yourself, I will absolve you) (95–97). The priest's dismissal of María is also the poem's punchline. The exasperated and discomfited priest, to get rid of María, gives her absolution without assigning her penance, which is what María wanted all along. Like the author of this poem, the priest and María are not depicted as Spaniards. Villergas's reputation too is moot in this poem. Instead, readers engage with the form, content, and genre of the poem free from Villergas's cultural signification.

In addition to the poem's disassociation from Villergas's authorship in *El Clamor Público*, this reprint disassociates "La Confesión" from other representative examples of poetic satire. In 1847, nine years before appearing in *El Clamor Público*, "La Confesión" was included in a Spanish anthology titled *Album de Momo. Colección de lo Mas Selecto que se Publicó en La Risa ó Sean Composiciones Jocosas en Prosas y Verso* (Momo's Album. Collection of the Most Select Published in Satire: Jolly Compositions in Prose and Poetry). Titled after Momus, the Greek mythological personification of satire, this anthology published poems by a cast of Spanish-born men. Their names are listed in the title page: "Hartzenbusch, Gil y Zárate, Zorrilla, Rubí, Breton de los Herreros, Villergas, Bonilla, Baldoví, Ribot, Príncipe, Diana, Asquerino, Lafuente (Fr. Gerundio), Lopez Pelegrin (Abenamar), Canseco y otros escritores" (and other writers). Representative lists, such as this one, function as authenticators of patriarchal literary traditions, emphasizing a shared race, gender, country, and nationality (i.e. white, male, Spain, and Spaniard). This anthological list strategically ties Spanish white men to traditional poetic satire. Cohen posits that anthologies create a vision of "tradition seen through the complex editorial machinery: the editor's authenticity guaranteed the authenticity and authentication of materials, and a poem's inclusion in the anthology therefore determines its genre."[44] Thus, the appearance of "La Confesión" in *Album de Momo* guarantees the poem's authenticity not only as satire but as one of the "most select" in this genre.

In the case of *Album de Momo*, the anthology is a nation-making artifact that is bound to its place of publication and the identities of the poets included. Reprinting "La Confesión" without a byline removes the poem from this nationalizing context, which I read as an act of aesthetic resistance that reimagines literary and national borders in Ramírez's newspaper. Shedding the cultural signification of this anthological list in *El Clamor Público*, the poem's reprint is not elevated to the status of exemplary Spanish satirical poetry. Without Villergas's byline, "La Confesión" is simply one of more than forty satirical poems that appear in *El Clamor Público*'s full run. No longer a part of an exclusive Spanish tradition of satire, as the anthology suggests, *El Clamor Público*'s unbylined reprint appears de-anthologized and reimagined within the pages of *El Clamor Público*, allowing readers to envisage the poem's setting and personae anew, an imaginative practice that for some facilitated metaphysical certainty.

Akin to the cases where *El Clamor Público* omits bylines, the edits of poem titles do not disrupt the comical and ironic effects of satirical poetry even when these edits result in discursive and narrative gaps. For example, on July 26, 1856, *El Clamor Público* reprinted, without a byline, the Cuban poet Francisco Javier Balmaseda's (1823–1907) satiric poem "Contestacion de las Mugeres [sic]" (Women's Reply) under the title "Pobre Hombres! . . . ¿Sera Verdad? –Mugeres [sic]" (Poor Men! . . . Is it True, Women?). *El Clamor Público*'s reprint title disassociates the poem from its original book format. Balmaseda's poem was originally published in *Rimas Cubanas* (1846) as part of a series of poems entitled "Hombres Y Mugeres" (Men and Women).[45] In this collection, "Contestacion de las Mugeres" is a response to a poem that appears before it titled "El Calendario en Verso" (Calendar in Verse), a disingenuous poetic tribute to women.[46] "El Calendario en Verso" satirically categorizes women by their names and what their names say about their character. For example, "Son falsas las Agustinas, / Y feas las Bonifacias" (Agustinas are dishonest, and Bonifacias ugly) (21–22). Following the same syntactical pattern as "El Calendario en Verso," the twenty-three stanzas of "Contestacion de las Mugeres'" categorize the character of men based on their names:

Son los Prósperos lunáticos,	Prósperos are lunatics
Incultos los Victorianos	All Victorianos are uncultured
Tramposos los Marcelinos	Marcelinos are cheaters
Y los Paquitos fanáticos (91–94)	And Paquitos are fanatics

The reprint title, "Pobre Hombres! . . . ¿Sera Verdad? –Mugeres" does not frame the poem as a reply to a previous poem. Thus, the dialogic relationship between "El Calendario en Verso" and "Contestacion de las Mugeres," part of the poems' original composition, does not exist in *El Clamor Público*. Instead of a satirical dialogue where both sides (men and women) have their say, the reprint title frames a unilateral response in *El Clamor Público*. In the first half of the reprint title, "Pobre Hombres!" (Poor Men!), men are satirically painted as victims. The latter half of the title, "¿Sera Verdad? –Mugeres [sic]," asks women if the speaker's allegations are true. In neither part does the title gesture to a previous poetic dialogue between "Hombres Y Mugeres," as Balmaseda's *Rimas Cubanas* intended. Yet the jocular tone of the poem remains.

El Clamor Público's reprint title disassociates the poem from Balmaseda himself. Georg Stanitzek argues that "the title—often associated metonymically with the author, thought to be traceable to him or her—is an object of shared authorship, and this fact changes the category of authorship itself in a significant way."[47] In other words, a poem's title is a transactional paratextual zone of contacts and contracts between the editor and poet. In the case of Ramírez's reprint of Balmaseda's poem, the new title traces the poem's authorship to not one but two authors, Balmaseda and Ramírez.

The above examples show how, in the case of *El Clamor Público*'s edited reprints, the genre of satire, for the most part, remains intact, in that removing bylines and editing titles did not disrupt the punchlines of the poems—that is, the inherent humor and comedy of the verses. This is not the case, however, for other genres that relied on bylines and titles as markers of their generic classification. In these cases, when Ramírez edited and retitled poems, he also created new frameworks for reading poems and understating their genre. Gérard Genette claims that a title has a communicatory function that is similar to a message delivered to an addressee:

> The titular situation of communication, like any other, comprises at least a message (the title itself), a sender, and an addressee . . . The title's (legal) sender, of course, is not necessarily its actual producer . . . [At times] the publisher suppl[ies] the title.[48]

With Genette's concept of the titular situation of communication in mind, we may consider Ramírez as a type of "sender" or title provider. In this sense, retitling poems also sends a new message to readers. Let us take as an example *El Clamor*

Público's reprint of José Zorrilla's (1817–93) "Canción" (Song) and the generic and content-based messages that Ramírez's new title sends to readers.

Published under the new title "El Prisionero" (The Prisoner) on October 17, 1857, Zorrilla's poem is about a lovestruck prisoner behind bars who sings about his beloved. The speaker hopes that his song will reach his lover's ears: "Si a tu oído, vida mía, / Mi canción llegar pudiera / Yo sé bien que no muriera / Al rigor de mi pasión" (If this song could reach your ears, my love, / I know well that / I won't die from the rigors of my passion) (15–18). The poem's original title, "Canción," is a generic category for a poem to be sung or played with musical accompaniment. It emphasizes the poem's form, that is, its musical qualities: a regular rhythm and rhyme that is a feature of the speaker's chorus, opening and closing the poem:

> Triste canta el Prisionero   Sadly, the prisoner sings
> Encerrado en su prisión,   Locked in his prison,
> Y a sus lamentos responde   And his sad chain
> Su cadena en triste son.   Responds to his laments
> Ábrele; ¡oh Viento! Camino   Open: oh Wind! A path
>   a la voz. (1–5)   for the voice.

El Clamor Público's new title shifts the poem's emphasis from form to content. No longer accenting the poem's musicality, "El Prisionero" frames the sentiment of the speaker's song: "Triste canta el Prisionero" (Sadly, the prisoner sings) (1). The chains of his imprisonment are mockingly in concert with the speaker's yearning to be free, as they "respond to his laments" (3). Emphasizing the melancholic prisoner, the new title draws attention to the speaker's subjectivity and "voz" (voice), describing both as imprisoned, perhaps as the same, whilst the speaker begs the "Wind" for freedom (5). *El Clamor Público*'s new title gives agency to the prisoner in a way that the original title does not. Framing the poem, the title makes the prisoner central to the poem and not just his song. It is, after all, his repeated commands (the poem's chorus) which echo throughout until the final line: "Ábrele; ¡oh Viento! Camino a la voz" (Open: oh wind! A path for the voice) (5).

Some of *El Clamor Público*'s new titles pull apart the original titular situation of poems and, as a result, create new genres. As Genette would argue, the function of the title as a threshold into the poem raises the issue of poetic genre. Genette states that changing the title of a work "presents what is actually a new text" and "may equally well indicate the text's form . . . in a traditional and generic way (Odes, Elegies, Novellas, Sonnets)."[49] For example, on December 22, 1855, *El Clamor Público* reprinted the Spanish writer Esteban Manuel de Villegas's (1589–1669) poem "Al Céfiro: Oda Sáfica" (To the Zephyr: Sapphic Ode) under the title "A Aquella" (To That One [feminine]/To Her). The original title of the poem, "Al Céfiro: Oda Sáfica," highlights Sapphic versification, a poetic form named after the poet Sappho. By removing the original title, the reprint's new title, "A Aquella," subordinates the literary and intellectual culture tethered to Sapphic poetry. The new title instead presents the poem in informal discourse. The informal "A Aquella" refers to a generic subject position that does not identify the addressee except as female, thus making the poem highly adaptable for *El Clamor Público*'s readers. Unlike the reprint title's informal discourse, the poem is written in a highly formal mode. The first stanza reads:

Dulce vecino de la verde selva	Sweet inhabitant of the green forest,
Huésped eterno del abril florido,	Eternal companion of flowery April,
Vital aliento de la madre Venus,	Vital breath of Mother Venues,
Céfiro blando. (1–4)	Thou mild Zephyr.

The poem's juxtaposition of informal and formal discourses allows for the speech patterns of *El Clamor Público*'s readers to exist in a Sapphic ode. The re-signifying cultural forms within less formal registers of Spanish, in a sense, informalized the formal traditional imagery of "flowery April" (2) and "mild Zephyr" (4) in the poem, making them relevant and accessible to broader readerships.

Ramírez's editorial practices have the most visible impact on *El Clamor Público*'s dedication poems. Many of these reprints, when heavily edited, disconnect the poets and/or personae in conversation. Commonly found in Spanish-language newspapers throughout the nineteenth century, the dedication poem was a performance of admiration between the poet and addressee that, for effectiveness and clarity, depended upon a chartable dialogue between them. As Vanessa Ovalle Perez argues, the dedication served poets as a vessel for a collaborative ars poetica, a dialogue between two poets who admire each other's style and skill and as a result build political and cultural solidarity.[50] Specifically focusing on the gendered dynamic of *poetisas* (poetesses) writing in Spanish-language newspapers in San Francisco, Ovalle Perez proposes that the dedication

> made possible not only [women poet's] precarious and gendered performance of Latin American solidarity, *panlatinidad*, but also set the stage for the articulation of a collaborative ars poetica in which these women contemplate their creative process and assert their identities as *poetisas*.[51]

Setting their own distinctive dual stages for *panlatinidad* and creative appreciation, *El Clamor Público*'s dedication reprints are conversations between poets, readers, and/or indiscernible love interests.

The dedication genre mainly relies on a poetic addressee often included in the title of the poem. When this poetic addressee is removed and/or edited, the genre of the poem is also truncated. For example, on December 19, 1857, Ramírez reprints the dedication poem "A Mi Amigo Don Juan Arguedas" (To My Friend, Juan Arguedas), a sonnet by the prominent Romantic Ecuadorian poet Numa Pompilio Llona (1832–1907). *El Clamor Público*'s reprint, however, appears with a new title, "El Becerro de Oro" (The Golden Calf). As the original title implies, Pompilio Llona's poem was dedicated to his contemporary, Juan Arguedas, a Peruvian Romantic poet and diplomat. In Pompilio Llona's *Cantos Americanos*, he states that "A Mi Amigo" "[f]ué escrito … en contestación a otro [soneto] que mi amigo Don Juan Argueda, me había dirigido el día anterior por el periódico *Comercio de Lima*" ([w]as written … as a response to another sonnet by my friend Don Juan Argueda, which was published the day before in the newspaper *Comercio de Lima*).[52] *El Clamor Público*'s publication does not include or mention Argueda's sonnet, thus omitting the poetic exchange between these poets. Argueda's titular name is replaced by a line from the poem's final line: "Esta postrado ante el BECERRO DE ORO!" (He is prostrate before the GOLDEN CALF!) (14). It is worth noting that even if Juan Argueda's name was irrelevant to *El Clamor Público*'s intended audience, the omission of his name, or any name for that matter, would have expunged the addressee, altering how readers entered the poem. In other words, what was originally a sonnet dedicated to a friend becomes a religiously coded sonnet ("El Becerro de Oro") in *El Clamor Público*'s reprint. The dedication was an important genre for Ramírez for it was the only one he wrote in, in *El Clamor Público*. Ramírez's singular interest in the dedication may be read as an admission to something worth developing in this genre.

From Chicanx Editor to Poet

Of the 230 poems published in *El Clamor Público*'s full print run, my survey shows that only one, a dedication titled "A Mi Maria Antonia," was penned by Ramírez. "A Mi Maria Antonia" appeared only with Ramírez's initials "F. P. R." on September 11, 1855. An analysis of this poem gives us a better sense of Ramírez's own poetic style and taste and how they shaped his reprint practices. Ramírez's writing style is straightforward and conversational, even when contemplating the complex agonies of love. Here is the poem in full along with my translation:

No sé—pero el pensamiento	I don't know—but my thoughts
Me dice que ambos sufrimos,	Tell me that we both suffer,
Y que en un mismo tormento	And that in the same torment
Nuestras almas consumimos.	Our souls we consume.
No sé porqué se encadena	I don't know why my sad luck
Mi triste suerte a tu suerte,	Is imprisoned to your luck

Si no es que una misma pena	If it's not the same lament
Nos lleva a una misma muerte.	That takes us to the same death.
Infeliz!—en tu mirada	Unhappy!—In your gaze
Leo tu triste fortuna,	I read your sad fortune,
Y se que eres desgraciada	And I know that you are unhappy
Por que el pesar te importuna.	Because sorrow bothers you.
Tú, que ayer no mas vivías	You, who only lived yesterday
Tan hermosa entre placeres,	So beautiful among pleasures,
Y que inocente atraías	And how innocent you
La envidia de las mujeres	Attracted the envy of women
Tú sufres mucho . . lo veo . . .	You suffer a lot . . . I see . . .
Sufres, como yo, el martirio	You suffer, like me, the martyrdom
De acariciar un deseo	Of caressing a desire
Que tan solo es un delirio.	That is only a delusion.
Tú pensáste, criatura,	You thought, gentle creature,
Que un amor amor alcanza,	That love reaches love,
Y que visto que en amargura	And that I saw that in bitterness
Se ha deshecho tu esperanza.	Your hope has been undone.
Yo también sufrí un engaño! . . .	I too suffered a deception! . . .
Tambien yo tuve ambiciones	I too had ambitions
Y en el mar del desengaño	And in the sea of disappointment
Se ahogaron mis ilusiones.	My illusions were drowned.
Yo las ví cuando murieron . . .	I saw them when they died . . .
Las ví en indolente calma,	I saw them in indolent calm,
Cuando al abismo cayeron	When they fell into the abyss
Desde el fondo de mi alma!	From the bottom of my soul!
. . . .	. . . .
. . . .	. . . .
. . . .	. . . .
. . . .	. . . .
Si nuestras almas amaron	If our souls loved
Con funesta idolatría,	With baleful idolatry,
Si el alma que se soñaron	If the soul that they dreamed of
Era una luz que no ardía.	Was a light that did not burn.

Sí pues tú tienes tu pena	Yes, well, you have your pain
Y yo tengo mis dolores,	And I have my pains,
Y la muerte nos condena,	And death condemns us,
Y llorar nuestros amores.	And [we] cry our loves.
Ven—acércate a mi lado	Come—come to my side
Y nuestras penas lloremos:	And we will cry our sorrows:
Yo también soy desgraciado . . .	I too am unhappy . . .
Los dos nos consolarémos. F. P. R.	We will both comfort each other. F. P. R.

In twelve rhyming quatrains, Ramírez's speaker shows us that he is a good reader of emotions: "Leo tu triste fortuna, / Y se que eres desgraciada" (I read your sad fortune / And I know that you are unhappy)" (10–11). Griswold del Castillo argues that the "painful sentiments expressed in love poems and songs reflected the poetic conventions of the period."[53] The speaker's pain and suffering mirror the pain and suffering of the poem's addressee, "Maria Antonia," who the speaker claims is "desgraciada / Por que el pesar te importuna" (unhappy / Because sorrow bothers you) (11–12). The speaker links Maria Antonia's suffering to his own, expressing empathy for her sentiments: "Tú sufres mucho .. lo veo . . . / Sufres, como yo" (You suffer a lot .. I see . . . / You suffer like me) (17–18). This is a twinned suffering which the speaker ambiguously describes as absolutely consuming the lives of him and his love interest.

Ramírez's poetic style is importantly informal, emitting a casual sense of familiarity to his readers. The regular use of the informal "Tú" instead of the formal "Usted" throughout the poem suggests that the speaker's relationship with Maria Antonia, and by extension to readers of the poem, is familiar and undecorated by the formalities of respect and custom. The consecutive use of the monosyllabic "Tú" at the beginning of stanzas 4 through 6 creates accented beats of address: "Tú, que ayer no mas vivías" (You, who only lived yesterday) (13); "Tú sufres mucho .. lo veo . . . " (You suffer a lot .. I see . . .) (17); "Tú pensáste, criatura" (You thought, gentle creature) (21). This accented informal "Tú" parallels the speaker's lyrical pronoun, "Yo," in stanzas 7, 8, and 12: "Yo también sufrí un engaño! . . . " (I too suffered a deception! . . . " (25); "Yo las ví cuando murieron . . . " (I saw them when they died . . .) (29); "Yo también soy desgraciado . . . " (I too am unhappy . . . " (47). The grammatical mirroring of "Tú" and "Yo" links the speaker to Maria Antonia, rhetorically solidifying their twinned pains of lost love. Furthermore, "Tú"/"Yo" also connects the speaker to *El Clamor Público*'s readers who may have seen themselves and/ or their own relationships in the poem. After all, as Ovalle Perez argues, "the content of the [dedication] cements the idea that the structure of the poem is fashioned for an intended person or persons."[54]

If, as Griswold del Castillo declares, early Chicanx poems displayed the "day-to-day relations between the sexes," then one might read "A Mi Maria Antonia" as a dedication to Ramírez's own love interest.[55] I have found no biographical evidence that confirms a love interest by that name connected to Ramírez, however. Maria Antonia may be a stand-in for another woman or for all lovers plagued by "un deseo / Que tan solo es un delirio" (a desire / That is only a delusion) (19–20). The poem's absence of language—its discursive omissions and gaps—reflects this lack of information about Ramírez's mysterious love interest. This absence is best captured in the poem's excessive use of ellipses.

In the poem, ellipses represent a longing and meditative state, a search for answers that begins with a drowning descent of the speaker's illusions: "Se ahogaron mis ilusiones // Cuando al abismo cayeron. / Desde el fondo de mi alma!" (My illusions were drowned. // When they fell into the abyss / From the bottom of my soul!) (28, 31–32). Following these lines appears a stanza-long ellipsis that visually represents the descent into the "the bottom of [the speaker's] soul" (29–32). This discursively elliptical stanza empties itself of the rhymes, beats, and imageries of the poem, encouraging readers, perhaps, to imagine or customize them. In a sense, the ellipsis provides a visual silence, a blank canvas for meaning-making possibility. In thinking about the use of ellipses in *poetisas'* poems, Ovalle Perez claims that while newspaper poets

> could have intended to include the lines of ellipses [in their poems], it is also possible the newspaper editor inserted them (perhaps in place of verses that were cut for space). Either way, for readers, the ellipses could represent a visual absence connoting a geographical and bodily separation.[56]

As both poet and editor, Ramírez would have had more control over the typesetting and publication of his poem, which makes the intentionality of his ellipses perhaps clearer and more deliberate. Taking the use of ellipses as an aesthetic choice by Ramírez, the ellipsis is a bridge between stanzas 8 and 10. The important thematic link results in a joining of souls between the speaker's individual soul "mi alma" (my soul) in stanza 8 (32) and his love interest's, which in stanza 10 he refers to as "nuestras almas" (our souls) (37). The stuff that links their souls is in a sense ineffable. It is a type of time passing in symbolic beats that are the dots of time. The speaker does not provide answers or remedies for their suffering, only companionship and sympathy. At the poem's end, the speaker calls to Maria Antonia, "Ven—acércate a mi lado / Y nuestras penas lloremos" (Come—come to my side / And we will cry our sorrows) (45–46). They are joined by a type of consolatory reciprocity, a collective "we" which is both their unity and mirrored desolation. The poem's penultimate line brings back the ellipsis to show a somber lack of language for the speaker's poignancy: "Yo también soy desgraciado . . . " (I too am unhappy . . .) (47). Rhetorically, this sentimental performance is a courting ritual, which the speaker hopes will win over Maria Antonia as implied in the final line: "Los dos nos consolarémos" (We will both comfort each other) (48).

In 1971, the Chicanx editors of the magazine *El Grito: A Journal of Contemporary Mexican-American Thought* reprinted Ramírez's "A Mi Maria Antonia" as an example of nineteenth-century Mexican American poetry.[57] It is an interesting choice given how many poems were reprinted and therefore reimaged in *El Clamor Público*. Although most were not authored by Mexican American poets, these reprint poems too represent a vital part of the tradition of Mexican American poetry in the Southwest, a tradition of reclamation, rewriting, and access that deserves more attention. After all, with no byline or bibliographic record, it was nearly impossible for readers to distinguish poems written by Mexican Americans and reprints by Latin American and Spanish poets which Ramírez heavily edits.

THE IMAGINED UNIVERSALITY OF A MEXICAN AMERICAN EDITOR

The formation of Mexican American poetry in *El Clamor Público* goes hand in hand with Ramírez's editorship of poems and his desire to create a paper that was both local and universal. In this sense, *El Clamor Público*'s poems in part account for Ramírez's attempt to achieve what Mariano Siskind calls "the contradiction between the desire for universality and the marginal conditions of enunciation [that point] to the anxiety and frustration of a split subject."[58] Ramírez's split subjectivity of Mexican American is a hyphenated border split between the imperial and the imperialized. This subjectivity is the cultural, political, social, and geographical circumstance of his publication, allowing Ramírez to keep track of the political and intellectual needs of his readers which, in a sense, were his own.

Informing his reprint choices, this split subjectivity of Mexican American allowed Ramírez to concretize an "imagined universality," or what Siskind deems a "world of undifferentiated symmetric relations among equivalent literary cultures."[59] In other words, in the pages of a radical newspaper, the traffic in reprint poems did not subvert the local culture in the service of cosmopolitan ideals. Gruesz points this out in her important treatment of *El Clamor Público*'s poetic offerings, arguing that *El Clamor Público*'s

> regular juxtaposition of previously published poems by noted writers with local, vernacular texts may complicate attributions of authorship, but that very confusion also helps bolster the authority of local producers, reinforcing the significance of their efforts by putting them on the same plane as international luminaries.[60]

With well-known poets reprinted alongside lesser and unknown writers, the disjointed nature of American literary culture enables, as in the case of *El*

Clamor Público, a democratized material space of comparable literary cultures where readers encounter both local and universal literary traditions on an intellectual and aesthetic level playing field.

Ramírez's choice of reprint poems shows that he was not invested in the imitation of national-popular materials, voices, and images of the US and Anglophone world. His desire to reprint poems recognized a common modernizing anxiety: sustaining an identity, culture, and people that is consistently under attack. At the same time, his reprints interrogate the cultural hegemony of Spanish and Latin American modern culture and the aesthetic or conceptual materials that bear the traces of Latin America's asymmetrical social relations. Extending across national boundaries, *El Clamor Público*'s transamerican poems are not just reprints. They are new and innovative forms of cultural production that facilitated a sense of belonging and subject-position stability for Californios. The reprint lives of these representative poems serve as evidence for the popularity and, to an extent, the significance of poetry to Californios of this period.

Conclusion

The poems in this chapter reflect a long tradition of writing, publishing, and reprinting Spanish-language poems in the western hemisphere, part of a mostly unknown but rich history of poets and editors who have contributed to the literary and cultural production of the United States. These poems evince how frontier editors like Ramírez enacted their own poetics of paratextuality of editing reprints in order to curate and customize poems that centralize Hispanophone readers' cultural and aesthetic interests. These transamerican poems are not contained by nation-based poetics, requiring us to think beyond a nationalist literary and intellectual culture in order to theorize specific print practices which, by nature, are borderless and nationless.

As shown in this chapter, unbylined reprints decenter authorship from the poem, distorting and at times erasing authorial connections as well as nationalist and cultural signifiers. Unbylined Spanish poets like Zorrilla and Villergas, and their cultural and social connections to Spain, are obscured in *El Clamor Público*'s publications. The same can be said about the print origins of Latin American poems by Numa Pompilio Llona and Francisco Javier Balmaseda, whose verses are unbound from the nation-making artifact of the anthology and book. While in these cases poems shed national signifiers, in other cases the poems' genres were transformed. The process of lifting poems from their original publications and reprinting them with new titles altered the poems' original message and genre, ultimately creating new versions of the same poems and at times new genres. In the case of *El Clamor Público*'s satirical reprints, we see how even when these poems are reprinted without bylines or with new titles, the genre of satire, for the most part, remains unchanged. This is not the case for many of *El Clamor Público*'s dedication reprints, which omitted a characteristic component of the genre, the poem's addressee. These reprint practices of unbylined reprints and edited titles are vital components of the (un)formation of authorship and genre in the mid-century Southwest Hispanophone press, which facilitated a specifically pan-Hispanic transcultural literary culture.

The process of reprinting made many of *El Clamor Público*'s poems authorless, at times nationless, and genre-bending. Many of these verses exist in a liminal space of bibliographic relevance and irrelevance, prevailing in this specific form only in *El Clamor Público*'s printscape. This liminal textual space allowed readers to imagine a poet like themselves, Californio, Hispanic, nonwhite, living at the margins of Latin America, as writer and creator. Ramírez's decision to alter certain poems for his public suggests an editorial impulse to shape the aesthetic principles of poems, showing us a crucial link between print culture and aesthetic cultural production. Reprinting poems in newspapers was a creative way for editors like Ramírez to affirm to themselves and their communities a Hispanophone Latinx literary culture that was both local and transnational, personal and public, and American and transamerican.

Ramírez's editorship allows us to imagine a new form of US cultural history, one that dethrones the fiction of American literature as nation-bound works with only monolingual and Anglocentric origins.[61] This is imperative not just for conceptualizing the print culture and writing of Hispanophone people in the US, people that categorically do not fit within the simplistic parameters of language and nation, English and the US. This is also crucial for conceptualizing a more comprehensive understanding of nineteenth-century poetry in the US, which included the voices of Hispanic editors, poets, and readers.

The culture of reprint poems, as McGill demonstrates, was ubiquitous in mid-nineteenth-century newspapers. In the case of Ramírez's editorship, we see how this culture allowed a young frontier editor to curate verse that, like his news, he felt was important and worth reading. This curation determined a specific poetic taste and value for his readers based on their cultural needs and customs. Taking on the pervasive practice of reprinting poems during the worst financial crisis in the nineteenth century, the Panic of 1857, the following chapter shows how reprint poems contribute to systems of value- and taste-making. The reprint afterlives of poems about money, railroads, and "hard times" reflect surrounding and paratextual conversations regarding similarly important issues. In 1857, reprint poems occasioned by the panic became cultural expressions of fiscal anxiety grounded in the conditions of the working class.

NOTES

1. Nicolás Kanellos, "*El Clamor Público*: Resisting the American Empire." *California History* 84, no. 2 (2006): 10.
2. Gruesz, *Ambassadors of Culture*, xii.

3. Paul Bryan Gray, *A Clamor for Equality: Emergence and Exile of Californio Activist Francisco P. Ramírez* (Lubbock: Texas Tech University Press, 2012), xvii.
4. John R. Chávez, *The Lost Land: The Chicano Image of the Southwest* (Albuquerque: University of New Mexico Press, 1984), 1.
5. Rosina Lozano, *An American Language: The History of Spanish in the United States* (Oakland: University of California Press, 2018), 5.
6. Gray, *Clamor for Equality*, 6.
7. Gray, *Clamor for Equality*, 22.
8. Gray, *Clamor for Equality*, 21.
9. Luis Leal, "Truth-Telling Tongues: Early Chicano Poetry," *Recovering the U.S. Hispanic Literary Heritage*, ed. Ramón Gutiérrez and Genaro Padilla (Houston: Arte Público Press, 1993), 52.
10. Gray, *Clamor for Equality*, 21.
11. Paul Bryan Gray, "Francisco P. Ramirez: A Short Biography," *California History* 84, no. 2 (2006): 20.
12. Richard Griswold del Castillo, *Los Angeles Barrio, 1850–1890: A Social History* (Berkeley: University of California Press, 1979), 91.
13. Luis Leal, "Pre-Chicano Literature: Process and Meaning (1539–1959)," *Handbook of Hispanic Cultures in the United States: Literature and Art*, ed. Francisco Lomelí, general eds. Nicolás Kanellos and Claudio Esteva-Fabregat (Houston: Arte Público Press, 1993), 71.
14. Leal, "Pre-Chicano Literature," 71.
15. Anna Brickhouse, *Transamerican Literary Relations and the Nineteenth-Century Public Sphere* (Cambridge: Cambridge University Press, 2004), 8.
16. Meredith McGill, *American Literature and the Culture of Reprinting, 1834–1853* (Philadelphia: University of Pennsylvania Press, 2007), 7.
17. McGill, *Traffic in Poems*, 108.
18. Kanellos, "*El Clamor Público*," 12.
19. Kanellos, "*El Clamor Público*," 12.
20. Chávez, *Lost Land*, 50–51.
21. Kanellos, "*El Clamor Público*," 12.
22. Kanellos, "*El Clamor Público*," 12.
23. Griswold del Castillo, *Los Angeles Barrio*, 134.
24. Griswold del Castillo, *Los Angeles Barrio*, 134.
25. Griswold del Castillo, *Los Angeles Barrio*, 134.
26. Raúl Coronado, *A World Not to Come: A History of Latino Writing and Print Culture* (Cambridge, MA: Harvard University Press, 2013), 30.
27. "Notes [to the Articles within This Issue]," *California History* 84, no. 2 (2006): 69.
28. Francisco P. Ramírez, *El Clamor Público*, April 7, 1855.
29. Kanellos, "*El Clamor Público*," 12.
30. Coronado, *World Not to Come*, 28.
31. Coronado, *World Not to Come*, 28.
32. Coronado, *World Not to Come*, 28.
33. Ryan Cordell, "Reprinting, Circulation, and the Network Author in Antebellum Newspapers," *American Literary History* 27, no. 3 (2015): 436.

34. Cordell, "Reprinting," 418.
35. "*El Clamor Público*'s Poems: An Interactive Map" is a digital map that displays the original publication locations of ninety-eight of *El Clamor Público*'s poems. These poems were initially published in Mexico (28), Spain (26), Portugal (1), Puerto Rico (2), Cuba (13), Peru (2), Colombia (8), Ecuador (2), Nicaragua (1), Argentina (1), Chile (2), Venezuela (2), the United States (4), England (3), France (1), Portugal (1), and Italy (1). Spain and Mexico were *El Clamor Público*'s largest source for reprints. The twenty-six poems originally published in Spain are by Spanish poets, and the twenty-eight poems originally published in Mexico are authored by Mexican poets. The map is interactive and functions as an archive, housing jpeg images of poems from *El Clamor Público*. Several symbols on the map describe the poems' publication and geographical provenance. The newspaper icon that only appears in California shows the four poems that were originally published in *El Clamor Público*. The printer icon represents the reprint poems' original place of publication. The quotation icon shows the original place of publication of the poems' epigraphs.
See <https://www.google.com/maps/d/viewer?mid=1BHIF9Bcw-1D26z8HH5UPbFy3Sl CP5Sme&ll=38.32091644769891%2C-51.51408904999994&z=3> (last accessed July 26, 2023).
36. Ratner, "Paratexts," 735.
37. Using Google Books, HathiTrust, and the Chronicling America Database to run keyword searches of words, lines, and phrases from *El Clamor Público*'s unbylined poems shows that, in many cases, unattributed poems are by well-known and widely published poets including, to name a few, Spanish poets Juan Bautista Arriaza (1770–1837), Juan Martínez Villergas (1817–94), Salvador Bermúdez de Castro Díez (1817–83), Juan Eugenio Hartzenbusch (1806–80), and José Selgas (1822–82); and Mexican poets Guillermo Prieto (1818–97), Fernando Orozco y Berra (1822–69), Juan Díaz Covarrubias (1837–59), Juana Inés de la Cruz (1648–95), Francisco Granados Maldonado (?–1872), and Marcos Arróniz (?–1859).
38. Katherine Bode, "Thousands of Titles Without Authors: Digitized Newspapers, Serial Fiction, and the Challenges of Anonymity," *Book History* 19 (2016): 285.
39. Bode, "Thousands of Titles," 284.
40. Cohen, *Social Lives*, 92.
41. Cohen, *Social Lives*, 86.
42. Ricardo Navas Ruiz, *El Romanticismo Español* (Madrid: Cátedra, 1982), 34.
43. All translations are mine.
44. Cohen, *Social Lives*, 147.
45. Francisco Javier Balmaseda, *Rimas Cubanas* (Habana: Tipografia de Don Vicente de Torres, 1846), 131.
46. "El Calendario en Verso" (Calendar in Verse) appeared in later anthologies as "Los Hombres" (Men).
47. Stanitzek, "Texts and Paratexts," 33.
48. Genette, *Paratexts*, 73.
49. Genette, *Paratexts*, 77.
50. Vanessa Ovalle Perez, "Voicing a Transnational Latina Poetics: The Dedication Poems of Amelia Denis and Carlota Gutierrez," *J19: The Journal of Nineteenth-Century Americanists* 8, no. 2 (2020): 297.

51. Ovalle Perez, "Voicing," 297.
52. Numa Pompilio Llona, *Cantos Americanos: Coleccion de Poesias de D. Numa P. Llona* (Paris: P.-A. Bourdier, 1866), 223.
53. Griswold del Castillo, *Los Angeles Barrio*, 72.
54. Ovalle Perez, "Voicing," 306.
55. Griswold del Castillo, *Los Angeles Barrio*, 72.
56. Ovalle Perez, "Voicing," 307.
57. *El Grito* was edited by Octavio I. Romano-V., Nick C. Vaca, and Herminio Ríos in Berkeley, California from 1967 to 1974. The journal published both scholarship and creative work by Mexican Americans from across the US.
58. Mariano Siskind, *Cosmopolitan Desires: Global Modernity and World Literature in Latin America* (Evanston, IL: Northwestern University Press, 2014), 9.
59. Siskind, *Cosmopolitan Desires*, 125.
60. Gruesz, *Ambassadors of Culture*, 105.
61. Brickhouse, *Transamerican Literary Relations*, 4.

3

THE REPRINT LIVES OF "PANIC POETRY"

No topic seems more un-poetic than money. Yet the historical record shows that numerous poems about money, class, and finance were published during what panic scholars call the worst financial depression of the nineteenth century: the Panic of 1857. Many of these poems appeared in newspapers and not in books or magazines, accounting for a pervasive reprint culture among wide-ranging publics. Within a paratext of news and advertisements connecting readers to some of the most pressing questions and concerns of the time, these poems were a core impulse in the formation of a poetics of information in the mid-nineteenth century.

As demonstrated in the previous chapter, reprinting poems was a regular practice in the production of antebellum newspapers. These poems represent what Meredith McGill calls a "literature defined by its exuberant understanding of culture as iteration and not origination."[1] Mid-century reprint poems were legal and generally a part of the cultural norm. Their proliferation throughout the nineteenth century was, as McGill posits, "proof of democratic institutions' remarkable powers of enlightenment."[2] Perhaps more than any other medium, newspapers proliferated this culture of iteration on a mass scale. Newspapers on average circulated more broadly and across social classes. This was in part because, unlike bound volumes and magazines which were more expensive to produce and often limited to a subscription demographic, newspapers were cheaper, accessible, and widely available. Ellen Gruber Garvey notes that "newspapers constituted a new category of media: cheap, disposable and yet somehow tantalizingly valuable, if only their value could be separated from their ephemerality."[3] While Garvey reconciles the newspaper's ephemerality and value by studying the cultural significance of scrapbooks, this chapter turns to the frequency of iteration, that is, the scale of reproduction and ground covered by reprint poems within specific networks and printscapes.

In this chapter, the culture of reprinting poems meets the historical phenomenon of the Panic of 1857. I demonstrate that the reprint life of panic poems during the Panic of 1857 was a far-reaching national phenomenon. Drawing examples from popular dailies and weeklies in 1857, I examine the reproduction of three popular panic poems: "The Lay of the Directors," "Lines by Buster" (both anonymously published), and "Hard Times" by Alfred "Alf" F. Burnett (1824–84). I analyze the poems in terms of their potential for what Shira Wolosky calls "public speech," that is, their open engagement with "issues of public concern, offering . . . an avenue for participation in social and political debate."[4] As forms of public speech, the panic poems in this study participated in social and political debates regarding finance, specie payments, railroad bonds, and poverty. The poems' specific use of railroad and bank speech made them particularly valuable to the media market of the time. In their reprint afterlives, these poems contributed to discursive networks of cultural production, disseminating information that was current, intertextual, and poetic.

The three poems in this chapter gained social value through robust reprinting and circulation. Collectively, they were reprinted in fifty-four popular dailies and weeklies and circulated in twenty-two states and fifty-five cities and townships between July 23, 1857 and January 9, 1858. This robust reprint culture created what Ryan Cordell calls a "feedback loop," that is, when "texts circulated because of their perceived value to readers while that perceived value was often tied to a given piece's wide circulation."[5] Cordell demonstrates that reprinting caused an escalation of value since readers assumed that widely reprinted newspaper content was reprinted because it was beloved. The paratext of these poems can help us to better understand this escalation of values, that is, why these poems stand out among the trove of mid-century newspaper poems published during the Panic of 1857; and how they participated in social and political debates and gained a renewed sense of significance in the public through robust circulation. Ultimately, this chapter encourages reading practices that are attuned to shifting networks, printscapes, and publics. The panics of past, the industrialization of the 1850s, and the threat of Civil War already taking hold of the public consciousness generated social and cultural distrust that in many cases served as the crucial historical context for the poems in this chapter.[6]

The Panic of 1857

The railroad industry suffered great financial loss during the Panic of 1857. In the years leading to the panic, the railroad industry was steadily growing. Migration to western states and territories, especially in Kansas, created a demand for transportation. As the railroads became profitable, the banks seized the opportunity to provide railroad companies with large loans.[7] After 1850, Ohio Life Insurance and Trust Company started offering high-interest-rate loans to railroad companies. Many New York banks followed its lead. Historian Scott Reynold Nelson argues that "every railroad that needed ready capital kept a New York City office in order to borrow from Ohio Life or any of the other New York banks that specialized in on-call loans for bonds."[8] The railroad market created value out of loose charters and speculation, with Ohio Life being the main source of revenue. When railways did not pay their loans, trust companies sold their bonds to the highest bidder. Railroad bonds were deeded federal land grants, which meant that their underlying value rested on mortgaged land. The Central Pacific, Union Pacific, Texas and Pacific, Santa Fe, Northern Pacific, and Great Northern received the vast majority of the land grant aid.[9] Some railroad barons acquired these land grants secretly, violating state charters that prevented railroads from owning or borrowing from other railroads.

These events essentially led to rapid escalation of market value and a subsequent crash. When the New York branch of Ohio Life collapsed on August 24, 1857 due to bad investments in agricultural exports to Europe, it precipitated a stock market crash and a social panic that led to hundreds of bank closures. "Poor administration of railroad and banks alike," Jay Sexton posits, "intensified what initially appeared to be an isolated instance of mismanagement. Railroad stock and confidence in the nation's monetary institutions plummeted."[10] Soon after, news of the bank closures spread quickly through the telegraph and periodicals, prompting investors to anxiously withdraw their money from banking institutions, causing the beginning of the panic. Prices of railroad stocks were driven above their intrinsic value, causing a stock market bubble.[11] Businesses also began to fail, and hundreds of workers were laid off.

There is a chartable correlation between the inflationary value of reprint poems and market crashes. Reprints of "The Lay of the Directors," "Lines by Buster," and "Hard Times" skyrocketed at the height of the Panic of 1857, when railroad shares and bank notes were particularly unstable. Out of the fifty-four reprints I surveyed, thirty-one of them appeared in October alone, when the panic reached boiling point as unemployment and bank failures rose.[12] Except for the month of November, which saw twelve reprints, no other month in 1857 saw more than three reprints of the three poems.

We should expect to find more panic poems in newspapers during a financial crisis. However, the scale on which these poems were reprinted is a sign of their social urgency in the public sphere. Given that the majority of newspaper material, whether news, ads, editorials, or poems, was reprinted only two or three times, the number of reprints for the poems under study is distinctive in this period.[13] For example, my survey shows that in 1857, other newspaper poems about the panic, including "The Times" (*Plattsburgh Republican*, October 31, 1857), "The Battle of Life," "Give Me the People" (both in the *Belmont Chronicle*, June 2, 1857), and "Confidence and Credit" (*The Liberator*, December 11, 1857) were not reprinted outside of their original publication, thus not acquiring social value through vast circulation.

"Panic Poetry"

"The Lay of the Directors" and "Lines by Buster" initially appeared together in the New York *Evening Post* in a column entitled "PANIC POETRY" on the front page of the October 2, 1857 issue (see Figure 3.1 for the general layout of the newspaper).[14] In the years between the Panic of 1857 and the Civil War, the New York *Evening Post* was one of only a few Democratic newspapers in New York. Its editor, William Cullen Bryant, championed the working-class poor and disenfranchised and furnished support from literary societies for labor unions. This newspaper catered in part to a social group of New York merchants who read and put out advertisements in the paper.[15] Although both poems were originally printed together in the *Evening Post*, they were reprinted separately in thirty-three newspapers in 1857. Before analyzing the circulation of these poems within the newspaper system, it is worth studying the poems' content within their original printscape in the *Evening Post*.

"The Lay of the Directors"

"The Lay of the Directors" is a call-and-response poem that uses railroad and financial discourse to rebuke railroad directors, describing them as deceptive and gluttonous financiers. The following is a transcription of "The Lay of the Directors" as it initially appeared in the *Post*:

> [For the Evening Post.]
> The Lay of the Directors
> *Respectfully Dedicated to the Directors of the — R. R. Co., by a Victimized Stockholder.*
>
> Who, when the times were good and bright,
> And speculation at its height,
> Made Railroad shares appear all right?
>   Directors.
>
> Who, when my money was paid in,
> Assured me that the road must win
> A large percentage on the "tin?"
>   Directors.

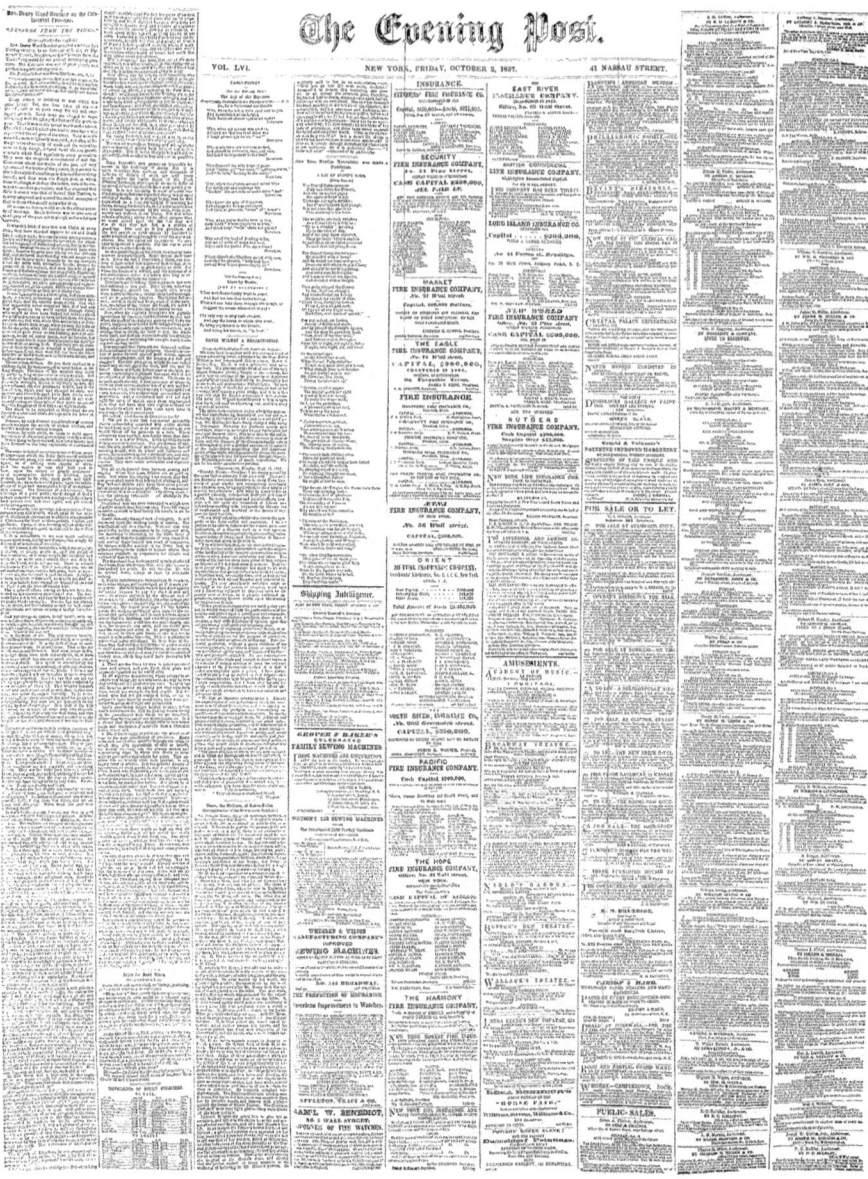

Figure 3.1 Front page, *The Evening Post*, October 2, 1857. Library of Congress. Public domain.

Who made the costs increase so fast,
And shared in contracts, long and vast,
And filled their pockets to the last?
      Directors.

Who flattered me with hopes of gains
From "branches," "air-lines," "lightning trains,"
And "feeders," leading to the mains?
      Directors.

Who, when the chance seemed rather blue
For dividends and earnings too,
"Cooked" the accounts to make them "do?"
      Directors.

Who know the arts of financiers,
And charge fat fees as endorsers,
And turn, at pleasure, "bull" or "bears"?
      Directors.

Who, when grave doubts arise in this,
Seek lands "where ignorance is bliss,"
And think large "sells" there not amiss?
      Directors.

Who swell the load of floating debts,
And set all sorts of traps and nets,
Who catch the public with their frets?
      Directors.

Whom should stockholders guard with care,
Lest they be cheated, "hide and hair,"
And all their hopes prove empty air?
      Directors.

The word "Lay" in the title categorizes the poem as a type of song and/or ballad. Since the sixteenth century, "lay" has described lyrical poems "usually dealing with matter of history or romantic adventure."[16] The poem's subtitle, "Respectfully Dedicated to the Directors of the — R. R. Co., by a Victimized Stockholder," satirizes the lay by first framing the poem as a dedication to railroad directors and, second, by offering a byline for the poem. As a byline, "a Victimized Stockholder" refers to the poet/speaker as both an individual and a metonym for the suffering bourgeois. This "Victimized Stockholder" is critical of a generic railroad company, the "R. R. Co.," and its dishonest financiers. Every stanza emphasizes the deception of directors with a series of anaphoric questions that begin with the pronoun "who(m)" and end with the epistrophe "Directors."[17] These rhetorical questions double as grievances against the "Directors of the — R. R. Co.," who have "Victimized [the] Stockholder." For instance, in the first stanza, the speaker claims that "when the times were good and bright . . . [railroad directors] made Railroad shares appear all right," leading the stockholder into investing in the railroad industry (1–3). Then, after "assur[ing the speaker] that the road must win [,] . . . made the costs increase so fast" (6–9).

In "The Lay of the Directors," public speech, the quoted words and phrases, may be considered a type of slang, symptomatic of a railroad- and finance-specific discourse of the Panic of 1857. By slang, I mean "[t]he special vocabulary or phraseology of a particular calling or profession; the cant or jargon of a certain class or period."[18] Michael Adams argues that "slang is language of a group with a shared interest but not a shared purpose."[19] Slang, according to Irving Lewis Allen, developed, in part, from the discourse of the economy. In *The City in Slang: New York Life and Popular Speech* (1993), Allen explains that the

> story [of slang] begins in history and is resolved primarily in the economic and social workings of the Great City. Popular speech and slang about city life in New York, or for that matter in any large city, anywhere in the world, or in any language, derives ultimately from the economic engine of the metropolis.[20]

The slang in "The Lay of the Directors" derives from a failing railroad industry and its impact on a contemporaneous suffering bourgeois class. Thus, slang in poetry reveals social classes, employment specialties, diverse lifestyles, as well as consumer cultures.[21]

"The Lay of the Directors" is part of the US poetic tradition of using slang for specific cultural and social effects.[22] In the nineteenth century, poets including Walt Whitman, James Whitcomb Riley, and Bret Harte routinely used slang, dialect, and vernacular in their writing, increasing their poems' accessibility and popularity. In her study of nineteenth-century hymnal songs, Claudia Stokes argues that vernacular lyrics "were typically characterized by features that enabled them to be accessible to a wide span of the public."[23] In *Schoolroom Poets: Childhood, Performance, and the Place of American Poetry, 1865–1917*, Angela Sorby claims that poets like Harte and Riley employed slang in their poems to incorporate "'high' and 'low' culture into a precarious balancing act that was further destabilized by racial, ethnic, and class anxieties."[24]

In "The Lay of the Directors," slang is a performance of railroad literacy. The quoted language in the poem suggests that select words and phrases are cited from other sources. These citations imply that the speaker's victimization is an epistemological problem based on a lack of information, a fate that the speaker wants readers to avoid. The quoted slang creates distance between the quoted words and the speaker (the "Victimized Stockholder"), suggesting that the speaker does not understand the slang, and this is why they can be so easily duped. This discursive distance is evident in the poem when the speaker claims stockholders are "flattered . . . with hopes of gains, / From 'branches,' 'air-lines,' 'lightning trains,' / And 'feeders,' leading to the mains" (13–15).[25] These words and phrases reveal an inconsistency of terms as the speaker names trains and railroad lines without differentiation. The speaker continues, claiming that directors falsely promise "hopes of gains" to convince stockholders to invest (13). Instead of fulfilling their promises, railroad directors "swell the load of floating debts / And set all sorts of traps and nets / [To] catch the public with their frets" (29–31). The metaphor of setting "traps and nets" shows how stockholders are trapped in a net of debt, "fret[ting]" for their release (31). The poem ends with a warning to the stockholder: "guard with care, / Lest they be cheated, 'hide and hair'" (33–34). The blame and liability of fraud falls on the epistrophic "Directors," which in each stanza is source of the anguish of the "Victimized Stockholder." By the end of the poem, the word "Directors" becomes nearly synonymous with deception and fraud.

Readers encountering this poem in the pages of the *Post* would not have failed to notice a paratext of relevant news and ads that, like the poem, repeats the word "Directors" (see Figures 3.3 and 3.4). This paratext contextualizes the poem's slang, providing readers with actual examples of victimization. For example, to the left of the poem's column is a lengthy jeremiadic sermon by the clergyman and social reformer Henry Ward Beecher entitled "Lessons from the Times" (see Figure 3.2).

The sermon contextualizes the moral accusations the speaker makes against directors. Beecher opens with a hermeneutic reading of Matthew 16:2–3: "O, ye hypocrites! ye can discern the face of the sky; but can ye not discern the signs of the times?"[26] After much proselytizing, Beecher claims that there is a "relaxation of moral integrity" connected to "the management of stocks" and explicitly blames the railroad board of directors for this moral relaxation: "The board of Directors . . . have permitted themselves to employ their power for selfish ends, by unscrupulous methods . . . it is one thing to buy and sell legitimately, and another to buy and sell as gamblers do."[27] As a paratext of "The Lay of the Directors," Beecher's sermon balances the poem's satirical tone with a sober and biblical timbre. This balance opens up a paratextual reading where the directors "Who know the arts of financiers, / And charge fat fees as endorsers, / And turn, at pleasure, 'bull' or 'bears'" are not simply unscrupulous but sinful against God (21–23).

The discourse of cheating directors in the poem and Beecher's sermon is crystalized in a series of paralleling fire insurance ads, which—resembling the poem's own line breaks—list their companies' "Directors" (see Figure 3.3).

Figure 3.2 "Lessons from the Times," *The Evening Post*, October 2, 1857. Library of Congress. Public domain.

Figure 3.3 Fire insurance ads, *The Evening Post*, October 2, 1857. Library of Congress. Public domain.

THE REPRINT LIVES OF "PANIC POETRY"

In this printscape, "Directors" is intertextual, reciprocally gesturing between the ads and the poem. When reading across the page, the proximity and intertextuality of ads and poem prompt a cautious reading of the ads, lest, like the speaker in the poem states, readers "be cheated, 'hide and hair'" (34). The likelihood of correlating the victimizing railroad directors with the insurance directors in the ads is more than feasible for readers of the *Post*, including, for example, merchants shopping for fire insurance to protect their businesses. For these readers, "The Lay of the Directors" paints the fire insurance directors, even if indirectly, as untrustworthy financiers who "set all sorts of traps and nets" (30). As "The Lay of the Directors" made the rounds, it was recontextualized within new printscapes for new publics, allowing the poem to generate value through circulation in the popular press.

The Reprint Afterlife of "The Lay of the Directors"

The newspaper-exchange system altered reprints of "The Lay of the Directors" in ways that shifted the poem's relationship to printscapes and networks. In 1857, "The Lay of the Directors" was reprinted in at least twelve newspapers in eleven cities and townships.[28] For example, on November 3, 1857, the *Wheeling Daily Intelligencer* reprinted the poem. Self-promoted as "a liberal and independent journal," the *Wheeling Daily Intelligencer* was a Republican daily that went on to characterize western Virginia as a free state before the Civil War.[29] The *Intelligencer*'s broad circulation, exceeding 3,000 in the 1860s, aided Wheeling's status as the capital of Virginia from 1863 to 1870. The ads and columns in the 1857 issues illustrate the paper's diverse readership of dry goods merchants, farmers looking to rent land, members of Congress, wet nurses in need of employment, and players of the Sparta Academy Lottery of Georgia.

In newspapers, value can be measured by the amount of time and labor editors, writers, and readers invested into a piece of writing. The *Intelligencer*'s reprint shows this value-making labor through the reassembly of the form and content of "The Lay of the Directors." The reprint, for example, is not published with the original title, "The Lay of the Directors," but under the heading "PANIC POETRY." "PANIC POETRY" citationally gestures to the original publication column in the New York *Evening Post*, exemplifying what Cordell calls the "network author," an idea that "accounts for the ways in which meaning and authority accrued to acts of circulation and aggregation across antebellum newspapers," even though the *Intelligencer* does not cite the newspaper title, as was common.[30] The *Intelligencer*'s new title frames the poem in more general terms. No longer just about "Directors," as in the original, the reprint title invokes the panic more broadly.

The editorship and circulation of this reprint models a collective authorship rather than an individual one, showing how the *Post* and *Intelligencer* respectively

99

labored at different times to compose and circulate, and recompose and recirculate this poem. For instance, likely considering the newspaper's public, the *Intelligencer*'s reprint of "The Lay of the Directors" changes the original dedication from "Respectfully Dedicated to the Directors of the—R. R. Co." to "Respectfully Dedicated to the Humbug and Credulity Railroad Company," creating for readers a new discursive threshold into the poem's content (see Figure 3.4).

Furthermore, with no lack of short poems making the rounds, one must account for the labor of intentionally editing a poem to fit on the page, instead of publishing a shorter one. Many of the *Intelligencer*'s readers would have encountered this poem for the first time as a reprint. For them, as was the case for many newspaper readers, the reprint was the original poem.[31] Figure 3.4 shows that the *Intelligencer*'s reprint omits four stanzas from the original poem, an editorial decision that speaks, even if indirectly, to the print-worthiness of certain stanzas over others. The *Intelligencer* only reprints stanzas 1, 2, and 5, leaving out much of the original content of the poem and creating, essentially, a new poem. In omitting stanzas 3–4 and 6–9, the reprint leaves out most of the slang words, which are a major component of the original poem. The reprinted stanzas (1, 2, and 5) feature only two slang words: "tin" (money or cash) and "cooked" (implying manipulation) (7, 11).[32] The omitted stanzas (3–4 and 6–9), on the other hand, contain nine slang words and idioms: "'branches', 'air-lines', 'lightning trains,'" "feeders," "'bull' or 'bears,'" "where ignorance is bliss," "sells," and "hide and hair" (14, 15, 23, 26, 27, 34). This poetic abridgment altered the poem's form and content in significant ways, but it does not drastically modify the precarious tone of the poem nor how readers engaged with and

Panic Poetry—Respectfully dedicated to the Humbug and Credulity Railroad Company, by a victimized stockholder:

> Who, when the times were good and bright,
> And speculation at its height,
> Made railroad shares appear all right?
>   Directors,
>
> Who, when money was paid in,
> Assured me that the road must win
> A large percentage on the "tin?"
>   Directors.
>
> Who, when the chance seemed rather blue
> For dividends and earnings too,
> "Cooked" the accounts to make them "do?"
>   Directors.

Figure 3.4 "Panic Poetry," *The Wheeling Daily Intelligencer*, November 3, 1857. Library of Congress. Public domain.

understood the poem's message. Although the poem is shorter, the speaker's warning about the corruptness of railroad directors is present. The *Intelligencer*'s candid dedication title, "Respectfully Dedicated to the Humbug and Credulity Railroad Company," appears to do the work of the missing stanzas by describing, before the body of the poem, the nature of the "Railroad Company" as "humbug and credulity." In the nineteenth century, "to humbug" meant "to deceive by words" while "credulity" meant to be "easily deceived."[33] Thus, a "Humbug and Credulity Railroad Company" is one that is both easily deceived and deceptive in return, a sham that readers should not trust.

Like the edited reprint poem, the newspaper page is a dynamic printscape molded and remolded by the shifting interests of publics. In the *Intelligencer*, the poem's paratext is made up of news and advertisements concerning the Panic of 1857 and railroads, revealing social relations of financial cataclysm. For example, like the poem, reports and ads in the *Intelligencer* depict winners and losers of the panic, that is, how while some suffered financially others prospered. In the third column, for example, the word "panic" appears again, this time in the context of a "Heiskell and Swearingen" advertisement for "silks and velvets" (see Figure 3.5).

Published during the peak of the panic, the ad notifies the public that the company's "stock of Fall and Winter Goods . . . have been purchased since the 'GREAT PANIC,' which has had the effect of reducing the prices of goods lower than they have been for many years."[34] In this context, "panic" does not suggest

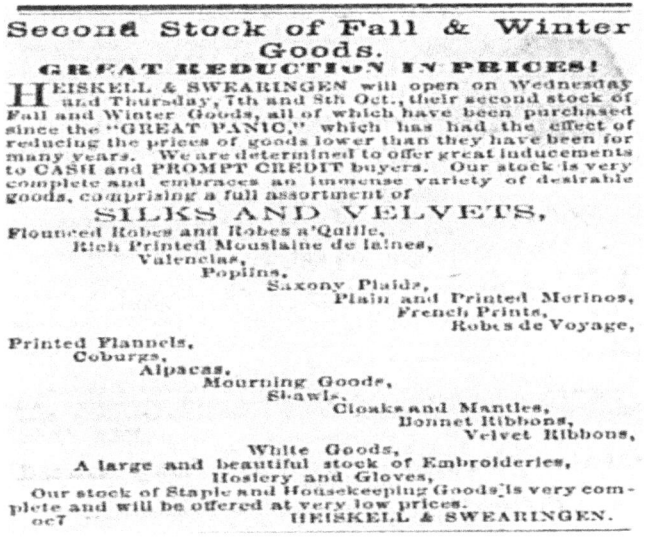

Figure 3.5 "Second Stock of Fall & Winter Goods," The *Wheeling Daily Intelligencer*, November 3, 1857. Library of Congress. Public domain.

financial ruin and fiscal anxiety. Instead, it implies a financial opportunity for customers looking to save money on material that has deteriorated in value.

The phrase "'GREAT PANIC'" appears in quotations either to show that the phrase is borrowed or as a hyperbolic gesture drawing attention to the ad's relevance to the financial panic. Akin to the short stanzas of the poem, which indent the last line, the ad's form fashions a series of indented line breaks that descend on the page from left to right, suggestive of a downward spiraling economy. The visual correlation of sliding texts with the depressing economy provides readers with a graphic representation of the panic in an ad about silks and velvets, ultimately showing us a potential synchronicity on the page influenced by an altered reprint. As seen in the examples above, a poem's paratext is a snapshot of its printscape. It is not a fixed or universal printscape for interpreting the poem, but a dynamic and constantly changing one that augments the meaning-making possibilities of the poem within various contexts.

"Lines by Buster"

Like "The Lay of the Directors," the companion poem "Lines by Buster," which appeared as part of the *Post*'s "PANIC POETRY" column, is a form of public speech that participated in social and political debates of 1857 by using slang that has a historical referent in the insolvency of banks.[35] The following is a transcription of the poem as it initially appeared in the *Evening Post* on October 2, 1857 (see Figure 3.2):

> [For the Evening Post]
> Lines by Buster,
> [NOT BY GOLDSMITH.]
> When merchants fondly trust to paper,
>   And find too late that banks betray,
> What art can help them through the scrape, or
>   Suggest the means wherewith to pay?
>
> The only way to stop each croaker
>   And pay the banks to whom they trust;
> To bring repentance to the broker.
>   And wring his bosom, is, "to bust?"

The use of bank slang in the poem is most prominent in the title, "Lines by Buster." The *OED*'s definition of "buster" is "[a] person who or thing which 'busts' a specified thing, or causes it to break or burst."[36] "Buster" derives from the phrase to "go bust," which means to go bankrupt.[37] The poem has two bylines. The first is in the form of a satirical title, "Lines by Buster," which suggests that the poem is in the voice of a speaker on the verge of "bust[ing]" (i.e. bankruptcy) (8). The second byline appears in brackets, "[NOT BY GOLDSMITH.]," implying this byline was added by someone who is not the poet. In this sense, the bracketed byline functions as a paratext informing the reader that the poet should not be confused with the eighteenth-century Irish poet Oliver Goldsmith (1728–74). "Lines by Buster" is a parody of Goldsmith's "When Lovely Woman Stoops to Folly." As such, it represents what Faith Barrett has termed "a poetics of parody," that is, a poem that pushes us to re-examine "the rhetorical conventions of poetry" in the nineteenth century.[38]

During the panic, the generic heterogeneity of "Lines by Buster" was a remarkably pliable means of expression. The poem's indistinct author, for instance, is ambiguously omniscient, from both the eighteenth and nineteenth centuries, comical yet sober. Barrett argues that nineteenth-century poem parodies serve as a "keynote genre" for understanding the "tonal dualities between sincere and parodic."[39] The byline of "Lines by Buster," "[NOT BY GOLDSMITH.]," features this tonal duality between sincere and parodic by troubling the idea of a unified and legible author. While the byline parodically gestures to Goldsmith's name, it also sincerely signals a type of insolvency that is rooted in a literal goldsmith, as in "one who fashions gold into jewellery, ornaments, articles of place, etc."[40] In this context, the poem is "[NOT BY [a] GOLDSMITH.]," that is, "[NOT BY]" an ornamentor of gold. This reading invites a contextualization of the impact of drained gold reserves during the panic. Allan H. Meltzer explains that "[w]ithin a few weeks of the start of the 1857 panic, the bank's discounts doubled. The loss of gold was so great [that banks were] forced to make use of the temporary power to issue notes without gold backing."[41] Bank notes issued without gold backing give up the fiction of inherent value. Thus, like issued unbacked bank notes, this poem has no "Goldsmith," that is, an identifiable author. This anonymity surrenders the fiction of authorial value. Not backed by the name of a famous poet, like Goldsmith, the intrinsic value of "Lines by Buster" lies in the poem's content, which transforms Goldsmith's love poem into a parody that underwrites the cultural distrust of banks, an immediate concern to publics living through the Panic of 1857.

Although "Lines by Buster" mimics the form of "When Lovely Woman Stoops to Folly," its use of slang revises the content of Goldsmith's poem and achieves what the literary theorist Linda Hutcheon calls an "imitation characterized by ironic inversion, not always at the expense of the parodied text."[42] The ironic inversion in "Lines by Buster" extends throughout the poem. For example, in lieu of addressing a "lovely woman [who] stoops to folly / And finds too late that men betray," the speaker in "Lines by Buster" addresses "merchants [who] fondly trust to paper / And find too late that banks betray" ("When Lovely," 1–2; "Lines," 1–2). These inversions show that romantic relationships resemble business relationships and how for both relationships, betrayal plays a central role. The inversion of the poems' addressees from "lovely woman" to "merchants" emphasizes another formulation of the parody: "repetition with critical distance, which marks difference rather than similarity."[43] For instance, although the *Post*'s parody and Goldsmith's original share formal elements (both are made up of two rhyming quatrains in iambic beats), the speakers in both poems offer distinctive counsel to "merchants" and to the unnamed "woman," respectively ("Lines," 1; "When Lovely," 1).

Juxtaposing the line "fondly trust to paper" in "Lines by Buster" with Goldsmith's "lovely woman [who] stoops to folly" enables the discursive relationship between the words "folly" and "paper" ("Lines," 2; "When Lovely," 2). In Goldsmith's poem, "folly" means "want of good sense . . . or *personified*, [as a]n example of foolishness."[44] In "Lines by Buster," "paper" is slang for paper money, which is a site of intimacy. In Jonathan Senchyne's phenomenological study of the role of paper in creating meaning in the early nineteenth century, he argues that "[f]or readers and writers during this time, paper acted and was figured as a site of intimacy, where intriguing proximities and contact became possible within the materiality of paper, book, and print."[45] Although Senchyne's focus is not the materiality of paper money, paper, as a site of intimacy, also extends to consumers' familiarity with and trust in paper currency. It is, after all, the intimacy of paper, that is, "When merchants fondly trust to paper," that causes them to in turn trust the banks and eventually go bust ("Lines," 1). James L. Huston claims that during the Panic of 1857, "most state legislators concurred that their principal objective was to stop the reckless emission of paper money . . . The Panic had destroyed so much bank note circulation that many enterprises were left with worthless paper that no one would accept."[46] Thus, during the panic, "trust[ing] to paper" money was conceivably a type of "folly," that is, "[as a]n example of [fiscal] foolishness" ("Lines," 2; "When Lovely," 2).[47]

In "Lines by Buster" and Goldsmith's "When Lovely Woman Stoops to Folly," the addressees have been respectively betrayed by the "banks" and "men" ("Lines," 2; "When Lovely," 2). In order to remedy their betrayal, both speakers offer advice which, although different, may be characterized as self-destructive and counterintuitive. On the one hand, in "Lines by Buster," the speaker offers financial advice, claiming that the only "art" that can "help [these merchants] through the scrape, or / Suggest the means wherewith to pay" is "to bust," that is, "To become insolvent or bankrupt." (3–4, 8).[48] On the other hand, in "When Lovely Woman Stoops to Folly," the speaker offers romantic advice, claiming, "The only art her guilt to cover / To hide her shame from every eye . . . is to die" (5–8). Bankruptcy in "Lines by Buster" is a type of financial suicide that, like the real suicide in Goldsmith's "When Lovely Woman Stoops to Folly," brings a permanent end to "betray[al]" (2). A bankrupt man is also called "ruined"; so too the woman who "stoops" (or falls, which is another word for financial ruin) is ruined. The language of female value is much like the language of economic value. But while the ruined merchant/broker/bank can just start again, the woman in Goldsmith's poem has a more concretely fatal ending.

THE REPRINT LIVES OF "PANIC POETRY"

The social value of "Lines by Buster" is tied to the fact that it is a Goldsmith parody. Editing and/or cutting stanzas would have distorted the poem's genre and purge reprints of their parodic significance. This is perhaps why in all the reprints I surveyed, "Lines by Buster" appears unedited, save for its title, facilitating, as the shortest poem, the nineteenth-century editorial practice of reprinting poems in compact and limited textual spaces. In October 1857 alone, "Lines by Buster" was reprinted in twelve states and twenty-one cities and townships in the North, South, and (Mid)West.

The *Plattsburgh Republican* (1854–1920) reprinted "Lines by Buster" on October 31, 1857 under the citational title "PANIC POETRY."[49] The *Republican* reprint is unique among others because it includes an epigraph that reads, "Shakespeare long ago predicted this wild time among the Banks // 'I know a Bank whereon the wild thyme grows'" (see Figure 3.6).[50]

The first part of the epigraph seems to come from an editorial voice who introduces the second part from the King of the Fairies in Shakespeare's *A Midsummer Night's Dream*. In Shakespeare's original, the line reads: "I know a bank whereon the wild thyme blows / Where oxlips and the nodding violet grows."[51] The editorial voice playfully misreads Shakespeare's original, reading "bank" as a financial establishment rather than a sloping hill. According to Gérard Genette, the function of an epigraph is to provide the "echoes" of another work, that is, "the indirect support of another text, plus the prestige of a cultural filiation."[52] The echoes of *A Midsummer Night's Dream* and the

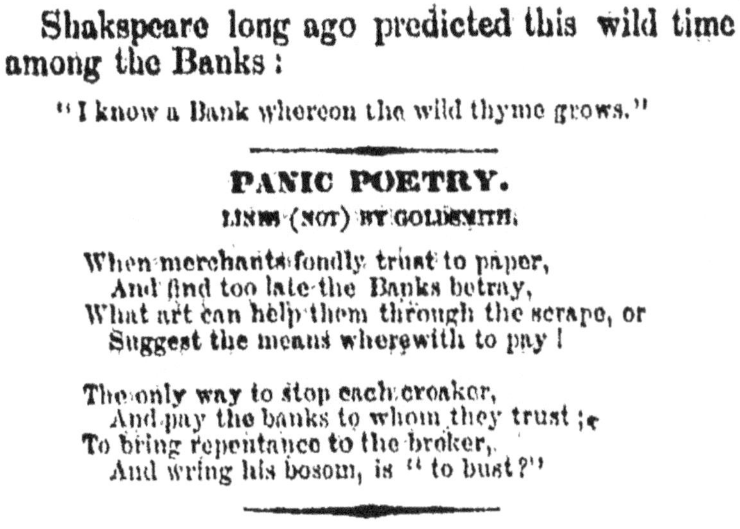

> Shakspeare long ago predicted this wild time among the Banks :
> "I know a Bank whereon the wild thyme grows."
>
> **PANIC POETRY.**
> LINES (NOT) BY GOLDSMITH.
>
> When merchants fondly trust to paper,
> And find too late the Banks betray,
> What art can help them through the scrape, or
> Suggest the means wherewith to pay !
>
> The only way to stop each croaker,
> And pay the banks to whom they trust ;
> To bring repentance to the broker,
> And wring his bosom, is " to bust?"

Figure 3.6 "Panic Poetry," *Plattsburgh Republican*, October 31, 1857. Library of Congress. Public domain.

105

cultural prestige of Shakespeare are, like "Lines by Buster," parodic. That is, they poke fun at the original for comical effects. Such discursive connections on the page remind us that the paratextual field of "Lines by Buster" can resituate not only the poem's placement but also the levels of parodic effect the poem deploys. For example, the epigraphical addition in the *Republican* creates a unique reprint where the echoes of Shakespeare and Goldsmith meet, showing us the comedic complexity of this reproduction. In the following section, I focus on how readings of "Lines by Buster" are especially tied to paratexts, which vary from newspaper to newspaper and from one public to the next.

Printscapes of "Lines by Buster" in Abolitionist Papers

The social value of "Lines by Buster" fluctuates from newspaper to newspaper and from one imagined public to the next. My survey reveals that in 1857, "Lines by Buster" was published in at least two abolitionist papers: the *Anti-Slavery Bugle* and the *Liberator*. In the Ohio-based *Anti-Slavery Bugle*, "Lines by Buster" is not simply a poem about economic injustice. In this new context, the reprint is grounded in the discourse of moral correctness and racial liberation. The *Anti-Slavery Bugle* was a weekly organ of the Ohio American Anti-Slavery Society (later the Western Anti-Slavery Society). For most of the paper's eighteen-year run, the *Bugle* was based out of Salem, Ohio, an active Underground Railroad station made up of a large Quaker population in Northeast Ohio. The *Bugle*'s circulation, however, extended outside Ohio in states such as Iowa, Illinois, Wisconsin, and Indiana. The minister and abolitionist Marius R. Robinson (1806–78) edited the *Bugle* from 1851 to 1861.[53]

The institution of slavery was essential for the economic progress of both Northern and Southern parts of the United States. In the years leading up to the Panic of 1857, for example, there was a cotton boom that benefited Northern economies as much as Southern ones. Sven Beckert and Seth Rockman argue that "[a]dvocates of national economic development presumed the reciprocal relationship of the slaveholding and non-slaveholding states, as well as the mutual interest of the slaveholder, manufacturer, and merchant."[54] Many Americans were aware of the capitalist network of slavery; as a result, abolitionist newspapers like the *Bugle* lambasted Northern self-righteousness. The *Bugle*'s motto, for instance—"No Union with Slaveholders"—underscores the reciprocity of racial capitalism, challenging the union of the US under the flag of bondage. Given that slavery was inseparable from the exchange of capital between the states, slavery capitalism, in essence, was American capitalism.[55] The *Bugle* showcased this interconnectedness of slavery and capitalism in its printscapes, often featuring "Lines by Buster" as a paratextual wedge. For example, on October 24, 1857, the *Bugle* reprinted "Lines by Buster" alongside a news item entitled "Assorting Brokers" (see Figure 3.7 for general layout).

THE REPRINT LIVES OF "PANIC POETRY"

Figure 3.7 "Assorting Brokers," *The Anti-Slavery Bugle*, October 24, 1857. Library of Congress. Public domain.

In the middle of "Assorting Brokers," the article criticizes the laws that protect bankers: "We do not deny that the law of the land protects them in their vocation."[56] However, just because it is law, the article continues, does not make the bankers' actions morally correct:

> The fact of their business being legitimate, moreover, does not make it respectable and proper. It is legal to establish negro-pens and to buy and sell slaves in our midst, and yet we should not like to engage in the business. There is no law against a banker receiving deposits from the poor and needy up to the hour before he closes his doors, and yet we cannot approve of such conduct.[57]

"Assorting Brokers" contextualizes the immorality of bankers within the institution of slavery, arguing that legal legitimacy does not constitute moral sanction. Using the language of commerce, the article posits that bankers and slaveholders are alike in that social codes and not just moral standing confirm their trade and practice. This rhetoric of injustice creates a new mode of discursive resonance for "Lines by Buster," one that decentralizes the poem's status as a parody of Goldsmith's "When Lovely Woman Stoops to Folly" and centralizes an abolitionist and rights-based context of slavery and money-handling.

Even among newspapers with similar political views, a reprint's printscape inflects unique discursive staging. For example, another abolitionist newspaper, William Lloyd Garrison's Boston-based *Liberator* (1831–65), reprints "Lines by Buster" on December 11, 1857, less than two months after the *Bugle*'s reprint (see Figure 3.8).

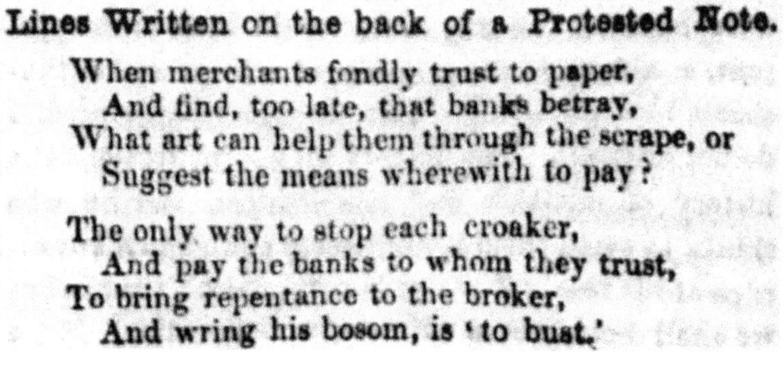

> **Lines Written on the back of a Protested Note.**
>
> When merchants fondly trust to paper,
>   And find, too late, that banks betray,
> What art can help them through the scrape, or
>   Suggest the means wherewith to pay?
>
> The only way to stop each croaker,
>   And pay the banks to whom they trust,
> To bring repentance to the broker,
>   And wring his bosom, is 'to bust.'

Figure 3.8 "Lines Written on the back of a Protested Note," *The Liberator*, December 11, 1857. Library of Congress. Public domain.

Garrison was aware of the reciprocity of slavery and capitalism and spoke out against it in the pages of his paper. Beckert and Rockman claim that "Garrison recognized the North as a 'partner in iniquity' and credited the Panic of 1837 with delivering a deserved ruin to those New York City mercantile firms engaged in commerce with the South."[58] The *Liberator*'s reprint appears under a new title, "Lines Written on the back of a Protested Note." A protested note is a promissory note that has not been paid by the maker at maturity. As a result, the note is legally *protested* by the holder of the note via a notarized sworn statement.[59] In the nineteenth century, people traded protested bank notes often without knowing they were bad until they tried to redeem them for legal tender. Not backed by cash, many of these notes became useless pieces of paper.

In "Lines Written on the back of a Protested Note," the materiality of the bank note is figurative, yet it calls attention to the literal contemporaneous circulation of paper money. During the months leading up to the *Liberator*'s reprint, the popular press regularly reported on insolvent notes, warning readers to guard against trading them. For example, on September 2, 1857, the *Summit County Beacon* (Akron, Ohio) prints a list of banks handing out "Discredited Bank Notes."[60] The article warns its readers, "Telegraphic information has been received that the following Banks have been refused by the Bankers of New York, and until further and reliable information can be obtained, we advise our customers to also decline taking them."[61]

The *Liberator*'s reprint title invites readers to imagine the material form and value of the paper the poem is printed on (see Figure 3.8). Through the literal proximity between the *Liberator*'s physical pages and its readers, readers were able to feel the materiality of the "Protested Note" and connect the poem's textuality to its physical form. The new title of "Lines by Buster" reintroduces the poem's content, staging a speaker who, perhaps out of frustration and disaffection, is inspired to "Writ[e] on the back of a Protested Note." In doing so, the "Protested Note" is both a synecdoche for paper money and the physical material through which the reader encounters the poem.

It is ironic that in the pages of the *Liberator* a discredited bank note becomes a vessel for advice about banks since a bad bank note gives up the fiction of monetary value. However, because the reprint recycles and circulates financial advice and information for readers, the material practicality of the insolvent "Protested Note" ostensibly acquires semantic currency. Michael C. Cohen argues that poems functioned as news conveying and elaborating newsworthy information: "The poem itself works as a news report of the event, a providential interpretation of it, and also a meditation on the social work of poems in communicating information and forming communities."[62] "Lines Written on the back of a Protested Note" works not only as news of the panic, but also as a consequence of it, that is, what happens "When," as the speaker claims, "merchants fondly trust to paper": their bank notes lose their monetary value and become discredited pieces of paper. The poem's informative lines fashion a type of epistemic value out of rhymed verse, that is, first-hand knowledge of how "to stop each croaker / And pay the banks to whom they trust" (5–6). Here, the speaker and not the commercial banks becomes the issuer of currency. Thus, instead of gold or silver coins, the *Liberator*'s readers redeem epistemic value from this protested note.

Straddling news and poetry, "Lines Written on the back of a Protested Note" is no longer just a parody in the *Liberator*. It is a news poem that communicates to readers the social value of a discredited bank note converted into a vehicle for viable information about failing banks across the country. Out of the twenty-four columns in the *Liberator*'s December 11, 1857 issue, not one includes news about the panic save for "Lines" and three other poems in the same column, "Confidence and Credit," "Rhymes for our Times," and "Parody on Hohenlinden." Consequently, in this issue, the topic of the panic becomes solely the subject of poetry. Given how common it was for newspapers, particularly Northern papers, to publish some news about the panic in this period, it is curious how the medium for news about the panic is verse and not prose. As panic-related information in the form of poems and news circulated, so did metaphors that were synonymous with financial turmoil. In addition to the word "panic," the phrase "hard times" acquired cultural currency during the Panic of 1857 in part due to the wide dissemination of a poem by the same title.

"Hard Times"

Like the *Evening Post* poems, Alfred "Alf" F. Burnett's poem "Hard Times" shows us that the use of slang to express common concerns about financial distress and panic became a staple of poems widely reprinted during the Panic of 1857.[63] Unlike the other poems in this chapter, however, "Hard Times" was initially printed a few years before the Panic of 1857, in the *Cincinnati Dollar Times* on January 5, 1855 with an authorial byline.[64] Before the Panic of 1857, "Hard Times" was only reprinted twice: once in the *Greenville Enterprise* (Greenville, South Carolina) on January 12, 1855 and another in the *Carroll Free Press* (Carrollton, Ohio) on February 15, 1855. It was during the Panic of 1857 when "Hard Times" began to significantly make the rounds in newspapers across the United States.

Although the popularity and reprint life of "Hard Times" did not commence until the Panic of 1857, the poem's author, Burnett, began making a name for himself long before its publication. Burnett was a soldier, poet, newspaper editor, and businessman, but was best known as a comic. Newspapers from the *Brooklyn Daily Eagle* (Brooklyn, New York) to the *Daily Commonwealth* (Topeka, Kansas) called Burnett "America's favorite humorist." His fame extended throughout the United States, England, and New Zealand.[65] Burnett was born in Suffolk, England, on October 2, 1824. In 1831, he immigrated with his father, Cornelius Burnett to Utica, New York.[66] Five years later in 1836, the family relocated to Cincinnati, Ohio, where his father opened a confectionery.[67] Burnett was an apprentice at his father's shop and learned the business while at the same time contributing poems to local newspapers and magazines. The editor of the *Daily Nonpareil* (Cincinnati, Ohio), Enos B. Reed, called Burnett "a rebellious writer . . . too ready, to pay that care and attention to the 'rules', which is considered, and justly so, to be indispensable to a correct writer."[68] Burnett's "Hard Times" exemplifies his unruly and unconventional approach to poetry.

"Hard Times" was among Burnett's most popular poems, reprinted in over twenty newspapers across the country.[69] Here is the poem as it appeared in the *Cincinnati Dollar Times*, on January 5, 1855:

Hard Times
"Hard Times" is now on every lip,
    And breathed from every tongue;
The Banks are cursed by one and all,
    The aged and the young.
The merchant has to close his doors,
    And throw his ledger by;
Such times he vows were never seen
    By any mortal eye.

The shopmen quit the counter's side
    For customers are so very few,
The times are now so very "TIGHT"
    It makes them all look "blue;"
The citizen in vain essays
    To make more than his bread;
A pound of which he now declares
    Won't weigh a pound of bread!

There's not a day but some one [*sic*] fails,
    Some house that goes to smash;
And names that once stood high on CHANGE,
    Are out for want of CASH.
Those who we tho't were MILLIONAIRES,
    And rich in shares and stocks,
Their "MILLION HEIRS" now disappoint;
    Fall and leave no "Rocks."

> "Hard times! Hard times! Was ever seen
>   Such times as hard as these!"
> This is the cry from morn till night,
>   In which each one agrees.
> A remedy I think I've found,
>   Say, how do you think 'twill do?
> "Pull off your coat, roll up your sleeves,
>   And work these hard times through!"

The title of the poem, "Hard Times," is an explicit allusion to Charles Dickens's novel *Hard Times* published in 1854, a novel that like the poem explores the social and economic conditions of the era. In four octaves, alternating between iambic tetrameter and iambic trimeter, the poem's speaker claims that "'Hard Times' is now on every lip, / And breathed from every tongue" (1–2). In the first two stanzas, the speaker provides examples of banks harming struggling businesspeople like the "merchant [who] has to close his doors" and the "shopmen [who] quit the counter's side" (5, 9). Business failures, the speaker declares, have grown to be a trend during the "hard times," for "There's not a day but some one [sic] fails" (17). In the final stanza, the speaker provides a "remedy" for this financial illness: "'Pull off your coat, roll up your sleeves, / And work these hard times through!'" (29, 31–32).

In Burnett's "Hard Times," slang reinforces the "hard times" to a seemingly in-the-know audience using shared expressions of financial hardship. Like "The Lay of the Directors," the slang in "Hard Times" appears in quotation marks: "TIGHT," "BLUE," "MILLION HEIRS," "ROCKS," and, the entire closing couplet: "Pull off your coat, roll up your sleeves, / And work these hard times through!" (31–32).[70] "Blue" (12) could mean both "to squander money" and also "extreme nervousness or dread, anxious depression."[71] In the context of Burnett's "Hard Times," the latter definition links financial panic to physical panic, to apprehension and social depression. "'MILLION HEIRS'" is a pun on "MILLIONAIRES" (23, 21). The speaker divides "millionaires" into two words, "million heirs," emphasizing the phonetic similarity between them. The pun "million heirs" also speaks to the dividends of stocks and shares, which the speaker hyperbolically claims are spread among a "'MILLION HEIRS'" (23). "Rocks" is slang for a "piece of money, *spec.* a dollar. In early use chiefly in *a pocketful of rocks*: a large amount of money."[72]

Like the two other panic poems in this chapter, Burnett's "Hard Times" had a significant reprint life. It was printed twelve times in eleven Southern newspapers between July 23, 1857 and November 12, 1857. The poem had a major reprint life particularly in the Carolinas, which saw eight out of the twelve publications.[73] The collapse of New York banks and the consequential panic on the East coast took a different shape in the South. Economic historians

Charles W. Calomiris and Larry Schweikart argue that the Southern banks were not as significantly affected by the panic: "Data for other Southern states show a remarkable degree of success in coping with the Panic. In Alabama, the Carolinas, Louisiana, Kentucky, and Missouri no banks failed."[74] Panic historian James L. Huston claims that in the aftermath of the panic, between 1857 and 1860, Southerners built far more railroad mileage than Northerners.[75] The relative success of Southern economies compels us to treat the afterlife of Burnett's reprint differently to that of "The Lay of the Directors" and "Lines by Buster," poems that are explicitly about failing banks and railroad companies and were predominantly reprinted in regionally Northern newspapers.

The expansive Southern afterlife of the reprints of "Hard Times" asks us to analyze the various paratexts of the poem in Southern newspapers not exclusively tied to the failure of railroad companies and the closure of banks, as seen in the previous example, but instead tied to the impact of financial decline on small businesses and the working class. After all, "Hard Times" was regularly reprinted in the South, showing us that the poem's content resonated with readers. By August 12, 1857, "Hard Times" was already circulating in the pages of three other Southern newspapers, including the *Yorkville Enquirer* (York, South Carolina, July 23); the *Fayetteville Weekly Observer* (Fayetteville, North Carolina, July 27); and the *Fayetteville Observer* (Fayetteville, Tennessee, August 6). The *Edgefield Advertiser* (Edgefield, South Carolina) reprinted Burnett's "Hard Times" twice in 1857, once on August 12 and another time on October 14.[76] This feedback loop evinces the poem's "perceived value" for the *Advertiser*'s intended public, offering two distinct paratextual fields for "Hard Times" in two different issues of the same newspaper.[77]

In the August 12 issue of the *Advertiser*, "Hard Times" received top billing. Burnett's poem was reprinted in the first column of the first section of the front page under the heading "Choice Poetry," bringing "Hard Times" to the fore of this issue. The August 12 issue printed a significant amount of news, ads, and editorials concerning temperance, the border wars in Kansas, and local news about enslaved people, Mormons, and agriculture.[78] However, the panic was not a central topic in this issue. Aside from the "Hard Times" reprint, the phrase "hard times" is mentioned only one other time in this issue, in a story about a New England shoemaker "who manages to make up for the hard times" even though his business is failing.[79] Two months after the August 12 reprint of Burnett's "Hard Times," the poem reappears in the *Advertiser* on October 14. This October reprint appears with an epigraph that explicitly mentions previous iterations of the poem, framing "Hard Times" within a broader reprint culture (see Figure 3.9).

The epigraph of "Hard Times" connects readers to the poem's iterative web of reprints, showcasing an awareness of the poem's feedback loop.[80] As Cordell argues, "[e]ach reprinted text linked those who read it to another newspaper

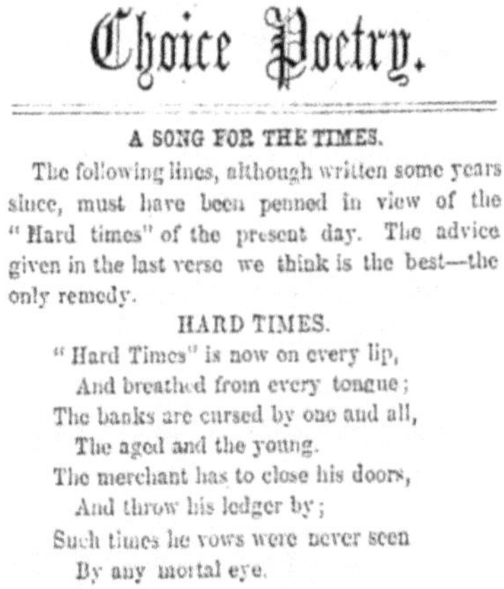

Choice Poetry.

A SONG FOR THE TIMES.

The following lines, although written some years since, must have been penned in view of the "Hard times" of the present day. The advice given in the last verse we think is the best—the only remedy.

HARD TIMES.

"Hard Times" is now on every lip,
And breathed from every tongue;
The banks are cursed by one and all,
The aged and the young.
The merchant has to close his doors,
And throw his ledger by;
Such times he vows were never seen
By any mortal eye.

Figure 3.9 "Hard Times," *Edgefield Advertiser*, October 14, 1857. Library of Congress. Public domain.

and other readers, within a complex system of paper links."[81] By drawing attention to the poem's feedback loop and its popularity among readers, the epigraph creates a sense of value and relevance for the poem. The modal verb "must" in the epigraph's first sentence assures readers that this poem is applicable to the current moment, that is, "the 'Hard times' of the present day."[82] The epigraph's second sentence guides the reading of the poem, emphasizing the significance of "[t]he advice given in the last verse."

Although the *Advertiser*'s August and October reprints of "Hard Times" are nearly identical vis-à-vis form and content, there are important distinctions between the two poems. Figure 3.10 shows the two reprints side by side. The slang words and phrases that in the initial reprint appeared capitalized are minusculed in the October reprint. Compared with their bold and loud counterparts in the August issue, in the October issue, "CHANGE," "CASH," "MILLIONAIRES," and "MILLION HEIRS" become soft echoes of the original, literally exemplifying a sonic feedback loop that like the panic itself diminished as the months went by.

The most important distinction between these two reprints is the speaker. In the August issue, the speaker uses the first-person singular, underlining an individual lyrical subject as the reasoning agent. In the October reprint, the "I" turns to a "we": "A remedy we think we've found" (29). Replacing the first-person singular with first-person plural creates a chorus of speakers in the October reprint that includes the *Advertiser*'s intended public. In this reprint, more than one subject is voicing the "remedy" in the closing couplet: "'Pull off your coat, roll up your sleeves, / And work these hard times through!'" (29, 31–32). The "we" in the October reprint also gestures to the editorial "we" in the poem's epigraph, that is,

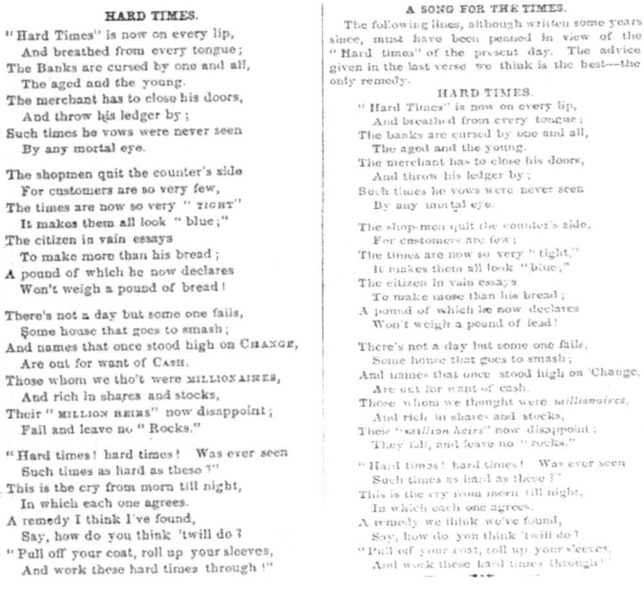

Figure 3.10 "Hard Times," *Edgefield Advertiser*, August 12, 1857 (left) and October 14, 1857 (right). Library of Congress. Public domain.

"The advice given in the last verse we think is the best—the only remedy," projecting the editors into the poem's body.[83] Lastly, "we" also points to the poem's feedback loop, that is, to a collective reading and appreciation of "Hard Times," particularly in the South, which commenced in 1855 and peaked in 1857. The editorial variations between the two reprints in the *Advertiser*, the lowercasing of slang words and phrases, as well as the shift from an individual to a collective speaker, are examples of how reprints are altered through circulation, creating new modes of engagement for the reader.

Conclusion

Nineteenth-century readers encountered panic-related poems in paratextually diverse yet overlapping ways. Whether critiquing the insolvency of banks, corrupt railroad companies, and/or the general hard times, the poems in this chapter contributed to complex networks of nineteenth-century panic discourses. Because "The Lay of the Directors," "Lines by Buster," and "Hard Times" were cultural expressions of the social anxieties of millions of nineteenth-century readers, they gained social value while paper money and bank notes were losing their intrinsic value. As such, these panic poems constituted a feedback loop in which their perceived value generated and fueled their reprint circulation.[84]

In their reprint afterlives, the three poems in this chapter contributed to discursive networks of cultural production, disseminating information that was current, intertextual, and poetic. They were printed next to news about regional and national issues like economic policies and debates, creating a shared economic responsibility among readers. Furthermore, their use of railroad, bank, and business slang made these poems culturally valuable and relevant to the information economy of the time.

"The Lay of the Directors," "Lines by Buster," and "Hard Times" constitute a newspaper tradition of publishing and reprinting occasional poetry, that is, poems composed to document and/or report on an event or occasion. During moments of crisis and social turbulence in the nineteenth century, occasional poems, like those above, often drew from the news cycle. At the same time, however, the news cycle also drew from them. For example, on November 7, 1857, the popular columnist Fanny Fern writes a piece entitled "The Hard Times" for Robert E. Bonner's *New York Ledger*, where she describes the Panic of 1857 as an infectious disease, a social epidemic generated by the growing public distrust of banks.[85] Fern claims, "I dread getting into an omnibus, or sitting down in a car or ferry-boat, lest I should catch the infections; for I will persist that a hopeful heart is the best antidote for times like these."[86] The three poems in this chapter capture the social angst in Fern's column, the contagion of financial precarity that plagued 1857. Fern's metaphor shows us how financial panic is like an infectious disease that can be contracted and passed to others through proximity. In the following chapter, Fern's metaphoric infection turns into a reality as an infectious disease ravages the city of New York. In this chapter, poems are occasioned not by money but by the social anguish of the cholera epidemic of 1866.

Notes

1. McGill, *American Literature and the Culture of Reprinting*, 4. McGill posits that antebellum literary ownership "cuts to the heart of republican ideology." McGill's important claim is partly based on Michael Warner's argument that in early America there was a mutual transforming relationship between print culture and republican political culture. In *The Letters of the Republic*, Warner claims that "an emerging political language—republicanism—and a new set of ground rules for discourse—the public sphere—jointly made each other illegible. Within this cultural vocabulary, print discourse made it possible to imagine a people that could act as people and in distinction from the state." Michael Warner, *The Letters of the Republic: Publication and the Public Sphere in Eighteenth-Century America* (Cambridge, MA: Harvard University Press, 1990), xiii. In his study of early American magazines, *The Rise and Fall of Early American Magazine Culture*, Jared Gardner presents a useful framework for thinking about the culture of iteration. He argues that literary culture "saw borrowings and recyclings as neither theft nor as homage but as something closer to what we today would call 'remix' culture—the means for

participating in a perpetually replenishing commons on which a new literary culture might be founded." Although Gardner is speaking about an earlier period, the practice of "borrowing and recycling [as] the means for participating in a perpetually replenishing" reprint culture is still very much a part of mid-century iteration practices. Jared Gardner, *The Rise and Fall of Early American Magazine Culture* (Champaign: University of Illinois Press, 2012), 39. It was, after all, the reprint practice of "borrowing and recycling" that allowed "The Lay of the Directors," "Lines by Buster," and "Hard Times" to acquire value as popular panic poems across the country.
2. McGill, *American Literature*, 3.
3. Garvey, *Writing with Scissors*, 2.
4. Shira Wolosky, *Feminist Theory Across Disciplines: Feminist Community and American Women's Poetry* (New York: Routledge, 2013), xix.
5. Cordell, "Reprinting," 418.
6. The Panic of 1857 was one of many financial depressions. The first major financial crisis of the century occurred in 1819 and persisted until 1821. Another wave of financial panic hit in 1837, and again the US confronted high unemployment rates and low wages and profits.
7. James L. Huston, *The Panic of 1857 and the Coming of the Civil War* (Baton Rouge: Louisiana State University Press, 1999), 3.
8. Scott Reynolds Nelson, *A Nation of Deadbeats: An Uncommon History of America's Financial Disasters* (New York: Random House, 2012), 134–35.
9. Lloyd J. Mercer, *Railroads and Land Grant Policy: A Study in Government Intervention* (New York: Academic Press, 1982), 141.
10. Jay Sexton, *Debtor Diplomacy: Finance and American Foreign Relations in the Civil War Era 1837–1873* (Oxford: Oxford University Press, 2005), 76.
11. Charles W. Calomiris and Larry Schweikart, "The Panic of 1857: Origins, Transmission, and Containment," *The Journal of Economic History* 51, no. 4 (1991): 830. Calomiris and Schweikart corroborate that although historians disagree on the origin of the Panic of 1857, "[s]ome facts were consistent with the view that the crisis was an unnecessary product of mismanagement or fear" (807). They claim that "[b]ankers and local businessmen feared their banks would be run to provide specie for other locales" (822). On October 10, 1857, American diarist George Templeton Strong (1820–75) contextualizes this fiscal fear in his journal: "The remedy for this crisis must be psychological rather than financial. It is an epidemic of fear and distrust that every one [*sic*] admits to be without real ground *except* the very sufficient ground that everyone is known to share them." *Writing New York: A Literary Anthology*, ed. Phillip Lopate (New York: Washington Square Press, 1998), 204. As a way of alleviating this psychological fear, newspapers editors advised the public to be financially cautious. On October 12, 1857, for example, Horace Greeley's *New-York Daily Tribune* cautioned, "The worst thing we have to Fear in this city is a panic. Should depositors be frightened into making a run on the bank, there would be danger."
12. Huston argues that "[t]he Panic of 1857 started to force discussion of concrete economic questions into the heated debates over slavery's expansion," debates which ultimately culminated in the Civil War. Huston, *Panic of 1857*, 66.

13. In his computational study of antebellum reprint material, Cordell uncovered nearly 40,000 reprinted texts. He argues that "[a] majority of these were reprinted only two or three times, but a significant minority were reprinted in twenty or more newspapers from the Chronicling America collection." Cordell, "Reprinting," 422. In comparison with the widely reprinted poems in this chapter, my survey shows that in 1857, other newspaper poems about the panic, including "The Times" (*Plattsburgh Republican*, October 31, 1857), "The Battle of Life," and "Give Me the People" (both in the *Belmont Chronicle*, June 2, 1857), were not reprinted outside of their original publication.
14. The alliterative neologism "panic poetry" tapped into the cultural and social anxiety of the Panic of 1857. My survey shows that before its initial appearance in the New York *Evening Post* on October 2, 1857, this phrase does not appear in newspapers. Between 1857 and 1861, panic poetry frequently appeared in newspapers either as the title or in the body of poems.
15. Frank Luther Mott, *American Journalism* (New York: The Macmillan Company, 1941), 258.
16. "lay, n.4," *OED Online*, June 2018 (Oxford University Press), <http://www.oed.com.proxy.lib.ohio-state.edu/view/Entry/106490?rskey=dpRCwm&result=4&isAdvanced=false> (last accessed July 17, 2018).
17. The use of epistrophes in "The Lay of the Directors" recalls the famous use of epistrophes in Henry Wadsworth Longfellow's 1841 poem "Excelsior," which, according to Christoph Irmscher, was widely parodied throughout the nineteenth century. Christoph Irmscher, *Longfellow Redux* (Champaign: University of Illinois Press, 2006), 62.
18. "slang, n.3," *OED Online*, July 2018 (Oxford University Press), <http://www.oed.com.proxy.lib.ohio-state.edu/view/Entry/181318?rskey=sEcq2p&result=3> (last accessed November 10, 2018).
19. Michael Adams, *Slang: The People's Poetry* (Oxford: Oxford University Press, 2009), 17.
20. Irving Lewis Allen, *The City in Slang: New York Life and Popular Speech* (Oxford: Oxford University Press, 1993), 4.
21. Allen, *City in Slang*, 6. Writing on the subject of "Slang in America," Whitman calls slang "a lawless germinal element, below all words and sentences, and behind all poetry." Slang, he continues, "produces poets and poems." In other words, for Whitman, slang can be considered the raw material of poems. Walt Whitman, "Slang in America," *Prose Works 1892*, ed. Floyd Stovall (New York: New York University Press, 1964), 572–77.
22. Brander Matthews, writing in *Harper's Magazine* on "The Function of Slang" (1893), defines slang as "[a] collection of colloquialism gathered from all sources, and all bearing alike the bend sinister of illegitimacy."
23. Claudia Stokes, *The Altar at Home: Sentimental Literature and Nineteenth-Century American Religion* (Philadelphia: University of Pennsylvania Press, 2014), 79.
24. Angela Sorby, *Schoolroom Poets: Childhood, Performance, and the Place of American Poetry, 1865–1917* (Durham, NH: University of New Hampshire Press, 2005), 74.

25. These slang words are defined as follow: "'branches'": "a road or railway"; "'air-lines'": "a straight line; a bee line. Hence Air-line ... as, air-line road"; "'lightning trains'": "lightning express trains capable of travelling 40 to 50 miles per hour"; "'feeders'": "a branch road, railway line, air service, etc." "branch, n.," *OED Online*, June 2018 (Oxford University Press), <http://www.oed.com.proxy.lib.ohio-state.edu/view/Entry/22600?rskey=bTHdl7&result=1&isAdvanced=false> (last accessed July 22, 2018); "The Locomotive Engineers in Council," *Brotherhood of Locomotive Engineer Monthly Journal* 3, no. 1 (January 1869): 498.
26. Henry Ward Beecher, "Lessons from the Times," *The Evening Post*, October 2, 1857.
27. Beecher, "Lessons from the Times."
28. "The Lay of the Directors" was reprinted in the following newspapers: *The Boston Evening Transcript* (Boston, Massachusetts), October 3, 1857; *Hartford Courant* (Hartford, Connecticut), October 6, 1857; *Chicago Tribune* (Chicago, Illinois), October 8, 1857; *Richmond Dispatch* (Richmond, Virginia), October 8, 1857; *The Boston Daily Bee* (Boston, Massachusetts), October 10, 1857; *Buffalo Weekly Republic* (Buffalo, New York), October 13, 1857; *The New York Reformer* (Watertown, New York), October 15, 1857; *The Highland Weekly News* (Hillsboro, Ohio), October 22, 1857; *The American Citizen* (Ironwood, Michigan), October 29, 1857; *New London Daily* (New London, Connecticut), October 31, 1857; *The Wheeling Daily Intelligencer* (Wheeling, West Virginia), November 3, 1857; *Dollar Weekly Mirror* (Manchester, New Hampshire), December 12, 1857.
29. "About the *Wheeling Daily Intelligencer*," Chronicling America Database, Library of Congress, <https://www.loc.gov/item/sn84026844/#:~:text=During%20this%20tumultuous%20era%2C%20the,Virginia%20on%20June%2020%2C%201863>.
30. Cordell, "Reprinting," 418.
31. In the context of newspapers, an original poem is written expressly for a newspaper's public, implying curation and exclusivity. In some cases, original poems were printed with a note explicitly flagging their novelty, as in the case of the initial publication of "The Lay of the Directors" in the *Post*. Many more poems omitted the source details, inviting readers to speculate about the origins of the poem. Like news items and ads published in newspapers which readers assumed catered to their values and interests, many readers approached poems, both reprints and originals, with the assumption that these too were printed because they catered to their specific values and interests.
32. "tin, n.," *OED Online*, June 2018 (Oxford University Press), <http://www.oed.com.proxy.lib.ohio-state.edu/view/Entry/202173?rskey=ebu2wq&result=1> (last accessed July 22, 2018); "cook, v.1," *Oxford English Dictionary*, July 2023 (Oxford University Press), <https://doi.org/10.1093/OED/7707709813>.
33. Rev. James Stormonth, *Etymological and Pronouncing Dictionary of the English Language* (Edinburgh: William Blackwood and Sons, 1881), 121, 415. See also "humbug, n. (and adj.)," *OED Online*, June 2018 (Oxford University Press), <http://www.oed.com.proxy.lib.ohio-state.edu/view/Entry/89319?rskey=kIbimX&result=1&isAdvanced=false> (last accessed July 17, 2018). "credulity, n.," *OED Online*, June 2018 (Oxford University Press), <http://www.oed.com.proxy.lib.ohio-state.edu/view/Entry/44134?redirectedFrom=credulity> (last accessed July 17, 2018).

34. "Second Stock of Fall and Winter Goods," *The Wheeling Daily Intelligencer*, November 3, 1857.
35. In the poem's adaptation of Goldsmith's original, for instance, "scrape" refers to "one who 'scrapes' or uses excessive economy, a miser"; it also means "to manage to 'get along' with difficulty, [i.e.] to scrape by"; "croaker" is slang for "a dying person beyond hope; a corpse," and "to bust" is a "vulgar pronunciation of the word *burst* [and was] very common" for the time. "To bust" means "to burst; to fail in business"; it also means to go bankrupt or declare bankruptcy. These slang phrases anchor and reinforce the parodic tone of "Lines by Buster."
36. "buster, n.," *OED Online*, June 2018 (Oxford University Press), <http://www.oed.com.proxy.lib.ohiostate.edu/view/Entry/25281?rskey=YINzai&result=1&isAdvanced=false> (last accessed August 14, 2018).
37. "buster, n.," *OED Online*.
38. Faith Barrett, "'What witty sally': Phoebe Cary's Poetics of Parody," *A History of Nineteenth-Century American Women's Poetry*, ed. Jennifer Putzi and Alexandra Socarides (Cambridge: Cambridge University Press, 2017), 106.
39. Barrett, "'What witty sally,'" 106.
40. "goldsmith, n.," *OED Online*, June 2018 (Oxford University Press), <http://www.oed.com.proxy.lib.ohio-state.edu/view/Entry/79803?redirectedFrom=goldsmith> (last accessed July 12, 2018).
41. Allan H. Meltzer, *A History of the Federal Reserve, Volume 1: 1913–1951* (Chicago: University of Chicago Press, 2003), 48.
42. Linda Hutcheon, *A Theory of Parody: The Teachings of Twentieth-Century Art Forms* (Champaign: University of Illinois Press, 2000), 4.
43. Hutcheon, *Theory of Parody*, 4.
44. "folly, n.1," *OED Online*, July 2018 (Oxford University Press), <http://www.oed.com.proxy.lib.ohio-state.edu/view/Entry/72576?rskey=rcE3tG&result=1&isAdvanced=false> (last accessed October 9, 2018).
45. Jonathan Senchyne, *The Intimacy of Paper in Early and Nineteenth-Century American Literature* (Boston: University of Massachusetts Press, 2020), 5.
46. Huston, *Panic of 1857*, 28.
47. "folly, n.1," *OED Online*.
48. "bust, adj.," *OED Online*, June 2018 (Oxford University Press), <http://www.oed.com.proxy.lib.ohiostate.edu/view/Entry/25270?rskey=AcTmtF&result=4&isAdvanced=false> (last accessed August 14, 2018).
49. Edited by R. G. Stone, the *Republican* was a four-page daily, measuring 20 × 40 inches, that ran from 1813 to 1916.
50. "Panic Poetry," *Plattsburgh Republican*, October 31, 1857.
51. William Shakespeare, *A Midsummer Night's Dream: The Oxford Shakespeare*, ed. Peter Holland (Oxford: Oxford University Press, 1994), 168.
52. Genette, *Paratexts*, 143.
53. According to the Chronicling America archive, "Other notable editors of the paper include Benjamin S. Jones and J. Elizabeth Hitchcock, the paper's first, and Oliver Johnson. James Barnaby served as the paper's publisher for almost its entire 18-year run." "About *Anti-Slavery Bugle*," Chronicling America Database, Library of Congress, <https://www.loc.gov/item/sn83035487/>.

54. Sven Beckert and Seth Rockman, "Introduction," *Slavery's Capitalism: A New History of American Economic Development*, ed. Sven Beckert and Seth Rockman (Philadelphia: University of Pennsylvania Press, 2016), 2.
55. The relationship between slavery and capitalism in North America predates the nineteenth century, dating back to the earliest enslavement and transportation of Africans to the region by the Spanish empire in the fifteenth century and the English empire in the sixteenth century.
56. "Assorting Brokers," *The Anti-Slavery Bugle*, October 24, 1857.
57. "Assorting Brokers."
58. Beckert and Rockman, "Introduction," 2. Throughout its thirty-four-year run, the *Liberator* regularly published anti-slavery poems by well-known abolitionist poets like Frances E. W. Harper, William Watkins, Elizabeth Chandler, and Sarah and Margaretta Forten. See Margaret Washington, "Frances Ellen Watkins: Family Legacy and Antebellum Activism," *The Journal of African American History* 100, no. 1 (2015): 59–86.
59. According to Henry Anson Finney, "In some cases the notice of dishonor may be made in an informal manner, by letter or by word of mouth. In other cases, prescribed by law, it is necessary to give notice of dishonor in a formal manner called protest." Henry Anson Finney, *Accounting Principles and Bookkeeping Methods, Volume 1* (New York: H. Holt and Co., 1924), 159.
60. "Discredited Bank Notes," *Summit County Beacon*, September 2, 1857.
61. "Discredited Bank Notes."
62. Cohen, *Social Lives*, 53.
63. According to the *OED*, the phrase "hard times" means "[o]f a period of time or (later) labour: characterized by adversity or hardship; grueling; (in weakened sense) arduous, tiring." "hard time, n.", *Oxford English Dictionary*, July 2023 (Oxford University Press), <https://doi.org/10.1093/OED/7206136416>. The usage of this phrase as meaning economic adversity dates to the eleventh century. Hundreds of newspaper poems published across the US from 1850 to 1861 contain the phrase "Hard Times" in either the title of the poem or in the body of the poem. For example, "The Cry of 'Hard Times'" by J. Bomber, Jr., printed in *The Altoona Tribune* on August 4, 1859; "Hard Times by Ned", printed in the *Evansville Daily* on April 1, 1859; and "The Banks," printed in the *Daily State Journal* on November 23, 1857. Like the *Evening Post*'s "panic poetry," these "Hard Times" poems are about business, banks, and poverty.
64. The *Cincinnati Dollar Times* was a Know-Nothing weekly newspaper edited and published by James D. Taylor (?–1871). Tyler Anbinder, *Nativism and Slavery: The Northern Know Nothings and the Politics of the 1850s* (Oxford: Oxford University Press, 1992), 25.
65. Alf Burnett, *Humorous, Pathetic and Descriptive: Incidents of the War* (Cincinnati: R. W. Carroll & Co., Publishers, 1874), iv.
66. Burnett, *Humorous, Pathetic and Descriptive*, iv.
67. Burnett, *Humorous, Pathetic and Descriptive*, v.
68. Burnett, *Humorous, Pathetic and Descriptive*, iv.
69. According to Enos B. Reed, Burnett's most famous poem was "The Sexton's Spade," which "gained [Burnett] world-wide celebrity." Burnett, *Humorous, Pathetic and Descriptive*, iv.

70. "tight, adj., adv., and n.2," *OED Online*, June 2018 (Oxford University Press), <http://www.oed.com.proxy.lib.ohio-state.edu/view/Entry/201925?rskey=ZA1Rk Q&result=2&isAdvanced=false> (last accessed July 22, 2018).
71. "blue, adj. and n.," *OED Online*, June 2018 (Oxford University Press), <http://www.oed.com.proxy.lib.ohio-state.edu/view/Entry/20577?rskey=DHnPvk&result =1&isAdvanced=false> (last accessed July 22, 2018).
72. "rock, n.1," *OED Online*, June 2018 (Oxford University Press), <http://www.oed.com.proxy.lib.ohio-state.edu/view/Entry/166697?rskey=B2V5sH&result=1&isAd vanced=false> (last accessed July 22, 2018).
73. Between January 1857 and January 1858, Burnett's "Hard Times" was reprinted twenty times in the following periodicals: *Yorkville Enquirer* (York, South Carolina), July 23, 1857; *Fayetteville Weekly Observer* (Fayetteville, North Carolina), July 27, 1857; *Fayetteville Observer* (Fayetteville, Tennessee), August 6, 1857; *Edgefield Advertiser* (Edgefield, South Carolina), August 12, 1857; *National Aegis* (Worcester, Massachusetts), September 9, 1857; *The People's Press* (Winston-Salem, North Carolina), September 25, 1857; *The Wisconsin Chief* (Fort Atkinson, Wisconsin), October 7, 1857; *Edgefield Advertiser* (Edgefield, South Carolina), October 14, 1857; *The Daily Journal* (Ogdensburgh, New York), October 22, 1847; *The Clarke County Democrat* (Grove Hill, Alabama), October 29, 1857; *Keowee Courier* (Pickens, South Carolina), October 31, 1857; *Reedsburg Herald* (Reedsburg, Wisconsin), October 31, 1857; *The Tarborough Southerner* (Tarboro, North Carolina), October 31, 1857; *The Greenville Enterprise* (Greenville, South Carolina), November 5, 1857; *Daily Evening Bulletin* (San Francisco, California), November 11, 1857; *Jacksonville Republican* (Jacksonville, Alabama), November 11, 1857; *Tuskegee Republican* (Tuskegee, Alabama), November 12, 1857; *Weekly Miners' Journal* (Pottsville, Pennsylvania), November 14, 1857; *Belmont Chronicle* (Saint Clairsville, Ohio), November 26, 1857; *Easton Gazette* (Easton, Maryland), December 5, 1857. This list of reprints reveals a few significant aspects about the reprint culture of Burnett's "Hard Times." For one, the poem saw a major reprint life in the South, particularly in the Carolinas. We also learn that the poem was reprinted as far west as San Francisco, which we have not seen in any of the previous panic poems. Similar to the other panic poem reprints, Burnett's "Hard Times" spiked in October, with seven reprints in that month. This, as I mentioned before, is not a coincidence but a result of the nadir of the panic.
74. Calomiris and Schweikart, "The Panic of 1857," 830.
75. Huston, *Panic of 1857*, 216–17.
76. Still in print today, the *Edgefield Advertiser* is the oldest newspaper in South Carolina. It commenced publication on February 11, 1836, also making it the oldest newspaper in South Carolina to publish uninterruptedly under the same nameplate. During the Panic of 1857, the paper was edited by William F. Durisoe (1805–unknown) and John Calhoun Simkins (1828–63).
77. Cordell, "Reprinting," 417.
78. Cordell, "Reprinting," 417.
79. "Hard Times and the Shoemaker," *Edgefield* Advertiser, August 12, 1857.
80. "Hard Times," *Edgefield Advertiser*, October 14, 1857.

81. Cordell, "Reprinting," 417.
82. "Hard Times," *Edgefield Advertiser*.
83. "Hard Times," *Edgefield Advertiser*.
84. Cordell, "Reprinting," 417.
85. Fanny Fern, "The Hard Times," *The New York Ledger*, November 7, 1857.
86. Fern, "Hard Times."

4

THE EPITEXTUAL SITES OF CHOLERA POEMS

The 1866 cholera epidemic marked the third time cholera struck the city of New York in the nineteenth century; previous epidemics had occurred in 1832 and 1849. With a population of over 1.1 million in 1866, one quarter of whom were immigrants, New York was starkly divided between the city's traditional elite class (Park Avenue bankers and traders) and predominantly Irish immigrants and African Americans. The latter lived in the city's most neglected quarters, which became the main site for contagion. Cholera's impact in 1832 and 1849 painted a frightening image of the disease for New York residents in 1866. Charles E. Rosenberg writes:

> The symptoms of cholera are spectacular; they could not be ignored or romanticized as were the physical manifestations of malaria and tuberculosis. One could as easily ignore a case of acute arsenical poisoning, the symptoms of which are strikingly similar to those of cholera. The onset of cholera is marked by diarrhea, acute spasmodic vomiting, and painful cramps. Consequent dehydration, often accompanied by cyanosis, gives to the sufferer a characteristic and disquieting appearance: his face blue and pinched, his extremities cold and darkened, the skin of his hands and feet drawn and puckered.[1]

Such symptoms appeared without warning and death followed soon after, in days or at times in mere hours.[2] Before the 1830s, numerous American cities dealt with poor sanitary conditions, which created the conditions for epidemic disease. In his history of sanitation, Martin V. Melosi posits that "[f]ew communities could boast of well-developed technologies of sanitation, and much of the responsibility for sanitation rested with the individual."[3] By 1865, sanitary reform advocates could justify their programs by pointing to the work of the prominent London anesthetist John Snow, who claimed that cholera propagated via contaminated water.[4] In 1849, Snow contested the force of tradition when he published a pamphlet titled "On the Mode of Communication of Cholera" outlining his hypothesis that cholera was not miasmic (not an airborne disease) and instead "reproduc[ed] itself in the bodies of its victims" via bacteria that derived from "the excreta and vomitus of cholera patients" often found in "a contaminated water supply."[5] Throughout the nineteenth century, Snow's refutation would go on to face skepticism from British and American medical communities that subscribed to the commonly held miasma theory.

As disease plagued the streets of the city of New York in 1866, cholera and its calamitous impact on society occasioned many newspaper poems. Readers encountered these poems in their preferred periodicals and next to their daily dose of newsprint. Thus, like many of the poems in this book, cholera poems are inherently paratextual. These poems reimagined and sometimes contributed to contemporaneous debates about sanitary reform, contagion, immigration, and preventative measures through verse that drew from the discourse of nineteenth-century epidemiology, in many cases shaping how reading publics understood and managed the disease.

In this chapter, I recover three popular cholera poems widely reprinted in New York during the 1866 epidemic: "The Voice of the Pestilence," "King Cholera," and "The Health Bill: A Talk Between Two Repubs at Albany." Collectively reprinted in over forty-four dailies and weeklies between August 25, 1865 and September 6, 1866, these poems exemplify what Shira Wolosky calls "the rhetorical intersections between poetry and public discourses."[6] Wolosky argues that nineteenth-century poetry was not "a self-enclosed art object that twentieth-century formalism projected."[7] Instead, poems in this period "directly participated in and addressed the pressing issues facing the evolving nation through its responses, circulation, and creative reflections on the rhetoric of national life."[8] The three cholera poems in this chapter exemplify this literary tradition through their engagement with and aestheticization of contemporaneous public discourses of cholera, including miasma theory, Christian charity, public health, immigration, and government. Through an analysis of the poems' relationship to their paratext of news, ads, editorial, and verse, the cholera poems in this chapter acquire historical contextualization and aesthetic significance. The paratext reveals how these poems reflected and reinforced specific middle-class social anxieties about "Eastern" disease, filth, poverty, and the non-white other, including Asians, Irish immigrants, and African Americans. Because cholera poems are occasioned by their cultural moment of disease, the paratext is necessary for understanding how these poems engaged with the political, social, and medical debates that concretized around cholera in the mid-nineteenth century.

So far, this book has centralized the poem's *peritext* (paratext published alongside and/or next to poems). This chapter expands the paratext to include the *epitext* (paratext published outside of the proximity of poems in other contemporaneous newspapers, books, and magazines). Gérard Genette defines the epitext as "any paratextual element not materially appended to the text within the same volume but circulating, as it were, freely, in a virtually limitless physical and social space. The location of the epitext is therefore anywhere outside the book."[9] The epitext is importantly made up of public discourses whose function, Genette posits, "is not always basically paratextual (that is, to present and comment on the text)."[10] The epitext instead has the potential to be paratextual, that is, it is "capable of furnishing us with paratextual scraps."[11] Thus, the epitext "is endlessly diffused in a biographical, critical, or other discourse whose relation to the work may be at best indirect and at worst indiscernible."[12] In the case of this chapter, the epitext is anywhere outside of the newspaper poem's direct proximity, that is, outside of the page, the newspaper issue, and even the newspaper medium. These epitextual sites consist of public discourses of cholera disseminated in news items, medical journals, illustrations, and other poems with direct, indirect, and at times indiscernible links to disease. They reveal how cholera poems initiated communicative practices among publics that made shared experiences about disease (contagion, transmission, containment, and other factors relating to health) legible and aesthetical.

In studying the paratextuality of public discourses during the cholera epidemic, I trace a network of newspaper writing that supplied readers with instruction and treatment based on practical and pseudo-scientific knowledge for thinking about the effects of disease. This multi-generic network emphasizes the corporeal effects of cholera on the human body and the body politic. Ultimately, what results is a network of cultural, biblical, legal, and epidemiological metaphors and references that hinge on the concept of miasma. Miasma theory posited that diseases like cholera, chlamydia, and malaria were caused by a miasma, that is, a noxious form of "bad air" that when inhaled contaminated people.[13] In 1866, miasma theory was a source of poetic creativity that allowed poets access to the popular and often misconstrued discourse of bad air and contagion in order to imagine the nature of cholera and how it related to other cultural aspects of readers' lives.

Entrenched in the discourse of airborne disease as a looming threat over the city of New York, cholera poems reveal that even though miasma theory was refuted by 1849, popular newspaper poems continued to circulate this fabulation well into the mid-nineteenth century. In the public imagination, cholera's source was miasma or poisoned air. For many, as Melosi argues, "[i]t was easier to visualize some sort of danger or inconvenience coming from noxious odors or putrefying wastes than from the mysterious appearance" of disease.[14] Not everyone, however, subscribed to this theory. Throughout the nineteenth century, the medical community was divided into two factions vis-à-vis the etiology of cholera: the "anticontagionists" and the "contagionists."[15] The anticontagionists claimed that bad air containing noxious fumes (miasma)—generated by unsanitary, unhygienic conditions, questionable morality, or irreligiosity—produced cholera.[16] The "contagionists," on the other hand, believed that cholera spread from physical contact between people. This latter group promoted quarantine measures against epidemics. Although not all contagionists and anticontagionists agreed on the predisposing causes of cholera, most physicians, according to both Rosenberg and Daniel Eli Burstein, shared opinions on "the proper means of prophylaxis."[17] For example, contagionists and anticontagionists directly linked sanitation to public health. Both groups agreed that inhabitants of filthy, ill-ventilated tenement apartments in working-class neighborhoods like the Five Points and Red Hook, Brooklyn were particularly at risk of contamination. Whether through physical contact in crowded apartments and/or effluvial filth due to inadequate waste disposal and access to clean drinking water, contagionists and anticontagionists believed that impoverished communities were most at risk of disease. As Rosenberg argues, most nineteenth-century physicians agreed that "[t]he poor who lived in such squalor were to be removed to clean, dry, and airy houses as soon as possible."[18] The means of prophylaxis often proved impossible, especially among poor immigrant communities who occupied dense wards with limited resources.

The cholera poems in this chapter, for the most part, employ anticontagionist discourse in their aestheticization of the wind, air, and breeze. Although the miasmic properties of cholera poetry were occasioned by disease, the wind, air, and zephyr are part of a Romantic literary tradition predating the major cholera outbreaks of the nineteenth century. To understand the public discourses of cholera poetry and how they were occasioned by disease, it is important to first distinguish them from the popular tradition of wind poetry in times of health and equilibrium.

Romantic Zephyrs

The wind, breeze, and air are tropes commonly found in Romantic poetry on both sides of Atlantic. Romantic poetry published between 1800 and 1830 personified the wind as *Zephyros*, the Greek god of the west wind, and/or a *zephyr*, a gentle or mild breeze.[19] For example, in Johann Wolfgang von Goethe's (1749–1832) poem "Gesang der Geister über den Wassern" (Song of the Spirits over the Waters), the wind is a "tenderest lover" that "from the deep tears foam-crested billows" (19–20). By the poem's end, the speaker converts the wind into a metaphor for the flow of destiny: "Fate of man mortal, how art thou like wind!" (22). In Percy Bysshe Shelley's (1792–1822) poems "Ode to the West Wind," "The Cloud," and "To a Skylark," the wind and air are endowed with sentient traits that personify the forces of nature. In "Ode to the West Wind," the west wind is "The trumpet of a prophecy," a Romantic spirit that the speaker wants to be possessed by: "Make me thy lyre, even as the forest is" in order to "Scatter . . . / my words among mankind!" (69, 57, 66–67). In "The Cloud" and "To a Skylark," the wind catalyzes the sublimity of a cloud and skylark, respectively. In "The Cloud," "the winds and sunbeams with their convex gleams / Build up the blue dome of air" that allow the cloud to "arise and unbuild it again" (79–80, 84). In "To a Skylark," the wind facilitates the natural beauty of the lark: "By warm winds deflower'd, / Till the scent it gives / Makes faint with too much sweet those heavy-winged thieves" (42–44). In both poems, the wind is a vessel and medium for the creation of the beautiful. It allows the cloud to "bring fresh showers for the thirsting flowers, / From the seas and the streams" and the skylark to "Pourest thy full heart / In profuse strains of unpremeditated art" ("The Cloud," 1–2, "To a Skylark," 4–5).

Even after the Romantic period, as Michael O'Neill claims, "there were Victorian poets who maintained a Romantic faith that there might be a deep correspondence between nature and the mind, between, for example, the natural wind and poetic inspiration."[20] In Emily Brontë's (1818–48) "The Night-Wind," the wind comforts the speaker: "The soft wind waved my hair; / It told me heaven was glorious, / And sleeping earth was fair" (6–8). In Christina Rossetti's (1830–94) "Who Has Seen the Wind?," the wind is an invisible agent of creation that animates the beauty of nature. The speaker asks, "Who has seen the wind? / Neither I nor you. / But when the leaves hang trembling, / The wind is passing through" (1–4). In these examples, the wind functions as a natural muse that allows the speakers to intimately know and aestheticize the forces of nature.

On the other side of the Atlantic, American poets too romanticized the wind as a kind of episteme for inspiration and creation. In William Cullen Bryant's (1794–1878) "Summer Wind," for instance, the speaker epitomizes the wind as a gentle zephyr that restores a dry and hot landscape.[21] The poem opens: "It is a sultry day; the sun has drunk / The dew that lay upon the morning grass" (1–2). The wind becomes a restorative agent that the speaker longs for in the following lines:

> Yet virgin from the kisses of the sun,
> Retains some freshness, and I woo the wind
> That still delays his coming. Why so slow,
> Gentle and voluble spirit of the air? (22–25)[22]

THE EPITEXTUAL SITES OF CHOLERA POEMS

Here, the speaker "woo[s] the wind," which is personified as a "gentle and voluble spirit" (25). Bryant's biographer Gilbert H. Muller argues that Bryant's "Summer Wind" is a groundbreaking poem because "[t]he images and rhythms shift from static, languid, oppressive heat to refreshing, almost homoerotic breezes willed or wooed into existence by the poet."[23]

Scholars have noted the omnipresence of the wind in nineteenth-century Aeolian harp poetry, another genre that focalized the trope of the wind and air. Named after the Greek ruler and god of the winds Aeolus, the Aeolian harp was a popular household item in the nineteenth century, a fact that in part explains its ubiquity in poetry. Aeolian harp poetry often features the wind as a musical composer of nature.[24] In Alison Byerly's study of the picturesque in nineteenth-century song, she argues that "the random expressiveness of the Aeolian harp, an instrument played by the wind itself, makes it a central metaphor for the Romantic imagination."[25] Poets saw musical instruments like the harp and lyre as creative tools that produced the kind of natural music they aspired to create.[26] For example, in José María Heredia's (1803–39) exilic poem "Ode to Niagara," the speaker invokes the lyre in order to compare the sublime majesty of Niagara Falls to his natal Cuba. The poem opens, "Dadme mi lira, dádmela: que siento / En mi alma estremecida y agitada / Arder la inspiración" (My lyre! Give me my lyre! My bosom feels / The glow of inspiration) (1–3). Here, the lyre is both a musical instrument and the poetic medium through which the speaker communicates his "glow of inspiration" for Cuba (3). Some poets conceptualized a figurative harp as their muse. John Hollander, for example, notes that "Henry David Thoreau kept in his journals over many years an ongoing prose-poem about what [Thoreau] called his telegraph harp—the Aeolian acoustical effect generated by telegraph wires in the wind."[27]

In the moments leading up to and during the cholera epidemic of 1866, the public discourse of miasma presented poets with new modes of engaging the longstanding conventions of wind and air as idealistic and musical gentle zephyrs. No longer a "refreshing, almost homoerotic breeze" as Muller says about Bryant's "Summer Wind," or a composer of prosody as in the Aeolian harp poems, the trope of the wind in "The Voice of the Pestilence," "King Cholera," and "The Health Bill: A Talk Between Two Repubs at Albany" functions as an ever-present agent of miasma in an age of contagion.

Miasmatic Origins of "Asiatic Cholera" in "The Voice of the Pestilence"

"The Voice of the Pestilence" was a popular poem historically grounded in the epidemic of 1832. It was first published in 1831 in the English poet Alfred Domett's (1811–87) collection *Poems*, with the byline "By a young friend of the author," implying that the poem was not authored by Domett himself.[28]

Inquiring about the authorship of "The Voice of the Pestilence" in *Notes and Queries* (1891), W. F. Prideaux writes, "I believe it is supposed in some quarters that the 'young friend' was Robert Browning, but I am unable to detect in the verses any semblance to that poet's peculiar style."[29] According to some bibliographic records, Domett and Browning were intimate friends during the initial publication of "The Voice of the Pestilence." Harry B. Smith, the editor of *A Sentimental Library* (1914), writes:

> It is not unlikely that Browning was the author of ["The Voice of the Pestilence"] ... The poem ... is in form, rhythm, and even in rhymes, an imitation of Shelley's "Cloud" [*sic*]. It is known that the dominant poetic influence upon Browning at this period was that of Shelley.[30]

Although "The Voice of the Pestilence" and "The Cloud" use similar diction, including "Nursling," "shores," and "ocean," these poems can best be described as mirror opposites. They share an inverted resemblance in terms of form and content. "The Voice of the Pestilence" is primarily written in dactylic trimeter while "The Cloud" is in anapestic tetrameter. The former is about the catastrophic impact of miasmatic cholera and the latter about the restorative powers of a zephyrous cloud that "bear[s] light shade for the leaves when laid / In their noonday dreams" (4–5). I have found no definitive evidence that confirms or denies Browning's authorship. All the newspaper reprints of the poem I surveyed appear without any authorial byline.

Although "The Voice of the Pestilence" was published in 1831 (i.e. the year before the first major cholera outbreak in the city of New York and in London), this poem became a site for creating, responding to, and repurposing the discourse of miasma theory in 1866. Between August 25, 1865 and July 5, 1866, "The Voice of the Pestilence" was reprinted in twenty newspapers across the United States from Albany, New York to San Francisco, California.[31] In nearly every reprint, the poem appears with variations of the following epigraph: "This splendid poem was written in 1831, on the approach of the cholera from the East toward the western parts of Europe, and it is appropriate to its renewed apparition and western progress, as mentioned in recent journals."[32] The poem's epigraph gestures to a feedback loop generated by other periodicals. Because the return of cholera reoccasions the "appropriate[ness]" of "The Voice of the Pestilence" for new publics, this epigraph ascribes a value to the poem that goes beyond the poem's initial publication in 1831.

"The Voice of the Pestilence" aestheticizes Orientalist notions of cholera's origins, which are a distinct feature of cholera poetry. As such, this poem is part of an Orientalist poetic tradition that restructured the East for a Western public. As Edward Said forcefully argued in 1978, nineteenth-century poets including

> William Beckford, Byron, Goethe, and Hugo restructured the Orient by their art and made its colors, lights, and people visible through their images, rhythms, and motifs. At most, the "real" Orient provoked a writer to his vision; it very rarely guided it.[33]

As part of this Orientalist tradition, "The Voice of the Pestilence" drew from public discourses that stereotypically tethered the origins of disease to an inscrutable East that threatened Western civilization.

The readers, editors, and publishers of "The Voice of the Pestilence" understood the word "Pestilence" to mean "Asiatic cholera." For example, when John Pierpont reprinted the poem in his schoolroom book, *The American First-Class Book; or, Exercises in Reading and Religion* (1856), he included an annotation for the word "Pestilence" directly citing "The Asiatic cholera."[34] This Orientalist association was common in the period. Most nineteenth-century cholera literature, regardless of its genre, described cholera as "Asiatic" from as early as 1817, when cholera spread rapidly from the Indian subcontinent to Russia via trade routes over land and sea. Soon after, the disease reached the rest of Europe, North America, and the rest of the world. For much of the nineteenth century, origin narratives about cholera emerging and escaping the global South and terrorizing the West circulated broadly in the Anglophone press. However, as Anjula Fatima Raza Kolb explains, 1817

> was also the year that the East India Company requisitioned the Sundarbans, declaring the mangrove forests company property and ramping up logging operations, during the course of which the . . . colonial troops, spread the infection far beyond its normal endemic region in their tasks of conquest.[35]

Because the transmission of cholera was not associated with Europeans, epidemiologists did not link its spread with the colonial empire. Instead, Orientalist tales deemed the early outbreaks in India to be a result of poor living conditions.[36] "Asiatic cholera" stuck throughout the nineteenth century, racializing the disease in the minds of Westerners.

In eighty lines, "The Voice of the Pestilence" aestheticizes the racialized origins of "Asiatic cholera" and its calamitous impact on Western society. The poem entangles complex allusions to miasma theory and biblical scripture to illustrate cholera as an Orientalist monster that moves with destructive force "from the South to the North" (21). The poem opens with a series of miasmatic metaphors, wherein the speaker details the deathly movements of a personified pestilence that "Breathless[ly takes] the course" toward "Northern" shores, leaving behind a pestilential "Stream on the sulphurous air!" (8, 79). In the second stanza, the speaker shifts from the third person to the lyrical "I," ascribing what the title calls "Voice" to the Pestilence: "But swifter than all, with a darker pall / of Terror around my path, / I have arisen from my lampless prison— / Slave of high God's wrath!" (13–16). The phrase "Slave of high God's wrath!" is a reference to the Epistle to the Romans: "For he is the servant of God, an Avenger who carries out God's wrath on the wrongdoer."[37] Joan D. Hedrick reminds us that in early America, "[e]pidemics [were] evidence that God's wrath was rising."[38] Thus, in the poem, Pestilence could be read as a type of consequential holy punishment for wrongdoing. However, the poem does not characterize Pestilence as a "servant of God" as one reads in Romans but rather a "*Slave* of God's high wrath," implicating the institution of slavery and bodies that are culturally and legally othered (16, emphasis mine). In "The Voice of the Pestilence," the reference to a "Slave" historically grounds the personification of Pestilence in the horrors of slavery, particularly the pestilential conditions that enslaved Africans faced in the belly of cargo ships during the Middle Passage. In her study of the cultural impact of widespread disease and death during the Romantic period, Emily Senior argues:

> The grim environment of the slave ship was one of brutal, cramped and unsanitary conditions which meant that contagious fevers, fluxes (dysentery and bowel complaints), measles, smallpox, influenza and parasites could spread above and below deck with exceptional speed.[39]

The poem's reference to a "Slave" conjures this transatlantic voyage from East to West, which exacerbated both social and biological diseases. The morally corrupt transportation of human cargo and the literal transmission of pestilence are coupled in this poem, illustrating how both are diseases that "[Do] trample the [social and cultural] atmosphere" (12).

In the third stanza, the Pestilence describes its awakening in greater detail, emphasizing its Orientalist origins and crusade from under the earth and into the atmosphere:

> A deep Voice went from the Firmament,
> And it pierced the caves of Earth—
> Therefore I came on my wings of flame
> From the dark place of my birth!
> And it said: "Go from the South to the North,
> Over your wondering ball—
> Sin is the King of that doomed Thing,
> And the sin-beguiled must fall!" (17–24)

The imagery of the Pestilence's approach "on my wings of flame / From the dark place of my birth!" resonates with nineteenth-century theories of cholera originating in atmospheric disturbances, a discourse that is grounded in Orientalist epistemes of disease (19–20). As Kolb reminds us, the so-called "father of Indian cholera literature," assistant surgeon and secretary to the Medical Board of the Bengal Presidency James Jameson, "produced one of the earliest accounts of the epidemic in the colonial archive."[40] He was one of the first to point to atmospheric disturbances as the root of cholera transmission in his account of the 1817 outbreak in India. In his influential *Report on the epidemick cholera morbus*, Jameson links the transmission of cholera in India to changes in temperature, that is, "easterly winds; very hot days: and great variations of temperature between the day and night."[41] These changes, he continues, "very strongly evinc[e] that unvarying connection of the Epidemick with marked vicissitudes in the atmospherical temperature, and an unsettled state of the weather."[42] Jameson's report orientalized the study of colonial disease by collapsing cholera's etiology with Jessore, a district in the southwestern region of Bengal, which he describes as "the place in which the disorder first put on a very malignant form, . . . a crowed, dirty, ill ventilated town surrounded by thick jungle."[43] His convictions about atmospheric distemperature in the Indian subcontinent inscribed an Orientalist tropical landscape in the study of cholera.

Jameson's work had a lasting influence on subsequent writers of cholera literature. As David Arnold posits in *The New Cambridge History of India*, this influence "possibly explains why so many [epidemiologists] clung to climatic or environmental explanations long after these had been jettisoned in Europe."[44] In 1866, many newspapers still linked cholera to rapid changes in the atmosphere and temperature. There were different phrases for describing these atmospheric changes, including "atmospheric deposits," "atmospheric decomposition," and "the great atmospheric cause."[45]

Contemporaneous epidemiological discourse of "Asiatic cholera" was rooted in Jameson's colonial and Orientalist notions of disease, which implicated the climate of the Indian subcontinent in cholera's etiology and transmission. On January 27, 1866, Horace Greeley's *New-York Daily Tribune* printed an article entitled "Epidemic Cholera: Pathological Conclusions. The 'Propositions' of the Famous Dr. James Johnson."[46] Like Jameson, Johnson had deep ties to England. He was the editor of *The Medico-Chirurgical Review* and a physician to William IV. In "Epidemic Cholera," he argued that "'Asiatic cholera' arises from 'atmospheric distemperature', and is diffused through, and conveyed by, the air."[47] We see the discourse of atmospheric distemperature in "The Voice of the Pestilence," where cholera is directly related to rapid changes in the temperature and environment of orientalized colonial spaces. In the poem, this "atmospheric distemperature" is the hellscape imagery of "spires of volcanic fires / [that] Stream on the sulphureous air" and "wings of flame" which, in later parts of the poem, are linked to "the jungles of Jessore" (6–8, 19, 51).

In the middle of the third stanza, the "Voice ... from the Firmament" instructs Pestilence to "'Go from the South to the North, / Over your wondering ball'" (17, 21–22), referring to the global South and the global North. These lines are indicative of how, as Kolb argues, "the patterns of disease transmission create the material and bodily conditions under which textual transmission can be seen to follow the course of the disease itself, a discursive 'Westward progress' from colonial outpost to metropole."[48] The Pestilence's directionality connects "the dark place of [Pestilence's] birth" to the miasmatic discharges of bodies and places that are outside or beyond clear national borders (20). As the Pestilence moves from "the jungles of Jessore" to the North, "the nations [are] aghast for dread, / Lo! I have passed, as the desert blast— / And the millions of Earth lie dead!" (51, 32–34). Following the course of the disease itself, the textual transmission of the threat of "Westward progress" reflects fearmongering paratexts in medical reports and newspapers articles about cholera's "Asiatic" origins that date to Jameson's *Report on the epidemick cholera morbus*. Kolb argues that "[i]f cholera indeed has a disposition for Jameson, it was somewhere between the 'foul fiend' ... and ... a figure of colonial vengeance, which is prefigured in the report's confounded attempt to grapple with the meaning of the epidemic's Westward tendencies."[49]

In 1865, scaremongering reports about cholera's "Westward tendencies" made headlines in newspapers, including titles like "Rapid Advance of the Cholera Westward" and "Progress of the Cholera Westward" in the *Pittsburgh Daily Commercial* and the *New York Times*, respectively.[50] In a front page column titled "The Coming Pestilence: Ravages of the Cholera. Its Westward Progress" on August 29, 1865, the New York *Evening Post* grapples with cholera's westward tendencies, claiming:

> The latest intelligence from Europe confirms the apprehension that the Asiatic cholera, in its most malignant form, is on its march, and advancing steadily westward ... It ... came thither, as at former periods, from India, for so many centuries its home and first starting-place.[51]

These alarming reports of cholera's westward vengeance rehearse Orientalist patterns of disease transmission, evincing that in the era of global contagion, India is the source of chaotic disease and westward malignity.

The fearmongering discourse of Western infiltration and alarm is thrown into sharp relief in the fifth stanza of "The Voice of the Pestilence," where the speaker describes in more detail the Pestilence's effluvia. The speaker claims, "My throne is the boundless air— / My chosen shroud is the dark plumed cloud / Which the whirling breezes bear!" (46–48). The "boundless air," "dark plumed cloud," and "whirling breezes" describe an atmospheric distemperature ripe for sickness, resembling popular nineteenth-century epitextual personifications of

Figure 4.1 Robert Seymour, "Cholera 'Tramples the Victor and the Vanquish'd Both,'" *McLean's Monthly*, October 1, 1831. National Library of Medicine Digital Collections. Public domain mark 1.0.

the disease (46, 47, 48). For example, in the October 1, 1831 issue of *McLean's Monthly*, the British illustrator Robert Seymour (1798–1836) famously illustrates the spread of cholera as a skeletal figure, "shroud[ed] . . . [in a] dark plumed cloud" (46) (see Figure 4.1).

Like "The Voice of the Pestilence," Seymour's illustration was published in response to the 1831 cholera epidemic in London. Both the illustration and poem characterize the disease as a powerful force that "tramples" the atmosphere, causing havoc among "the Victor and the Vanquish'd Both." It is a war against cholera that the soldiers beneath Cholera's skeletal feet are losing. Their weapons are ineffective against the disease, a conceit, no doubt, for Western civilization's unsuccessful tactics in the war against cholera.

"The Voice of the Pestilence" concludes with an ominous warning to Western publics: "Harken, harken, my coming shall darken / The light of thy festal cheer: / In thy storm-rocked home on the Northern foam, / Nursling of Ocean—hear!" (77–80). The poem concludes where the second poem in this chapter, "King Cholera," begins. In "King Cholera," cholera has already made its transoceanic voyage and commences to spread in "thy storm-rocked home on the Northern foam" (79). Set in the cityscape, "King Cholera" reveals important connections between the public discourses of disease and middle-class social anxieties about poverty, immigrants, and filth, which acquire historical significance when read alongside the poem's epitext.

The Disease of Poverty in "King Cholera"

"King Cholera" shows important intersections between periodical poetry and the public discourses of the Industrial Revolution. The poem was first published anonymously on August 26, 1865 in *Mrs. Grundy*, a weekly humor magazine based in the city of New York that printed articles, poems, jokes, illustrations, and letters addressed to the fictive "Mrs. Grundy," often about political and economic issues in the city.[52] Like the other poems in this chapter, "King Cholera" was not a self-enclosed art object. After its initial appearance, the poem was reprinted in twenty-two newspapers from Keene, New Hampshire to San Francisco, California between September 8, 1865 and September 8, 1866.[53] Through its circulation, "King Cholera" directly participated in and addressed pressing issues of class, sanitary reformation, and immigration in a time of disease-induced social panic. When we read "King Cholera" along its epitext of cultural images and texts about class inequities in metropolitan centers, contagion, and cholera death maps, the poem gains the necessary contextualization and aesthetic significance required to read it as nineteenth-century readers did. Before getting into the content of "King Cholera," one epitextual site worth exploring is John Leech's etching "A Court for King Cholera," which informs the cultural provenance of the poem's title.

The poem's title, "King Cholera," was part of a discursive network of metaphors used in newspaper articles and illustrations to conceptualize cholera's power and, as it were, dominion over human bodies. One the most well-known illustrations of "King Cholera" is Leech's "A Court for King Cholera" published in *Punch Magazine* on September 25, 1852, just a few years after the 1849 cholera outbreak in the city of New York and in London (see Figure 4.2).

"A Court for King Cholera" portrays a satirical representation of the urban impact of the Industrial Revolution, linking overcrowded living conditions to the spread of cholera. In Figure 4.2, a crowd of old and young in tattered rags gather in a filthy and busy street. The tenement apartment windows in the background frame curious, inscrutable effigies poking their faces out toward a street pulsing with activity. On the far-right side of the illustration, a coffin is hoisted above a city dweller's head as somber faces move to and fro. To the left of the etching, a child does a headstand on top of a pile of squalor as an elderly woman and boys inspect rubbish. This is the image of metropolitan poverty or, as the title implies, the court of "King Cholera." Analyzing the *Punch* cartoon as part of a set of communicative practices that made shared experiences meaningful, Suzanne Nunn argues that "this image reflected and reinforced specific middle-class social anxieties about dirt, disease, the poor and the Irish, and

THE EPITEXTUAL SITES OF CHOLERA POEMS

Figure 4.2 John Leech, "A Court for King Cholera," *Punch*, September 25, 1852. Licensed under the Creative Commons Attribution 4.0 International (CC BY 4.0).

fully engaged with the medical, political, and social debates that crystallized around cholera in the mid-nineteenth century."[54] Leech's image emphasizes the compactness of the city, the margin-to-margin traffic of people unable to physically distance. It is an example of how social class exacerbates cholera among the poor who occupy crowded and filthy places.

"A Court for King Cholera" illustrates the impact of cholera among society's most vulnerable. While affluent citizens could escape congested city streets during outbreaks, the poor were confined to dense and unsanitary wards. Melosi posits:

> In New York, about one-third of the 27,000 residents fled during the 1805 epidemic. The poor, who were unable to flee, usually suffered the most. To make matters worse, economic activity ground to a halt during epidemics as merchants and other business owners took flight, leaving workers at least temporarily unemployed.[55]

Thus, as cholera spread in dense and impoverished metropolitan wards predominantly made up of poor immigrants, so did the level of poverty and unemployment, causing a cycle of poverty and disease among the city's most neglected communities.

Like Leech's illustration, the poem "King Cholera" offers a look at class inequities in metropolitan centers, revealing to readers a correlation between disease and poverty or, more accurately, the disease of poverty. Here is the poem in full:

"King Cholera"
[Respectfully Dedicated to the City Fathers]

i

A dreadful Whisper comes from the East
Of a Raging Monster Gaunt and grim,
Making of Men a Vampire-Feast,
Highest and lowest, greatest and least—
All that he finds are food for him!

ii

And ever Westward he holds his way,
Marching with slow, insidious tread,
His Victims struggle, and weep, and pray,
But naught can his horrible Hunger stay
Till his path is strewn with a Thousand Dead!

iii

Squalor he loves, Filth, and Crime:
What shall we do to avert his Wrath?
Can we not purge our City in time,
With Charcoal, Water, and sprinkled Lime
And leave no place for his hideous path?

iv

Or, will our Rulers no danger know
Till at our door King Cholera halts,
While Dead-carts hither and thither go,
And the thick air shudders with Cries of Woe,
And everywhere gape the Burial-Vaults?

v

Take heed of warning now—take heed
While still there is time our Homes to save!
For everywhere ripens to the Poisonous Seed
On which King Cholera loves to feed,
That our City may be but a mighty Grave!

> vi
> Cleanse, O Fathers! These Gutters and Styes,
> Festering Kennels and filthy Slums,
> Reeking under the Dog-day Skies,
> For—if their Stench must still arise—
> What shall we do when King Cholera comes?

Nearly every "King Cholera" reprint includes the dedicatory epigraph "[Respectfully Dedicated to the City Fathers]," a bracketed dedication to city officials who have the political influence to change health codes and laws. The brackets suggest that these "City Fathers" could be replaced and/or edited to reflect who is in charge.

In the first stanza, rehearing Orientalist transmission narratives, the speaker describes cholera as "A dreadful Whisper com[ing] from the East" and a "Raging Monster" who "Mak[es] of Men a Vampire-Feast" (1–3). In the second stanza, the speaker claims:

> And ever Westward he holds his way
> Marching with slow, insidious tread,
> His Victims struggle, and weep, and pray,
> But naught can his horrible Hunger stay
> Till his path is strewn with a Thousand Dead! (5–10)

In the context of newspapers, the imagery of Cholera's insidious westward movement that leaves a "path ... with a Thousand Dead!" correlates with the rising number of cholera-related fatalities in the city of New York (10). Epitextual sites of contemporaneous cholera death maps frequently published in newspapers contextualize cholera's "horrible Hunger" and its impact on the city's most vulnerable communities (9). For instance, on July 23, 1866, the *Herald* printed two cholera death maps detailing the appearance of cholera in 1832 and 1836 (see Figure 4.3).

The maps traced a rather unclear type of path that suggested a miasmatic transmission of cholera and, more importantly, implicitly warned readers of where cholera cases occurred. According to the *Herald*, the map on the left was "sketched for the purpose of enabling strangers to perceive the evidence of non-contagion, as well as of local origin."[56] The black circles on the map identified the parts of the city where the disease "suddenly appeared," suggesting that these outbreaks occurred simultaneously without human contact.[57] The anticontagionist article goes onto link cholera to the "filthy state of several of these points, or of the intemperate, dissolute and abandoned habits of the inhabitants of some of them, or of the proverbial filth of the streets ... in most

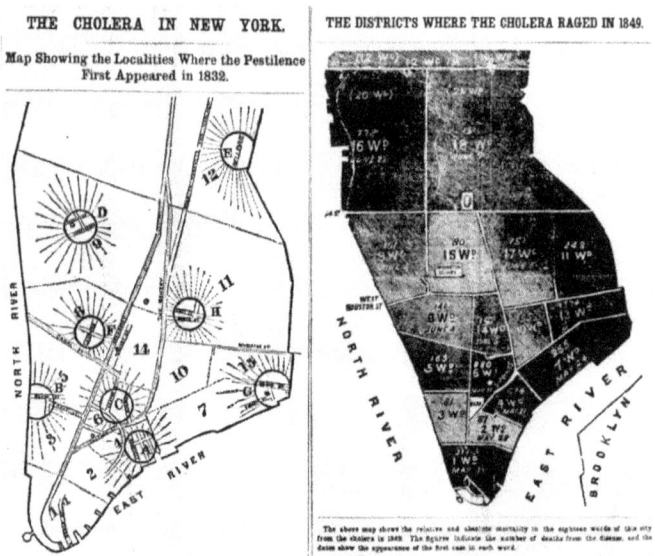

Figure 4.3 "Map Showing the Localities Where the Pestilence First Appeared in 1832" and "The Districts Where the Cholera Raged in 1849," *New York Herald*, July 23, 1866. Library of Congress. Public domain.

locations."[58] The map on the right "shows the relative and absolute mortality in the eighteen wards of the city from the cholera of 1849."[59] The map provides the number of cholera deaths and the dates when the disease first appeared in each ward. The concentration of cases in the lower part of Manhattan, neighborhoods with significant Irish immigrant and African American populations, reveals that the most marginalized in society suffered the greatest from epidemic disease. The poem's imagery of a "path ... strewn with a Thousand Dead" acquires cultural and historical significance in the *Herald*'s maps (10). It is a grim path of Irish immigrant and African American populations, the most vulnerable and under-resourced communities in Lower Manhattan.

This sepulchral path is more directly contextualized in another epitextual site published in the *New York Sun* titled "Cholera Report." Published on July 23, 1866, the same day as the *Herald* publication, the *Sun*'s report includes short descriptive prose pieces for twenty patients in the city of New York who showed symptoms of cholera. These pieces contain the names of the patients and the physicians who reported on their conditions, and the patients' home addresses. Here are a few examples:

> The following is the report since Saturday.
> At 8:12, Joseph Russell, of 141 Duane Street, was reported by Dr. Van Kleek to be sick of cholera. He is doing well.

THE EPITEXTUAL SITES OF CHOLERA POEMS

> Dr. McCauley, reported Mary Daniels, age 49, to be sick of cholera at 49 Mott Street. She was taken on Friday night at 8.A.M. Saturday she was on collapse and died in the afternoon.
>
> At 2.P.M. Saturday. Dr. Tomelier reported James Halliday, 13 [illegible] Street, rear, to be sick of cholera.[60]

What made these snippets newsworthy content is that in addition to informing readers of who was infected, they also provided details (addresses, names, conditions) regarding where the disease was concentrated. Like the *Herald*'s cholera maps, the *Sun*'s report traced the path of cholera's transmission, implicitly cautioning readers to stay away from Lower Manhattan.

Drawing similar attention to cholera's destructive path, "King Cholera" explores the disease's etiology and miasmatic movements in the third stanza. Here, the speaker emphasizes the city's unsanitary conditions, which are a source of disease: the "Squalor he loves, Filth, and Crime" (11). At the end of this stanza, the speaker satirically inquires about preventative measures for cholera's arrival, ridiculing city officials' lack of preparation: "What shall we do to avert his Wrath? / Can we not purge our City in time, / With Charcoal, Water, and sprinkled Lime / And leave no place for his hideous path?" (12–15). Although many nineteenth-century sources reported that charcoal was a prophylaxis against the transmission of cholera, the speaker comically suggests charcoal only to show how desperate citizens are driven to extreme measures to protect themselves from disease.[61] In the fourth and fifth stanzas, the speaker more earnestly turns to sanitary reform as a preventative measure:

> Or, will our Rulers no danger know
> Till at our door King Cholera halts,
> While Dead-carts hither and thither go,
> And the thick air shudders with Cries of Woe,
> And everywhere gape the Burial-Vaults? (16–20)

The speaker cautions "Rulers" not to respond sluggishly to the cholera outbreak (16). Melosi reminds us that "[e]pidemics forced the government to deal with public health, at least from crisis to crisis, but the absence of regularized preventive action had to do with limited knowledge about contagious diseases."[62] The thought that city officials were not doing enough to prepare their constituents for another outbreak was in the minds of many newspaper readers. On March 10, 1865, the *New York Times* reported:

> Science has demonstrated with the clearness of noonday that thousands of human beings, the greater part of them innocent, helpless children, are every year deprived of life in this city by effluvia that might be prevented.

Why has it not been prevented? . . . Why have not better laws been made, better men put in trust?[63]

Similarly, on November 13, 1865, the *Brooklyn Daily Eagle* published an article titled "Preparations for the Cholera," calling "on the authorities to take immediate steps to save our citizens from unreasonable panic by giving them, with the least possible delay, the reassuring knowledge that their lives stand protected by thorough measures of sanitary reform."[64] Mirroring the public demands in these articles, the fifth stanza of "King Cholera" asks "the City Fathers" to "Take heed of warning now—take heed / While still there is time our Homes to save!" before "our City may be but a mighty Grave!" (21–22, 25). The fifth stanza's sepulchral imagery of the city as a "mighty Grave," together with the "Dead-carts" and the "Poisonous Seed" in the previous stanzas, conjure a collective image of an unprepared city in the throes of contagion (25, 18, 23).

In the final stanza of "King Cholera," the speaker once more invokes the question of sanitary reform, summoning "the City Fathers" and asking them to

> Cleanse, O Fathers! These Gutters and Styes
> Festering Kennels and filthy Slums
> Reeking under the Dog-day Skies,
> For—if their Stench must still arise—
> What shall we do when King Cholera comes? (26–30)

In this stanza, the speaker requests what many New Yorkers wanted in 1866: a comprehensive health law that would protect the city from another cholera outbreak. Although the New York Board of Health was first established in 1805 during a cholera epidemic, it had little power and resources.[65] After the 1805 epidemic passed, the Board of Health also died out and the city council continued to take its usual passive role toward preventative measures. With cholera breaking out in Europe in 1865, the city of New York needed to prepare for another wave of disease. As the *Herald* reported on November 5, 1865, "Vigorous preparations are now being made by the Health Commissioners, Quarantine Commissioners and the other bodies to meet any emergencies which may arise regarding the presence of that fatal epidemic, the cholera, which now threatens to visit our shores."[66] In "King Cholera," the supplication "O Fathers!" invokes the Health Commissioners and Quarantine Commissioners cited in the *Herald*, as well other city leaders whom the public beseeched for protection against cholera. However, as the *Eagle* reported, there was public distrust toward the Board of Health's lackadaisical response to cholera: "The Public must have remarked that the tone of the Board, at the time, was one of languor."[67] Many residents "call[ed] on the authorities to take immediate steps," demanding that the Board of Health acquire ordinances that would grant them enough resources to visit private houses, to abate all nuisances within them, to cleanse privies, dig ash-pits, whitewash, distribute chloride of zinc, of iron, of lime, or other disinfectant, &c.; and, in conjunction with the city police, to bring all persons guilty of depositing foul water, garbage, ashes, &c, on the streets, to summary punishment.[68]

Such epitextual sites historically locate the imagery in "King Cholera" of "Festering Kennels and filthy Slums / Reeking under the Dog-day Skies" in the larger political questions of public health and sanitary reform (27–28). Partisan opinions regarding public health and sanitary reform were heated during the 1866 cholera epidemic. These debates are thrown into sharp relief in the final poem in this chapter, "The Health Bill: A Talk Between Two Repubs at Albany."

"The Health Bill: A Talk Between Two Repubs at Albany"

"The Health Bill: A Talk Between Two Repubs at Albany" is a satirical poem by the Irish American journalist, Union soldier, and poet Charles G. Halpine (1829–68), also known by his *nom de plume* Miles O'Reilly.[69] The poem was first printed on February 1, 1866 in the *New-York Citizen*, a weekly newspaper that ran from 1864 to 1873 and was published by the Citizens' Association of New-York, an organization of prominent New Yorkers who advocated for reforming New York's sanitation and public health.[70] When Halpine retired from military service in 1864, he moved to New York where he began to edit and later own the *Citizen*. The poem's title, "The Health Bill," refers to the Metropolitan Health Bill of 1866, the first bill in the state of New York that created comprehensive control of sanitary conditions.

"The Health Bill" acquires cultural and historical significance within paratextual partisan debates in the press about overhauling the old system of public health. This historical context consists of epitexts about public health debates that circulated in Republican-leaning papers like the *New York Times* and the *New York Tribune* and in democratic-leaning newspapers like the *New York Herald*. As a satirical poem, the poem relies on the politicization of sanitary reform and cholera in 1866 for comedic effect. Without this epitext, the comedic elements of the poem, the references to politicians and bills, are nearly indiscernible. For this reason, I want to first introduce the political debates that contextualize "The Health Bill" before getting into the poem's content.

After its initial publication in the *Citizen*, "The Health Bill" was reprinted in Robert B. Roosevelt's (1829–1906) collected works of Halpine's poems, *The Poetical Works of Charles G. Halpine* (1869), with the following note for "The Health Bill":

> This was a measure of reform carried by the Citizen's [sic] Association with the help of the Republicans, to take the control of sanitary matters in

> the city of New York from a body of political inspectors, several of whom testified before a legislative committee that they considered "hygiene" to be a "bad smell" or a "collection of dirty water," and give it to a medical board. Reference is made to Thomas C. Anton, president of the Metropolitan Board of Police, and Lyman Tremaine, attorney general.[71]

As editor of Halpine's poem, Roosevelt understood that not all of his readers in 1869 would be familiar with the specific political debates about cholera that importantly contextualize "The Health Bill." For this reason, he provides an epitext to the poem, a note that historically situates Halpine's words within overlapping public discourses of sanitary reform, miasma, and partisanship. In doing so, Roosevelt contextualizes the poem in a public conversation and discourse regarding political power between the Republicans and "political inspectors," some of whom subscribed to miasma theory while others did not. However, Roosevelt's epitextual note is limited by its own medium. As a note appended to the poem, it only provides a brief summary of the poem's provenance, an incomplete picture of its cultural significance. The note does not fully capture the contemptuous disputes between political parties that are a main feature of "The Health Bill." For a fuller picture, we must de-anthologize the poem and turn to contemporaneous debates in the press about sanitary reform.

Before New York passed the Metropolitan Health Bill in 1866, overhauling the old system of sanitation, the state legislature had failed to act on the bill the previous year in part because of fiery disputes among and between prominent Republicans and Democrats fighting over the consolidation and control of their political parties. The press served as a catalyst for these debates. For example, on January 31, 1866, James Gordon Bennett's Democratic-supporting *Herald* printed an attack on the Republican party, particularly aimed at the editor of the *Tribune*, Horace Greeley:

> The Health bill . . . after all the vociferations of Greeley and the *Tribune*, and the fact that its defeat last year was made the basis of a radical campaign in every Senatorial district—that bill is to-day in danger of the same end as last year at the hands of these radicals and under the direction of Greeley. The extraordinary reason of this is the intense importance attached to the Republican General Committee of New York City, and the strife which Greeley and his friends are engaged in to capture and control that important body.[72]

The *Herald* accused Greeley and the Radical Republicans of having ulterior political motives, which kept them from voting on the Health Bill. Greeley responded to this accusation in a *Tribune* article printed on February 14, 1866:

> The Health Bill now before the Legislature has had our support from the beginning, save in one particular—the Constitution of the Board of Commissioners appointed by it. The public understand us in this, and understand that our objection to the Bill in the shape it passed the Senate is simply and solely because complete control is thereby given, not to a *new* Board of Health Commissioners, but to the *old* Board of Police . . . the ruling influence in that old Board of Police is in sympathy with a certain political clique which we object to seeing clothed with this additional power.[73]

Greeley countered the *Herald*'s accusation by defending his party's conditional objection to the Health Bill. He claimed that the bill "has had our support from the beginning" apart from "the Constitution of the Board of Commissioners appointed by it."[74] The Constitution, according to Greeley, would give "complete control . . . to the *old* Board of Police" that is in league with "a certain clique" of conservative Republicans, including newspaper publisher and politician Thurlow Weed (1797–1885).

Halpine's poem satirizes such public debates about the Health Bill through a dramatic dialogue between "two Repub[lican]s at Albany." Through a series of questions asked by the first speaker and answered by the second, the poem reveals complex political divisions within the Republican party. The poem opens:

> "Shall we pass this great Bill for the Public Health?"
> "Why, that is no longer the question!
> But shall endless sources of power and wealth,
> And unlimited chances for public stealth—
> On the cholera-plea, and the Public Health—
> Be secured for our party's digestion?" (1–6)

The two Republican speakers claim that their real concern is not "pass[ing] this great Bill for the Public Health" but rather securing, for the Republican party, the power and influence that comes with control of the Board of Health (1). The question of power and influence regarding the Health Bill was a pressing issue of the time. An Albany correspondent for the *Brooklyn Daily Eagle* writes on February 19, 1866 that those who control the Board of Health will "have power to run a small kingdom, and can bleed the Treasury with unlimited freedom."[75] These "endless sources of power and wealth" are what the speakers hope to "secure for [their] party's digestion" (3, 6). In the second stanza, the two speakers continue their debate:

> "And if to our party this power is to glide,
> And these chances of wealth be won for us?"

"Why, the next question, then, we have got to decide
Is this: Shall we make it 'an equal divide'
Betwixt the Weed-Seward and the Radical side,
Or give all to Lord Thurlow, or Horace?" (7–12)

Here, the speakers contemplate how to "divide" this power and influence among members of their own party, including US Secretary of State William Henry Seward (1801–72); Seward's political advisor, Thurlow Weed; and the "Radical side," referring to a faction of Republican abolitionists, including Horace Greeley (10). Divisions within the Republican party over who gets control over the Board of Health are made clearer in the following stanza as the speakers draw attention to the 89th New York State Legislature:

The Senate think [sic] Weed should be given the whole,
And the Board of Police therefore packed on;
But the bully Assembly's as black as coal,
And the Radical rascals say "Thurlow's control
Is already too great for the good of his soul"
And they're down like Old Scratch on Tom Action. (13–18)

The speakers claim that the Radicals say that "Thurlow [Weed's] control / Is already too great for the good of his soul" (16–17). Weed endorsed a more conservative version of Republicanism. After Lincoln's assassination, he staunchly supported Andrew Johnson's presidency (1865–69). On October 9, 1866, the Democratic-leaning *Brooklyn Eagle* acridly remarked that Weed

has done more than any living man, by the countenance he has given to jobbery and corruption, to bring Republican representative institutions into disagreement. His name has been a synonym for corruption. His very presence in the vicinity of our public bodies, is accepted as all-sufficient proof that some scheme involving bribery and fraud is being attempted.[76]

The speakers in the poem go on to say that Radical Republicans are "down like Old Scratch on Tom Action" (18), alluding to Washington Irving's popular short story "The Devil and Tom Walker" (1824). In Irving's story, Tom makes a deal with the devil, Old Scratch, trading his soul for worldly possessions. The comparison between Radical Republicans and Old Scratch suggests that the Radical Republicans are willing to make a deal with Weed, that is Old Scratch, in order to pass the Health Bill. However, as the final stanza shows, irresolution ensues:

"So between them the Health Bill is dragged either way
And all kinds of fools' errands sent on?"

"Why, yes; but you'll find they'll agree some fine day
Not to lose such rich chances of pickings and pay;
And the Health Bill—at least so I hear Lyman say—
Will be given to lord Horace through Fenton." (19–24)

These closing lines are riddled with the names of political figures: Lyman Trumbull (1813–96), co-author of the Thirteenth Amendment; Horace Greeley; and New York governor and state senator Reuben Fenton (1819–85), requiring readers to be completely immersed in the news and nuances of the Health Bill. At the poem's end, Greeley is satirically deemed the victor of this debate via Fenton who, at the time, was serving his final year as governor of New York. But the real winners were the city of New York's long-suffering denizens who were in desperate need of a bill that would put sanitation before politics. Despite these political setbacks, the state legislature passed the Metropolitan Health Bill on February 26, 1866. With the efforts of the city of New York Department of Health and Mental Hygiene, this bill laid out the legal grounds for a comprehensive reform of sanitary laws to improve living and working conditions in New York. However, as the press made clear in the months after, the new bill did not protect all New Yorkers equally.

In the summer of 1866, as cholera cases spiked in Brooklyn, the *Brooklyn Daily Eagle* critiqued Brooklyn Mayor Samuel Booth and the president of the Health Commissioner's Office for "not performing the duties the Health Commission was created to perform."[77] After the establishment of the Metropolitan Board of Health, city aldermen refused to cooperate with the Board because of the latter's suspected unethical business dealings with Brooklyn "street contractors, or perhaps not wishing to annoy their constituency with too much investigation in their habits and sanitary condition."[78] Some newspapers argued that the aldermen and the mayor's oversight cost the lives of many poor Brooklyn residents. Outraged by the alleged corruption of city officials and the consequential number of lives lost to cholera, the *New York Times* reported:

> This was naturally the case in Red Hook district and the Sixteenth Ward. Here, accordingly the cholera already appears, and in every ward . . . where the Aldermen declined to work with the Board, there is the greater mortality. The most threatening appearance of cholera thus far is in Brooklyn, and though the pestilence does not break out generally, the deaths from neglect of sanitary precautions are on the increase. From the miserable jealousy of these Aldermen, or from baser motives, the poor people of the lowest quarters are left without public care to be carried off by dysentery fever and cholera. Indeed, it would seem that the pestilence is allowed to enter Brooklyn in order that some wicked street contractor or petty official may reap larger profit from his neglect of the public good.[79]

As the *Times* corroborates, when aldermen declined to cooperate with the Board, cholera casualties increased, affecting those living in "the lowest quarters" of society.[80] The questionable ethics of street contractors and the financial greed of aldermen exacerbated the transmission of disease in areas like Red Hook, Brooklyn that were underserved even before the Metropolitan Health Bill was passed. Red Hook was an urban waterfront neighborhood whose working-class population was made up predominantly of Irish and Italian immigrants and African American dockworkers, together with a transient population of sailors between voyages. As such, it was a prime location for the transmission of cholera.[81]

CONCLUSION

Cholera poems draw on, illuminate, and redirect public discourses of disease. In 1866, many newspaper poems were occasioned by cholera and its calamitous impact on society. These poems reimagined and sometimes contributed to contemporaneous debates about sanitary reform, contagion, and preventative measures through verse that drew from the discourses of epidemiology, shaping, in many cases, how reading publics understood and managed the disease.

This chapter has argued that during the city of New York's cholera epidemic of 1866, writing, publishing, circulating, and reading newspaper poems played an important role in disseminating public discourses of cholera. It is no mere coincidence that poems about cholera, pestilence, and sanitary reform were printed and reprinted as cholera approached and spread throughout the city. Occasioned by the epidemic, "The Voice of the Pestilence," "King Cholera," and "The Health Bill: A Talk Between Two Repubs at Albany" responded to concerns about cholera's "Asiatic" origins, contagion, and containment. Using the discourse of infection, "The Voice of the Pestilence" and "King Cholera" personify cholera, giving it a voice, shape, and origin. While these poems illustrate the calamitous impact of cholera, "The Health Bill: A Talk Between Two Repubs at Albany" exposes the internal mechanisms of sanitary reform within governing bodies and political systems, particularly the New York State Republican party of 1866. Through a satirical dramatic dialogue, this poem shows us how (bi)partisanship opinion about political influence and power shaped how city officials responded to the 1866 cholera epidemic. Together, the three poems in this chapter provide a historical narrative of the 1866 cholera epidemic that focuses on the city's efforts to prepare for and control the disease before it spread again. This narrative acquires historical and aesthetic significance through its epitext of contemporaneous news, medical articles, and illustrations.

Cholera poems are a part of the information-driven media culture of the nineteenth century. As cholera plagued the streets of New York, readers of newspaper poems encountered these poems in their preferred newspapers and next to their daily dose of newsprint. Such poetic encounters became a part of the regular cycle of information-driven print. Although distinguished from the prosaic news columns, these poems recycled similar public discourses informing the public of what they thought they knew about cholera and contagion.

In addition to contextualizing poems within complex public discourses and political debates, a poem's paratext can align a newspaper's politics with a poem's byline. The final chapter in this book turns to this phenomenon in the Spanish-language press. I analyze how paratextual sites politicized the public image of the Cuban-born transamerican poet Gertrudis Gómez de Avellaneda (1814–73), influencing how the public engaged with and interpreted her writing.

Toward the end of the nineteenth century, a significant Antillean Hispanophone population was exiled to the city of New York. There they escaped Spanish persecution in Cuba and Puerto Rico, the Spanish empire's remaining colonial territories. Many exiles established printing houses and newspapers in order to create communities among exiles with similar political and ideological desires. Within the pages of these newspapers, many Hispanophone editors published popular poems that often served their newspaper's political rhetoric of revolution. Avellaneda was one of the most frequently published poets in these papers. As a celebrity poetess with nationally recognized affiliations in Cuba, Spain, Puerto Rico, and the US, Avellaneda's poems and public image were bound up in the push and pull of nationalist discourses. Some newspapers claimed her as a Spanish loyalist and/or nationalist while others framed her as a feminist abolitionist—aligning her with Cuban freedom fighters. Crossing political divides, her newspaper poems show us an important component of paratextuality, how the poem's framework, at times, polices and censors the poet's reputation and cultural significance.

Notes

1. Charles E. Rosenberg, *The Cholera Years: The United States in 1832, 1849, and 1866* (Chicago: University of Chicago Press, 1962), 3.
2. Rosenberg, *Cholera Years*, 3.
3. Martin V. Melosi, *The Sanitary City: Environmental Services in Urban America from Colonial Times to the Present*, abridged edition (Pittsburgh: University of Pittsburgh Press, 2008), 11.
4. Rosenberg, *Cholera Years*, 6.
5. Rosenberg, *Cholera Years*, 193.
6. Wolosky, *Poetry and Public Discourse*, x.
7. Wolosky, *Poetry and Public Discourse*, ix.
8. Wolosky, *Poetry and Public Discourse*, ix.
9. Genette, *Paratexts*, 344.
10. Genette, *Paratexts*, 345.
11. Genette, *Paratexts*, 346.
12. Genette, *Paratexts*, 346.

13. John M. Last, *A Dictionary of Public Health* (Oxford: Oxford University Press, 2007), 178.
14. Melosi, *Sanitary City*, 14.
15. Daniel Eli Burstein, *Next to Godliness: Confronting Dirt and Despair in Progressive Era New York City* (Champaign: University of Illinois Press, 2006), 13. Burstein claims, "As nineteenth-century physicians learned more about contagion, many theories came to accept a modified miasma theory, which some medical historians term 'contingent-contagionism'. In this schema, diseases were caused by contagia. But these contagia . . . could take hold only in conjunction with foul air, unhealthy soil, noxious social conditions, intemperate personal lifestyle choices, or inborn constitutional weaknesses that undermined one's resistance" (13).
16. Burstein, *Next to Godliness*, 13.
17. Rosenberg, *Cholera Years*, 3.
18. Rosenberg, *Cholera Years*, 73.
19. G. K. Blank argues that Percy Bysshe Shelley's "Ode to the West Wind" is an exception to this characterization of the wind as zephyr. Shelley's "Ode" portrays the wind as "an invisible mover and carrier." For Shelley's speaker, the wind is simultaneously auspicious and menacing and draws its powers from a dual "unseen force." "Ode to the West Wind," 2. Blank calls the wind in Shelley's poem the "angel of death and life." G. K. Blank, "Shelley's Wind of Influence," *Philological Quarterly* 64, no. 4 (1985): 478.
20. Michael O'Neill, *The Cambridge History of English Poetry* (Cambridge: Cambridge University Press, 2010), 358.
21. According to William Cullen Bryant's biographer Gilbert H. Muller, Bryant's "Summer Wind" was first published in the *United Sates Literary Gazette* in 1824. Gilbert H. Muller, *William Cullen Bryant: Author of America* (Albany: State University of New York Press, 2008), 41.
22. Bryant, *Poems*, 62–63.
23. Muller, *William Cullen Bryant*, 42.
24. The Aeolian harp (or lyre) was a musical instrument invented by the German Jesuit Athanasius Kircher in 1650. Michael Ferber describes it as a "long, narrow wooden box with a thin belly and with eight to twelve strings stretched over two bridges and tuned in unison; it is to be placed in a window (or a grotto) where the wind will draw out a harmonious sound." Michael Ferber, *A Dictionary of Literary Symbols* (Cambridge: Cambridge University Press, 1999), 7.
25. Alison Byerly, *Realism, Representation, and the Arts in Nineteenth-Century Literature* (Cambridge: Cambridge University Press, 1997), 45.
26. Robert Stark, *Ezra Pound's Early Verse and Lyric Tradition: A Jargoner's Apprenticeship* (Edinburgh: Edinburgh University Press, 2012), 54.
27. John Hollander, "The West Wind and the Mingled Measure," *Daedalus* 111, no. 3 (1982): 146.
28. Alfred Domett, *Poems* (London: Henry Leggatt, 1833), 149.
29. W. F. Prideaux, "Domett and Browning," *Notes and Queries: A Medium of Intercommunication for Literary Men, General Readers, etc.*, Seventh Series, vol. 12 (London, 1891), 28.

30. Harry B. Smith, *A Sentimental Library: Comprising Books Formerly Owned By Famous Writers, Presentation Copies, Manuscripts, and Drawings* (Privately Printed, 1914), 17.
31. "The Voice of the Pestilence" was reprinted in the following newspapers: *Daily National Intelligencer* (Washington DC), August 25, 1865; *The Leavenworth Bulletin* (Leavenworth, Kansas), September 7, 1865; *Albany Evening Journal* (Albany, New York), September 9, 1865; *Macon Telegraph* (Macon, Georgia), September 9, 1865 (printed with a preface about the poem's original publication in 1831 "on the approach of the cholera from the East toward the western parts of Europe"); *East Saginaw Courier* (East Saginaw, Michigan), September 27, 1865; *White Cloud Kansas Chief* (White Cloud, Kansas), September 28, 1865; *Norwich Aurora* (Norwich, Connecticut), October 7, 1865; *Rutland Weekly Herald* (Rutland, Vermont), October 12, 1865; *Perrysburg Journal* (Perrysburg, Ohio), October 20, 1865; *The Union and Dakotaian* (Yankton, South Dakota), October 21, 1865; *San Francisco Bulletin* (San Francisco, California), November 1, 1865; *Providence Evening Press* (Providence, Rhode Island), November 2, 1865; *Western Reserve Chronicle* (Warren, Ohio), November 15, 1865; *The Madison County Courier* (Edwardsville, Illinois), November 23, 1865; *Urbana Union* (Urbana, Ohio), December 20, 1865; *The Perry County Democrat* (Bloomfield, Pennsylvania), April 26, 1866; *The Vermont Phoenix* (Brattleboro, Vermont), May 4, 1866; *The Enterprise and Vermonter* (Vergennes, Vermont), May 11, 1866; *The Summit County Beacon* (Akron, Ohio), June 7, 1866; *The Pittsfield Sun* (Pittsfield, Massachusetts), July 5, 1866.
32. "The Voice of the Pestilence," *Daily National Intelligencer*, August 25, 1865.
33. Edward Said, *Orientalism* (New York: Pantheon Books, 1978), 22.
34. John Pierpont, *The American First-Class Book; or, Exercises in Reading and Religion*, , revised and improved edition (Philadelphia: J. B. Lippincott & Co., 1856).
35. Anjula Fatima Raza Kolb, *Epidemic Empire: Colonialism, Contagion, and Terror, 1817–2020* (Chicago: University of Chicago Press, 2021), 46.
36. In his *Report on the epidemick cholera morbus*, James Jameson argues that "[cholera's] attacks were chiefly limited to the lower classes of the inhabitants; whose constitutions had been debilitated by poor, ungenerous diet, and by hard labour in the sun; and who were badly clothed and frequently exposed in low and found situations to the cold and damp air of the night . . . and rarely did it reach the European portion of the community." James Jameson, *Report on the epidemick cholera morbus, as it visited the territories subject to the Presidency of Bengal, in the years 1817, 1818, and 1819/drawn up by order of the Government, under the superintendence of the Medical Board* (Calcutta: Government Gazette Press, 1820), A1.
37. Romans 13:4.
38. Joan D. Hedrick, *Harriet Beecher Stowe: A Life* (Oxford: Oxford University Press, 1995), 148.
39. Emily Senior, *The Caribbean and the Medical Imagination, 1764—1834: Slavery, Disease and Colonial Modernity* (Cambridge: Cambridge University Press, 2018), 2.
40. Kolb, *Epidemic Empire*, 60.
41. Jameson, *Report on the epidemick cholera morbus*, 148.
42. Jameson, *Report on the epidemick cholera morbus*, 159.

43. Jameson, *Report on the epidemick cholera morbus*, 107.
44. David Arnold, *The New Cambridge History of India: Science, Technology and Medicine in Colonial India* (Cambridge: Cambridge University Press, 2000), 82.
45. "Atmospheric Deposits and the Cholera," *The New York Times*, December 17, 1866; "Asiatic Cholera of 1832," *The Brooklyn Daily Eagle*, July 19, 1866; "Causes and Treat of Cholera," *The Buffalo Commercial*, April 19, 1866.
46. "Epidemic Cholera: Pathological Conclusions. The 'Propositions' of the Famous Dr. James Johnson," *New-York Daily Tribune*, January 27, 1866.
47. "Epidemic Cholera."
48. Kolb, *Epidemic Empire*, 65.
49. Kolb, *Epidemic Empire*, 62.
50. "Rapid Advance of the Cholera Westward," *Pittsburgh Daily Commercial*, August 19, 1865; "Progress of the Cholera Westward," *The New York Times*, September 2, 1865.
51. "The Coming Pestilence: Ravages of the Cholera. Its Westward Progress," *The Evening Post*, August 29, 1865. This article exemplifies the scientific discourse popularized during the worldwide cholera epidemic of 1831–32. Rosenberg argues that "[t]hroughout the fall and winter of 1831–32, newspapers, magazines, and pamphlets reported in alarming detail cholera's westward spread." Rosenberg, *Cholera Years*, 13.
52. "King Cholera," *Mrs. Grundy*, August 26, 1865.
53. "King Cholera" was reprinted in the following newspapers: *The New Orleans Times* (New Orleans, Louisiana), September 8, 1865; *White Cloud Kansas Chief* (White Cloud, Kansas), October 26, 1865; *The Daily Age* (Philadelphia, Pennsylvania), November 17, 1865; *The Daily Standard* (Raleigh, North Carolina), November 18, 1865; *The Louisiana Democrat* (Alexandria, Louisiana), November 22, 1865; *Western Clarion* (Helena, Arkansas), November 25, 1865; *The Woodstock Sentinel* (Woodstock, Illinois), December 6, 1865; *Urbana Union* (Urbana, Illinois), January 17, 1866; *Centralia Sentinel* (Centralia, Illinois), February 22, 1866; *The West Virginia Journal* (Martinsburg, West Virginia), February 28, 1866; *The Wheeling Intelligencer* (Wheeling, West Virginia), March 12, 1866; *The Courier-Journal* (Louisville, Kentucky), March 15, 1866; *The Leavenworth Times* (Leavenworth, Kansas), March 27, 1866; *The Daily Constitutionalist* (Augusta, Georgia), April 19, 1866; *The Lancaster Gazette* (Lancaster, Ohio), April 19, 1866; *Daily Davenport Democrat* (Davenport, Iowa), April 30, 1866; *Quad-City Times* (Davenport, Iowa), April 30, 1866; *The Selma Times and Messenger* (Selma, Alabama), May 6, 1866; *The New Hampshire Sentinel* (Keene, New Hampshire), May 10, 1866; *The Evening Telegraph* (Philadelphia, Pennsylvania), May 26, 1866; *The San Francisco Examiner* (San Francisco, California), June 4, 1866; *American Citizen* (Canton, Mississippi), September 8, 1866.
54. Suzanne Nunn, "A Court for King Cholera," *Popular Narrative Media* 2, no. 1 (2009): 5.
55. Melosi, *Sanitary City*, 13.
56. "Localities Where the Pestilence First Appeared in 1832 and 1849," *New York Herald*, July 23, 1866.
57. "Localities Where the Pestilence First Appeared."

58. "Localities Where the Pestilence First Appeared."
59. "The Districts Where the Cholera Raged in 1849," *New York Herald*, July 23, 1866.
60. "Cholera Report," *The New York Sun*, July 23, 1866.
61. According to contemporaneous news sources in both the US and England, charcoal was used to prevent the spread of cholera around people and livestock. For example, a column in the *Field and Fireside* periodical (Raleigh, North Carolina) entitled "Charcoal for hog Cholera," reported on January 16, 1866 that "[b]ituminous coal is recommended as a preventive of hog cholera." Another column published in the *Leeds Mercury* (Leeds, West Yorkshire, England) on August 11, 1866 claimed, "Charcoal—and especially wood charcoal—possesses amongst other useful properties, an astonishing power of absorbing deleterious gasses." Erin O'Connor argues that in the nineteenth century, "certain occupations were thought to confer a kind of elemental immunity to cholera, building up a resistance in workers . . . charcoal manufacturers were thought to be comparatively immune." Erin O'Connor, *Raw Material: Producing Pathology in Victorian Culture* (Durham, NC: Duke University Press, 2000), 228.
62. Melosi, *Sanitary City*, 13.
63. "The Pulpit and Sanitary Reform," *New York Times*, March 10, 1865.
64. "Preparations for the Cholera," *The Brooklyn Daily Eagle*, November 13, 1865.
65. John Duffy, *A History of Public Health in New York City 1625–1866* (Hartford: Russell Sage Foundation, 1968), 159.
66. "Previous Ravages of the Cholera in New York," *New York Daily Herald*, November 5, 1865.
67. "Preparations for the Cholera."
68. "Previous Ravages of the Cholera in New York."
69. Charles G. Halpine, *The Poetical Works of Charles G. Halpine (Miles O'Reilly)*, ed. Robert B. Roosevelt (New York: Harper & Brothers Publishers, 1869), xiv.
70. The poem was also included in Halpine's collected works, *Poetical Works of Charles G. Halpine* (1869).
71. Halpine, *Poetical Works*, 342.
72. "The State Capital," *New York Herald*, January 31, 1866.
73. "Who is Partisan," *New York Tribune*, February 14, 1866.
74. "Who is Partisan."
75. "Our Albany Correspondence," *The Brooklyn Daily Eagle*, February 19, 1866.
76. "Thurlow Weed Defines His Position," *The Brooklyn Daily Eagle*, October 9, 1866.
77. "The Board of Health and Brooklyn," *The Daily Eagle*, July 20, 1866.
78. "Board of Health and Brooklyn."
79. "Brooklyn and the Cholera," *The New York Times*, July 20, 1866.
80. "Brooklyn and the Cholera."
81. Peter Eisenstadt, *The Encyclopedia of New York State* (Syracuse: Syracuse University Press, 2005), 1671.

5

GERTRUDIS GÓMEZ DE AVELLANEDA IN PUERTO RICO'S PARTISAN PRESS

The transamerican poet Gertrudis Gómez de Avellaneda (1814–73) was one of the most celebrated writers to emerge from the nineteenth-century Hispanophone world. Born in Puerto Príncipe (modern-day Camagüey), Cuba, she lived most of her life in Spain. Her father, Manuel Gómez de Avellaneda, was an aristocratic Spanish navy officer, and her mother, a wealthy creole of the landed gentry. Like many young women of the landed caste, Avellaneda received an unparalleled education. One of her tutors was the foremost Romantic poet of the Americas, José María Heredia (1803–39), whose influence on Avellaneda's writing is evident in poems like "A Washington" and "A Vista del Niagara."

Like many women writers of the mid- to late nineteenth-century, Avellaneda maneuvered in a literary landscape governed by an ideology of separate spheres that deemed women unfit for public letters. Yet, no other Hispanophone woman poet of her time was reprinted more in newspapers. As a popular poet and a woman in the public sphere, Avellaneda's literary talents were often measured against her gender. In fact, her gender and talents were rarely separated from critiques, celebrations, and reviews of her publications. For instance, the Spanish poet José Zorrilla writes of Avellaneda, "she was a woman—but undoubtedly only by an error of nature, which had absentmindedly placed a manly soul in that vessel of womanly flesh."[1] Zorrilla is one of the many Spanish writers who fault nature, or God, for misgendering Avellaneda, that is, for erroneously placing her in a woman's body. Critics like Zorrilla dispossessed Avellaneda of her body (both physical embodiment and literary corpus). Along with the gendered dispossession of her body, critics of her work regularly positioned and repositioned Avellaneda within opposing Spanish nationalist and Caribbean anticolonial discourses.

A paratextual reading of Avellaneda's gendered body is useful for better understanding her public image within the press's vying colonial and anticolonial discourses. The opposing discourses and power dynamics that contextualized Avellaneda's public image must be examined diachronically and synchronically to understand the semiotic relationship between text and reputation. The newspaper is the ideal artifact for horizontal and vertical readings of Avellaneda because newspapers provide paratexts and extended print runs. The logical and axiological contentions, inconsistencies, and contradictions that simultaneously included and excluded women writers like Avellaneda from participating in the public sphere and contributing to the discourse of nation-building—a discourse that subverted them to the patriarchal colonial power—required the continuous overturning of various social and cultural hierarchies.

In this chapter, I use a poetics of paratextuality as a type of decolonial option or, as Walter Mignolo defines it, a way of "confronting and delinking from coloniality, or the colonial matrix of power."[2] By using the term "colonial," I invoke Mignolo's definition of coloniality as the "darker side of modernity" which contributes to the legacy of the term "colonialism": "Modernity is a complex narrative whose point of origination was Europe" and in our specific case, Spain. It is "a narrative that builds Western civilization by celebrating its achievements while hiding at the same time its darker side, 'coloniality.'"[3] Coloniality and modernity go hand in hand, according to Mignolo. They cannot exist without each other in the Western world because they both depend on Eurocentric epistemes, that is, the "Western code."[4] Thus, in this chapter, "colonial" refers to Western modernity as much as it does to the historical/cultural/social phenomenon of colonialism and its axiological and logical forms of oppression and domination.

This chapter examines how print practices shaped and reshaped Avellaneda's poetics and public image within and among colonial spaces. Vying colonial and anticolonial discourses meet in the pages of newspapers where Avellaneda's works are published. These discursive differences amount to printscapes that frame her work and public image for complex social groups. Some of the works discussed in this chapter were culled from Spanish books and periodicals and reprinted in colonial contexts. Through the reprint process, certain manipulative editorial practices, including public censorship and political reportage, allowed newspapers to concomitantly create and recreate Avellaneda's public image for their audience.

My primary focus is the nineteenth-century Puerto Rican colonial press for two reasons: first, because, although Cuba and Puerto Rico were Spanish colonies throughout Avellaneda's lifetime (they were often called sister islands because of their converging interest in liberation from Spanish), a paratextual study of Avellaneda's work in the Puerto Rican colonial press has never been done. Avellaneda's popularity in Puerto Rico blurs the lines of Caribbean belonging in ways that can help us to better understand the rhizomatic networks of colonial/anticolonial projects; and second, the colonial island of Puerto Rico reveals an aperture through which to study Avellaneda's pan-Caribbean and transcolonial poetics in the Hispanophone press. In other words, Puerto Rico functions as a vantage point, a liminal space and colonial parallel, where Spanish nationalist discourses can be examined. Avellaneda's presence in the periodical press reveals a triptych image of colonial, anticolonial, and decolonial desires that linked the Hispanophone Caribbean to Spain and the United States. This transnational triangulation of print circulated poems, discourses, and political interests to English and Spanish readerships which contributed to Avellaneda's multifaceted image in the public sphere.

As a celebrity poetess with nationally recognized affiliations in Cuba, Spain, Puerto Rico, and the US, Avellaneda's poems and reputation were bound up in a dialectical push and pull of colonial, anticolonial, and decolonial desires. Like many writers of her time, she did not have control over her work once it was printed. Some newspapers portrayed her as a Spanish loyalist, while others framed her as a feminist abolitionist—aligning her with Cuban freedom fighters like the Afro-Cuban abolitionist and formerly enslaved poet Gabriel de la Concepción Valdés (Plácido) and the revolutionary architect of Cuban liberation José Martí. As a woman in the nineteenth century with disputed connections to the imperial metropoles and colonial territories, Avellaneda never had complete ownership of her public image. Her poems were printed, reprinted, and disseminated throughout the Hispanophone world without her consent or compensation. Reportage about the author speculated on her political views according to the partisanship agendas of the press. It is important to trace this messy contextualization of her work and reputation to better understand Avellaneda not so much as a nationalist poet but as a woman who maneuvered in a cacophonous landscape of voices advocating for different futures. Did she see herself as an anti/decolonial poet advocating for Cuba Libre or a Spanish nationalist loyal to Queen Isabella II and Spain, or both? Was she indifferent? The media played an under-studied role in shaping these very questions.

This chapter shows how the conservative and progressive press politicized and depoliticized Avellaneda for specific political ends. I examine how Avellaneda's image, reputation, and poems were filtered through the specific political needs and agendas of the partisan newspapers that published her. This created a knotted image of the writer throughout the Hispanophone world that we are still disentangling today. Ultimately, the paratext enables us to see the dispossession of Avellaneda's body, that is, how her embodiment (as a Cuban-born white colonial Spanish subject and citizen) and her body of work (as a kaleidoscopic projection of the vying discourses of the pan-Caribbean Hispanophone colonies) were regularly contextualized in the press for specific colonial/

anticolonial social groups. To understand this gendered landscape, we must understand Avellaneda's role in refuting it.

As a woman and celebrity, Avellaneda blurred the social lines between the public and private spheres. At the same time, she merged political and national lines, which have historically presented a categorical conundrum for students of literature and culture attempting to pin her down to a school of thought and/or national literary tradition. Beth Miller reads Avellaneda from a historical and feminist perspective. She argues that Avellaneda's "literary production is feminist for its time in some of its themes, plots, characters, and statements."[5] As a creole woman of means and fame, Avellaneda's career did not come without its fair share of gendered challenges. She maneuvered in a sexist patriarchal colonial culture and, as Miller argues, acquired endurance.[6] Through a feminist historiographical approach, Catherine Davies takes on an important set of questions about Avellaneda's literary reputation:

> Should she be credited to (or appropriated by) the cultures and literary traditions of the colony or the metropolis? Why not to both? Clearly what is at issue here is not Avellaneda's work as such but her status as a cultural icon and repository of colonial or anti-colonial sentiment.[7]

Her status as a repository for competing (anti)colonial futures importantly reveals how nation-formation is inherently a patriarchal project in which gender norms function as epistemic forces in the colonial and imperial spaces in which Avellaneda maneuvered. Davies posits that "consideration of the polemics that arose on account of Avellaneda may show us how cultural nationalism produced women as a social category in colonial Cuba and how [Avellaneda] negotiated subsequent contradictions."[8] Miller and Davies teach us that the social values of the cult of domesticity and nation-formation that shaped Avellaneda's public life share a patriarchal episteme that molded women into social categories in the service of cultural nationalism.

Avellaneda in the US Periodical Press

In the US press, Avellaneda was considered a major poet of the Americas. In articles published from New York to California, her poems were likened to the work of her mentor, José María Heredia, for its Romantic and Cuban characteristics. In their deep dive into Avellaneda's presence in the US press, María C. Albin, Megan Corbin, and Raúl Marrero-Fente argue that "[t]he U.S. newspapers increased public awareness among their readers of Gómez de Avellaneda's influential role as a literary and public figure engaged with the most salient issues [i.e. the Ten Years' War and abolitionism]."[9] Many US editors reprinted poems and published columns about the poet that introduced US readers to her work and celebrity status. For example, upon her arrival in the US in 1864,

Frank Leslie's Illustrated Newspaper (New York) and the *Daily Evening Bulletin* (San Francisco) noted the poet's arrival.[10] On July 27, 1864, the *Daily Evening Bulletin* printed:

> A Cuban Poetess—Señora de Avellaneda, a Cuban poet of celebrity, has arrived in New York from Havana. She has won a distinguished name in contemporary Spanish literature, both by her lyric and dramatic poetry and by her romances, particularly the historical one of Guatimotzin, the heroic defender of Mexican independence, against the Spanish conqueror, Hernán Cortez.[11]

In addition to noting her arrival in the US, numerous newspapers reprinted some of Avellaneda's popular poems. Her poem, "A Washington," a tribute to the first president where the speaker praises American republicanism as a model for other nations, was reprinted in New York's anticolonialist newspaper *La Verdad* on March 20, 1852 and in *El Clamor Público* on July 10, 1858.[12] In the context of US newspapers, Avellaneda's literary production unveiled the nature of Spanish tyranny (in the case of her poem "A Washington") and the terrors of slavery (in the case of *Sab*). *Sab* was particularly important in shaping Avellaneda as an abolitionist in the eyes of the progressive press in the US, Cuba, and Puerto Rico.

Published in 1841, eleven years before Harriet Beecher Stowe's *Uncle Tom's Cabin*, *Sab* is considered the first anti-slavery work of fiction published in the Americas and Spain. Although it was banned in Cuba, many copies were smuggled into the Hispanophone Caribbean. The book was also reprinted in periodicals in New York and Europe, gaining Avellaneda notice for her abolitionist writings. Scholars of *Sab* read the novel as evidence for "an early and genuine concern for the emancipation of [enslaved people], and ... one example of [Avellaneda's] lifelong commitment to the abolitionist cause."[13] In her comparative study of US and Cuban nineteenth-century poets, Anna Brickhouse examines the impact of *Sab*'s censorship in Cuba and New York. She argues that late in Avellaneda's life, "*Sab* had emerged again as anticolonial fodder," stoking the flames of revolution and abolitionism.[14] Brickhouse continues:

> Obviously aware of the potential impact of her novel, Avellaneda herself claims in a foreword that she wrote the novel purely for "amusement" and never intended to publish it, though many details in the novel, as well as the explanatory notes that accompany it, suggest that she intended all along to introduce Cuba and its folk customs to a foreign readership. Indeed, Avellaneda ambiguously disavows the ideas in *Sab* as "somewhat different" from those she holds at present; at the same time, however, she acknowledges having opted not to change them—but decline to specify "whether out of laziness or our unwillingness to alter something she wrote with real conviction."[15]

Avellaneda's cautious response to *Sab*'s political message is a symptom of what Davies calls the "contradictions of the political discourse (liberal individualism) as a gendered formation."[16] This was a double standard, Davies continues, meaning that "[m]en were free to make identity choices. Women, on the other hand, represented the unchanging, natural qualities of the nation, and therefore were denied progressive agency and citizenship."[17] On the surface, Avellaneda's disavowal of the abolitionist ideas in *Sab* sides with ambiguity, abstraction, indifference, and "the unchanging, natural qualities of the nation."[18] However, given the contradicting discourse of gendered formation of the period, a cautious response was the only publicly acceptable answer Avellaneda could offer.

The New York exile press did its part in playing up Avellaneda's abolitionist views in its publications. Through her involvement in the press, Avellaneda established transnational relationships with editors in the US. She was in contact with Cuban intellectuals and editors in New York, including Cirilo Villaverde, Miguel T. Tolón, Lorenzo de Allo, and Juan Ignacio de Armas, who, from May 15 to September 15 of 1871, serialized *Sab* in the Spanish-language periodical *La América* (renamed the following year to *La América Ilustrada*).[19] Lorenzo de Allo and Cirilo Villaverde were among the most frequent Cuban contributors to New York newspapers.[20] They were likely responsible for submitting Avellaneda's poems to be published in the bilingual New York paper *La Verdad*, the longest-running Cuban-operated newspaper published in New York between 1848 and 1860.[21] As Rodrigo Lazo posits, *La Verdad* was the "voice of the Cuban Council, a coalition of revolutionaries and planters from the island who saw annexation to the Unites States as a viable option for separating from Spain."[22] *La Verdad* circulated in the United States and, due to censorship, was smuggled into Cuba.[23] Avellaneda is the only woman writer published in *La Verdad*.[24] Her famous sonnets "A Washington" and "Al Partir" were reprinted in *La Verdad* on March 20, 1852 during the period when Villaverde edited *La Verdad*'s Spanish-language content. In the pages of *La Verdad*, Avellaneda's poems intersect with the newspaper's annexationist and abolitionist mission, clearly aligning the famous poet with the paper's political desires. Thus, in *La América* and *La Verdad*, her byline becomes inextricably tethered to anti-slavery and annexationist sentiments voiced by some of these papers' contributors and editors. Conversely, within the pages of Puerto Rico's conservative press, Avellaneda's poems were contextualized and reconfigured within a paratext of pro-Spanish propaganda.

Avellaneda in the Puerto Rican Conservative Press

While the anticolonial New York press claimed Avellaneda as one of their own, as a liberator and abolitionist writer central to the Cuban fight for annexation, independence, and abolitionism, some Hispanophone colonial newspapers painted her in a light that was more palatable to their readers. The abolitionist and Cuba Libre overtones in New York's exile press are wiped out in the reportage and reprint poems that appear in the pro-Spanish press. In colonial Puerto Rico, these overtones were replaced with a patriotic performance of Spanish colonial control of which Avellaneda was a part.

In Puerto Rico, the Spanish government utilized two major newspapers as a means of communication and colonial control: *La Gaceta de Puerto-Rico* and the *Boletín mercantil de Puerto Rico*. Both papers used Avellaneda's image and poetics to represent the colonial interests of Spain in Puerto Rico. The four-page *La Gaceta de Puerto-Rico* was the earliest Spanish colonial newspaper published on the island. Its earliest issues date back to 1806, marking the arrival of the first printing presses in Puerto Rico.[25] As the official newspaper of the Spanish Crown, *La Gaceta* served the readerly needs of the Spanish land- and slave-owning elites. According to the Library of Congress, which has made available one of the largest print runs of the paper, *La Gaceta* published local and international news, "speeches, arrival of vessels in San Juan, people arrested for illicit gambling, the lottery, and the escape and capture of fugitives."[26]

La Gaceta fused Avellaneda's private and public life through reports and reprint poems that seemed to align her poetics and personal life with the colonial project. For example, in a front page column titled "España" printed on July 28, 1846, *La Gaceta* announced the "marriage . . . [of] Mr. Sabater, current political chief of Madrid, and the well-known and acclaimed writer Doña Gertrudis Gómez Avellaneda."[27] News of Avellaneda's marriage ceremony and French honeymoon appeared alongside a paratext of news about the exiled "obispo de Barbastro" (Bishop of Barbastro), who has returned "á España en virtud de un decreto de la Reina" (to Spain by virtue of a decree of the Queen), the establishment of the Banco de Cádiz, and news of a society gathering "en el Real Palacio" (at the Royal Palace).[28] The imbrication of Avellaneda's private and public lives as colonial fodder can also be seen in the poems *La Gaceta* published. On April 20, 1858, *La Gaceta* reprinted a poem titled "Serenata: A su Alteza Real: la Serma. Sra. Infanta Duquesa de Montpensier: La Vispera de Su Cumpleaños" (Serenade: To Her Royal Highness, Mrs. Infanta Duchess of Montpensier, On the eve of her Birthday). Avellaneda dedicates the poem to the eponymous Duchess of Montpensier, Luisa Fernanda, the youngest sister of Queen Isabella II. The poem was later collected in Avellaneda's *Obras Literarias* in 1869. The poem's speaker serenades the Duchess with sentimental and adorning compliments to the royal family. Midway through the poem, the speaker asserts:

Luisa su nombre bendecir vea;	Luisa her name blessed be;
Y honra no habiendo que no le cuadre,	There's no honor that does not fit her,
La augusta hermana de Isabel sea	The august sister of Isabel be
De bella prole dichosa madre (49–50)[29]	Beautiful offspring of her happy mother

This poem is a colonial serenade that pays homage not only to Luisa but also to Queen Isabella II and their mother, Maria Christina of the Two Sicilies (1806–78). The deferential speaker illustrates a continuation of the royal Spanish line which inherently extends to Spain's colonies. Contextualized in *La Gaceta*, the poem performs an exaggerated faultless devotion, an old-world custom of polite deference over 5,000 miles away from Spain that models good colonial subjectivity.

Along with the poem's addressees and colonial overtones, *La Gaceta* provides a paratextual note that further depicts Avellaneda as a good colonial subject:

> This poem was read by Ms. Avellaneda to the Dukes of Montpensier on the occasion of her highness Doña's Luisa Fernanda's birthday, and the next day the princes sent the poet a rich gift consisting of a beautiful case with a rich jewel of shiny pearls and rubies of exquisite work.[30]

This formal exchange of goods—a poem and reading for precious jewels—is a performance of good colonial subjectivity printed and promoted in the pages of *La Gaceta*. This patriotic performance displays two important components of colonial subjectivity: (1) that the good colonial subject will be well compensated for honoring the royal family, and (2) that the Crown is enormously wealthy, no matter that the rubies and pearls were likely plundered from the very land on which Avellaneda was born. The pearls might as well be a metonym for Avellaneda herself, who was famously nicknamed "la Perla de Las Antillas" (the Pearl of the Antilles).[31] In *La Gaceta*'s context, the pearl is more than a sobriquet. It is also a colonial consequence of plundering Caribbean islands, people, and aesthetics in the name of Spain. *La Gaceta*'s paratextual note offers readers access to this patriotic performance and, most important, to a metonymic collapse of the poet and her plundered pearls, which begs the rhetorical question, was the poet a gift to Spain, or is Spain a gift to the poet? The vertical exchange of goods suggests the latter. The paratextual note applies value and ownership to Avellaneda's genius, implying that it too can be purchased or perhaps rewarded. At the same time, like Avellaneda, the colonial subject will benefit from the charity of the colonizer so long as the colonized works to sustain the colonial power. This is the logic that sustains colonization from a distance. *La Gaceta* is part of the colonial machinery of Spanish propaganda, and Avellaneda's poem was an ideal cultural artifact to strengthen the unequal cultural relationship between *caribeños* and *españoles*. However, not all of *La Gaceta*'s poems focused on the poet's relationship with Spanish royals. Some, like the following example, placed Avellaneda in conversation with poets who challenged colonial values like gender norms.

Avellaneda's celebrity presented newspapers with an opportunity to edit, as it were, the poet's public image. On May 14, 1861, *La Gaceta* reprints three of Avellaneda's poems: "A la Vírgen," "A Washington," and "A Sabater." The poems' byline, "La Avellaneda Poetisa" (The Poetess Avellaneda), appears in bold type, larger than the poems' titles, emphasizing the poet's name. A paratextual note at the end of the column, authored by the famous Spanish abolitionist and Romantic poet Carolina Coronado (1820–1911), complements the paper's emphasis on Avellaneda's celebrity (see Figure 5.1):

> Poets don't get your hopes up: Those who sing the most tender, soft, and sweet cannot produce sounds like "Contemplacion, A la Vírgen" [Contemplation, To the Virgin] and the quatrains of "A Sabater" [To Sabater]. Poetesses don't get your hopes up; those that sing briefly, loudest, energetically, and bravely, do not produce echoes like "A Francia" [To France], "Al Escorial" [To the Escorial] and "A Washington" [To Washington].
>
> A celebrated poet was able to exclaim when reading these last compositions: "This woman is a lot of man." Upon reading this for the first time, [and] thinking of what men have said about the author, I exclaim: There is a lot of woman in this man!
>
> Carolina Coronado.[32]

Coronado claims that Avellaneda was a poet in certain poems and a poetess in others, emphasizing Avellaneda's versatility as a poet that breaks gendered stereotypes about writing. In the second paragraph, Coronado inverts Bretón de los Herreros's famous phrase, "¡Es mucho hombre esta mujer!" [This woman is a lot of man], rewriting it as new statement, "es mucha mujer este hombre!" [There is

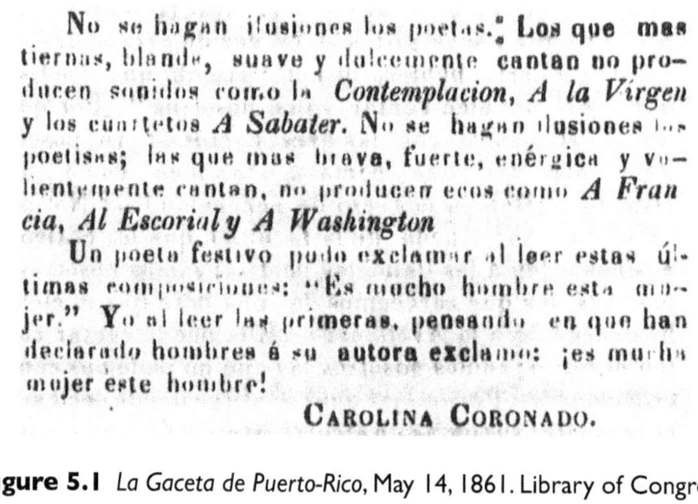
No se hagan ilusiones los poetas: **Los que mas** tiernos, blandos, suave y dulcemente **cantan no** producen sonidos como la ***Contemplacion, A la Virgen*** y los cuartetos ***A Sabater.*** No se hagan **ilusiones** las poetisas; las que mas **brava, fuerte, enérgica** y valientemente cantan, no producen ecos como ***A Francia, Al Escorial y A Washington***

Un poeta festivo pudo exclamar al leer estas últimas composiciones: "Es mucho hombre esta mujer." Yo al leer las **primeras, pensando** en que han declarado hombres á su **autora exclamo**: ¡es mucha mujer este hombre!

CAROLINA CORONADO.

Figure 5.1 *La Gaceta de Puerto-Rico*, May 14, 1861. Library of Congress. Public domain.

a lot of woman in this man!]. Bretón de los Herreros's original statement implicitly measures women against a portion of masculinity. By comparison, Coronado upends this gender dynamic, resisting the sex–gender system that the patriarchy deploys to categorize women's literary production. In Coronado's version, women are the ontological template, not men's equal but subtly above them; for it is a woman, Avellaneda, who defines men's poetic tastes.

The above examples of Avellaneda's appearance in *La Gaceta* show a complex colonial impression of Avellaneda's poems and public image, which she had limited part in painting. Patriotic performativity, as evinced in *La Gaceta*, can resist some colonial values like gender norms as long as this form of colonial resistance does not threaten the royal and colonial social order. The contextualization of Avellaneda for colonial propagandistic ends is also part of the print culture of the second largest Puerto Rican pro-Spanish newspaper, *El Boletín mercantil de Puerto Rico*.

Published in San Juan between 1839 and 1918, *El Boletín mercantil de Puerto Rico* was, along with *La Gaceta*, one of the most important newspapers for Spanish loyalists and merchants on the island. Starting as a bi-weekly and later changing to a daily, the *Boletín* was a Spanish organ that catered to the interests of Spain and Spaniards doing business in Puerto Rico. In his foundational study of the Puerto Rican press, *El periodismo en Puerto Rico*, Antonio S. Pedreira emphasizes the *Boletín*'s saliency as "a newspaper of transcendental significance in the history of newspapers in Puerto Rico."[33] From a colonial perspective, the *Boletín*'s news columns, editorials, and literary offerings illustrated the everyday life of Spaniards and their descendants on the island. This newspaper serves as an important resource for analyzing how the colonial pro-Spanish press framed Avellaneda concomitant with the political currents and interests of the colony.

As a merchant paper, the *Boletín*'s readers would have been made up in large part of the mercantile class: business owners, exporters, and planters. Many of the *Boletín*'s readers "grouped as conservatives in the Partido Conservador (1869), shortly after renamed Partido Incondicional Español (Unconditional Spanish Party)."[34] However (as I have argued elsewhere) partisan newspapers were often read by social groups outside of their intended political party.[35] In part because of the relative scarcity and cost of reading materials, any literate person with access to the *Boletín* would have read the paper. Like many merchant papers in the mid-century, the *Boletín* was not all business. It was a disseminator of culture, and its editors, as Kirsten Silva Gruesz would argue, acted as curators.[36] The *Boletín* regularly printed and reprinted poems, dramas, short stories, and literary reviews, and announced book publications and their prices, providing a glimpse of the literature that circulated in the colony during the last four decades of Spanish domination in Puerto Rico.

The *Boletín* was part of the periodical machinery that turned Avellaneda into a Romantic barometer, or, as I call it, the "Avellanedaen barometer," for measuring the prowess and cultural expectations or lack thereof of other women literary figures. The *Boletín* often marketed Avellaneda as a cosmopolitan poet, on equal footing with, and at times above, other women celebrity writers of her day. In 1871, the *Boletín* serialized essays from the five-volume *Obras Literarias de la Señora Doña Gertrudis Gomez de Avellaneda*. Published in Madrid between 1869 and 1871, *Obras* collected Avellaneda's poetry, fiction, autobiographical essays, and celebrity profiles. The *Boletín*'s selected reproductions describe Avellaneda as the ideal woman nationalist writer and publicly good colonial subject, that is, an apolitical and non-propagandistic poetess. On September 22, 1871, less than two years before her death, the *Boletín* reprinted selections from *Obras* authored by the Spanish writer and diplomat Leopoldo Augusto de Cueto (1815–1901), retitling them "Noticias Literarias" (Literary News). The article compares Avellaneda to the English novelist and poet Dinah Maria Mulock (also known as Dinah Maria Craik) (1826–87). Cueto writes:

> The only one of the writers of the sentimental analytic school that compares to Mrs. Gómez de Avellaneda is Miss Mulock, because, with her vigorous instinct, she recounts events with an unfettered and firm style, comments soberly, and does not abuse philosophical analysis.[37]

The fabricated barometrical link between Avellaneda and Mulock suggests that Avellaneda's own poetics, politics, and style (which served as a model for other women writers to achieve a measure of literary success) were polite, submissive, and non-critical.

Cueto focuses almost exclusively on Avellaneda's Romantic poems and ignores her more political and widely read abolitionist, anticolonial, and feminist work (including *Sab* and "A Washington"). He does not evaluate literary talents but rather attempts to reconcile domestic colonial values with women in the public sphere. Cueto goes on to argue that Avellaneda's and Mulock's sober and "not abusive" philosophical thinking result from their feminine natures:

> This creation of popular fantasy, skillfully reproduced by Miss Mulock, came to our memory as a delicate analogy of feminine natures, when reading Mrs. Gómez de Avellaneda's [novel] "La flor del ángel" [The Angel Flower], a deva flower very similar in shape to a bee.[38]

Cueto's analogy collapses "feminine natures" and the natural world. He likens women and their literary production to the deva flower and the bee, which are part of Romanticized nature. In addition to these "feminine natures," Cueto claims that Avellaneda's aesthetic sentiment distinguishes her from men: "Women understand and feel more delicately and intensely than men these fantastic illusions of the muse of the mountains, and Mrs. Gómez de Avellaneda has nothing to envy in this part the dreamy imagination of the northern races."[39] It is this myopic vision of Avellaneda as Romantic, sentimental, and non-political that writers like Cueto fixated on and that pro-Spanish newspapers reproduced.

To emphasize Avellaneda's aesthetics as non-political and pro-Spanish, Cueto uses the Avellanedaen barometer to compare the Cuban/Spanish poetess with celebrity writers who threatened the patriarchy. For example, later in the column, Cueto contrasts Avellaneda to George Sand (1804–76) by way of a rebuke of the popular French novelist's proto-feminist views:

> [Sand] can never dispense with her insane systematic designs, usually so uncertain, so that even [Pierre-Joseph] Proudhon, who is certainly not scrupulous and skittish in matters of daring and innovation, condemns with energy and even distaste her fierce desire for feminine emancipation without restraint and without measure, and all the inevitable consequences of this *rebellious bacchante* philosophy using the violent expression of Proudhon, namely: the absolute equality of both sexes; freedom in love, the ban on marriage; or in other words, envy and hatred of men, and spontaneous debasement of women.[40]

Cueto relies on the anarchist Pierre-Joseph Proudhon (1809–65), known for his anti-feminist views, to substantiate critiques about Sand's anti-patriarchal politics. Citing Proudhon, Cueto attempts to discredit Sands for "her fierce desire for feminine emancipation," which he equates with the "envy and hatred of men, and spontaneous debasement of women."[41] Cueto follows this by "add[ing] nothing to this tremendous judgment of the French critic," implicitly agreeing with Proudhon's position that feminist writers like Sand pose a threat to the social and gendered patriarchal order.[42] The article continues, referring to Avellaneda as antagonistic to Sand:

> Mrs. Gómez de Avellaneda is a novelist and not a propagator of risky and ambitious doctrines; she does not denaturalize the novel or the theater, which are literary genres destined for the refined and honest recreation of the people, and does not transform them into publications of upheaval and moral agitation.[43]

Cueto subscribes to a patriarchal Romantic aesthetics where politics and "literary genres" are irreconcilable for women. Unlike her contemporary Sand, Cueto affirms that Avellaneda does not work against this Romantic aesthetics. He assures his readers that Avellaneda is a woman writer and not a propagator of feminist ideology. Thus, she does not "denaturalize" her writing, a logic that assumes that nature in essence is always already patriarchal.[44]

Avellaneda is contextualized in the *Boletín*'s heteropatriarchal context of Romantic aesthetics to serve as a fabricated model for the comportment of women in the colonial public. Ultimately, Cueto offers a moral argument for examining Avellaneda's aesthetics: "The morality of the legends and novels of Mrs. Gómez de Avellaneda is frank, resolute, and healthy, which is offered by the sincere study of human nature, without hints of social doctrine and without fussiness of form."[45] For Cueto, this non-political study of human nature is the duty of women writers who wish to partake in nation-building: "Women . . . cultivate themselves and help civilization and ease the weight of patriotism through literature and the arts."[46] Cueto's article exemplifies how Romanticism was often used as a tool of censorship in Avellaneda's poetics. He emphasizes the Romantic beauties and affective devices of Avellaneda's writing to depoliticize her work and undermine the political potential of Romanticism.

Such efforts to depoliticize Avellaneda suggest her powerful influence in the public sphere and, most importantly, the threat she posed to not just the colonial order but the patriarchy all together. This powerful influence over the public and threat to the Spanish colony are facets of Avellaneda's poems and reputation that Puerto Rico's anticolonial press highlighted.

Avellaneda in Puerto Rico's Anticolonial Press

Avellaneda's poems were commonly printed and contextualized in newspapers that supported a liberated vision of the Antilles. The discourses that shape Avellaneda's paratext in anticolonial newspapers like *La correspondencia de Puerto Rico* and *La Democracia* were informed by a common struggle against Spain's nearly 350-year colonial rule over South America. In the early part of the nineteenth century, the Peninsular War (1808–14) weakened Spain's military and political control in Spanish America, creating a military opportunity for Latin America to sever ties with the colonial metropoles. Inspired by the American, French, and Haitian revolutions, Simón Bolívar ignited the Latin American Wars for Independence, which led to the liberation of most of Spain's colonies between 1808 and 1833.

In the mid-nineteenth century, Cuba and Puerto Rico remained as Spain's lone colonies in the western hemisphere. However, Puerto Rico's and Cuba's colonial governments gradually turned more despotic. Members of the planter class began to show discontent over Spain's heavy tariffs and taxes on most import and export goods. Plans for liberating Puerto Rico and Cuba began to form in the Antilles and abroad. In 1866, Puerto Rican patriots Ramón Emeterio Betances and Segundo Ruiz Belvis formed the Comité Revolucionario de Puerto Rico (Revolutionary Committee of Puerto Rico) while in exile in New York. Along with other members the Comité Revolucionario de Puerto Rico, Betances and Belvis coordinated the first major revolt against Spanish rule in Puerto Rico, "El grito de Lares," on September 3, 1868.[47] The Spanish Crown brutally suppressed Puerto Rico's liberation attempt. However, the insurrection had a lasting effect on the political and cultural imagination of Puerto Ricans. Just over 700 miles from Puerto Rico, three liberation wars between Cuba and Spain soon unfolded: the Ten Years' War (1868–1878), the Little War (1879–80), and the Cuban War of Independence (1865–98). With the intervention of the US military in the final year of the Cuban War of Independence, the Spanish Crown was defeated, and the signing of the Treaty of Paris officially brought an end to the war. Spain lost its remaining colonies in the western hemisphere, surrendering Puerto Rico to the United States and recognizing Cuba as an independent nation.[48]

These events forever altered the cultural-political landscape of the Puerto Rican periodical press. One change was the immense popularity and circulation of *La correspondencia de Puerto Rico* (1890–1943). *La correspondencia*'s editor and proprietor, Ramón B. López, was a bilingual writer who vehemently opposed US colonization and the annexation of Cuba. At one cent per issue, *La correspondencia* was the most affordable daily newspaper on the island, making it also the most widely accessible to the public. The newspaper covered regional and international news. López saw the US's occupation of Puerto Rico as deleterious to the island's liberation, often publishing scathing remarks about "the faults to be attributed to the American Government at present ruling Puerto Rico."[49]

Eight months after the Spanish–American War on August 22, 1899, *La correspondencia de Puerto Rico* published a column (likely authored by López) titled "Nuestra Glorias" (Our Glories) in which Avellaneda's nationality is used as a rhetorical device for anti-US expansionism. The article opens:

> An American newspaper, which already takes the annexation of Cuba as a fact, publishes a portrait and a biographical yawn of the great Cuban poet Doña Gertrudis Gómez de Avellaneda, who is reputed to be one of the most brilliant "American" glories . . . The word "American" is not used today but synonymous with Yankee, and by degree or by force we have to conform, because to tell the truth, the Yankees have illustrated it more than we, and we have never, protested against that monopoly, which, well considered, is a hidden but solid base for the absorption force of the entire continent.[50]

In the above column, the demonym "American" is a starting point for debating how imperialism converts national aesthetics into consumable goods that become the cultural spoils of war. Avellaneda is one example. Her name is a critical point of discursive contention for resisting the nationalization of the word "American," a word that carries a hegemonic weight and reveals an uneven exchange of power. López's anxieties about Avellaneda were warranted as more and more US newspapers printed columns about her life and work from the *New York Herald* to the *Los Angeles Times*.

López's column deconstructs the discourse of American expansionism as a way of resisting US cultural imperialism. He calls out the US's claim to the word "American" and Avellaneda's affiliation to this word. He explains that "American" is a rhetorical tool for the imperial project of manifest destiny: it "is a hidden but solid base for the absorption force of the entire continent."[51] This deconstructive interpretation is importantly anticolonial. López is particularly critical of how the word "American" lays cultural claim to continents and their icons, that is, North and South America and Avellaneda. In the final lines of this column, López aligns Avellaneda with anticolonial poets in the Americas and warns against Yankee cultural hegemony: "Apparently, the day is not far off when the conspirators [will] include Avellaneda, and Plácido, Zenea and Martí in the Yankee Parnassus."[52] Ahead of his time, López seems to be calling for a proto-Caribbean literary tradition that is introspectively critical of the US's colonial interest and agenda.

Avellaneda's profile in "Nuestras Glorias" is contextualized in *La correspondencia*'s anticolonial paratext, where the word "Americano/a" is freely used to describe anything based in and affiliated with the US. For example, to the left of "Nuestras Glorias" appears a column titled "La prensa americana" (the American press).[53] "La prensa americana" is an editorialized collection of reportage from mainland periodicals, including *El Journal de Nueva York* (*The New York Journal*), *El Daily Inter Ocean de Chicago* (*The Daily Inter Ocean*), *El Herald de Nueva York* (*The New York Herald*), and *El Toledo Blade* (*Toledo Blade*), reporting on current issues in Puerto Rico. Such a periodical assortment reveals that López drew information from a vast archive of Anglophone periodicals when curating the pages of his own paper. Readers of *La correspondencia* could essentially learn about how Puerto Rico figured in the imagination of US readers by reading in translation Yankee reports about Puerto Rico and its people.

The August 22, 1899 issue mainly reports on the 1899 San Ciriaco hurricane. Considered one of the longest and deadliest hurricanes to strike Puerto Rico, it killed nearly 4,000 people and left as many as 250,000 people without food and shelter.[54] López's "La prensa americana" is not simply a summary of US reportage of the hurricane. It is also an anticolonial critique of the US's commercialized interests. López posits that pervasive US reportage on the hurricane does not translate "to the aid of those in need":

> In short, it cannot be said that there is a single newspaper in the U.S. that has not extensively reported on the damage caused by the storm, and that does not excite the people to come to the aid of those in need with their subscriptions.[55]

The coverage of the hurricane in the US press suggests an overt interest in the sensationalization of natural catastrophes. The column tapped into the cultural imagination of US readers, imagining them justifying a rationale for expansionism based on Puerto Rico's vulnerability after the Spanish–American War and San Ciriaco hurricane, which occurred less than a year apart. López also understood the island's precarity and that in order for Puerto Ricans to receive aid, they needed to appeal to the moral judgment of the US government.

In an English-language column he wrote for the New York weekly, *The Independent* on November 29, 1900, López claims, "The large majority of Puerto Ricans are Americans at heart; all they desire now is that they may become Americans in fact as well as name."[56] Recalling the imperialist connotations of the demonym "American" in his earlier column, López describes two types of Americans, one of name and the other of fact. The former invokes an occupied people whose lives are determined by the consequence of war. The latter American of fact raises the still relevant question about Puerto Rican citizenship: Are the privileges and protections of US citizens bestowed onto Puerto Ricans? Is the occupation of Puerto Rico simply a manifestation of US imperialism? López's column implies that Puerto Ricans are American in name only. The fact of being American—citizenship, equal rights, and protection under the constitution—does not seem to extend to the Puerto Rican body politic.

La correspondencia's paratext contextualizes Avellaneda within these two Americas. She is conveniently "reputed to be one of the most brilliant 'American' glories," while Puerto Ricans are Americans only in name even during a natural disaster.[57] López's observations function as a metaphor for the uneven power relationships between the colonizer and colonized. Just like Spain did when it ruled over the Antilles, the US embraced Avellaneda, a literary icon with cultural value, while rejecting the common Puerto Rican. López was clearly wary of this exploitative relationship. He understood that manifest destiny was as much cultural as it was territorial. For López, Avellaneda's celebrity exemplified what US geo-cultural expansionism meant for the future of Puerto Rico and the Spanish Caribbean.

Cuban Sonnets in *La Democracia*

Similar to *La correspondencia*, the Puerto Rican liberation daily newspaper *La Democracia* (Democracy) (1890–1943) contextualized Avellaneda as a symbol of progressive politics. At the turn of the nineteenth century, the *Democracia* claimed the largest readership in Puerto Rico. Since its inception in 1890, this daily advocated for Puerto Rican self-governance. This is reflected in the news and poems it published. On October 2, 1901, twenty-seven years after Avellaneda's death, the *Democracia* printed three sonnets by Cuban poets: Avellaneda's "Al Partir," José Maria Heredia's "Inmortalidad," and Gabriel de la Concepción Valdés's (Plácido) "En la Muerte de Jesucristo" (see Figure 5.2). It is likely

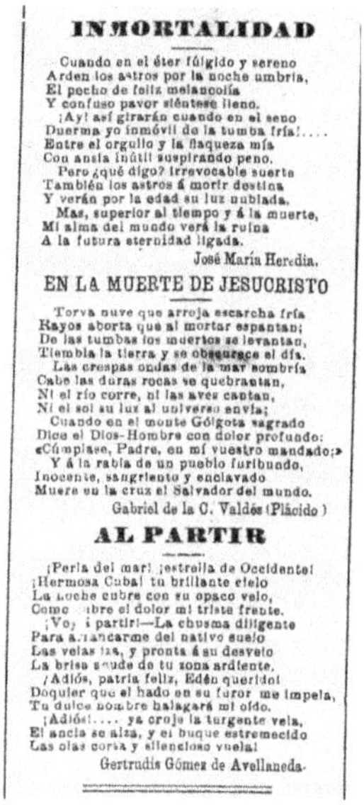

PARATEXTUALITY IN ANGLOPHONE AND HISPANOPHONE POEMS, 1855–1901

Figure 5.2 *La Democracia*, October 2, 1901. Library of Congress. Public domain.

that the *Democracia* anthologized these poems based on their shared genres and authorial connections to Cuba.

The proximity of the three sonnets to each other enabled readers to identify intertextual patterns between poems and create meaning-making possibilities. For instance, readers who read the three sonnets from top to bottom transferred formal- and content-based impressions from one poem to the next. In their original publication, each sonnet appeared with two quatrains and two tercets. The *Democracia*'s publication omits the stanzaic breaks in each poem, offering its readers what looks like a long, breathless poem. Thus, it is possible that some readers of the *Democracia* read the sonnets not as three separate poems but as one. Adapting such reading praxis can help us get a better sense of how the *Democracia*'s readers read and interpreted Avellaneda's sonnet alongside its anticolonial paratext of Heredia's and Plácido's poems.

The curation of these poems contextualizes Avellaneda's "Al Partir" within a discourse of Romantic departures and Cuban *patria*. The theme of parting reverberates in the column, echoing in the lines of Heredia and Plácido in ways that could only exist on the *Democracia*'s page. This poetic and collective parting offers an opportunity to examine critical distinctions and similarities between what Édouard Glissant calls errantry and exile. In his influential rhizomatic study of alterity and relational poetics, one of Glissant's arguments is that "[r]oots make the commonality of errantry and exile, for in both instances roots are lacking."[58] Errantry and exile share the meaning of migration with a critical difference: exile is forced migration while errantry, as Glissant says, is a type of "wanderlust."[59]

The speakers in the *Democracia*'s poems describe different types of departures. The first sonnet in the series is Heredia's "Inmortalidad." It begins with a pensive speaker:

Cuando en el éter fúlgido y sereno	When in the bright and serene ether
Arden los astros por la noche umbría,	The stars burn in the shady night,
El pecho de feliz melancolía	The chest of happy melancholy
Y confuso pavor siéntese lleno. (1–4)	And confused dread sits full.

The setting of the "shady night" invokes in the speaker a sublime sentiment of "happy melancholy / And confused dread" (3–4). Such feelings, the speaker later explains, will accompany him to "la tumba fría / Entre el orgullo y la flaqueza mía" (the cold grave / Between my pride and weakness) (6–7). In the poem, death is universal. It is the transcendental link between the speaker and Nature: "También los astros a morir destina / Y verán por la edad su luz nublada" (The stars too are destined to die / And they will see their cloudy light through age) (10–11). At the poem's end, the speaker links his own soul to the fate of stars: "Mas, superior al tiempo y á la muerte, / Mi alma del mundo verá la ruina / A la futura eternidad ligada" (More, superior to time and death, / My soul will see the ruin of the world / And be linked to future's eternity) (12–14). By the poem's end, the speaker's soul is made into a Romantic ruin linked to eternity.

In Frederick Luciani's study of Heredia's political exile in the US, he argues that the theme of immortality is one that Heredia regularly returned to in his work. His famous "Ode to Niagara," for example, "closes with the hope that the poet's verses will prove as eternal as the great cataract itself; the poet imagines a kind of after-death apotheosis in which he will continue to hear the 'echoes of his fame.'"[60] The difference between "Ode to Niagara" and "Inmortalidad" is the source or substance of immortality, that is, that which grants the speaker an eternal existence. In "Ode to Niagara," it is his "humble verse, / Might be like thee immortal" whereas eternity in "Inmortalidad" is more abstractly attributed to the speaker's "alma" (soul) ("Ode to Niagara," 95–96, "Inmortalidad," 13). Heredia's "verse" and "soul" are linked by their Romantic capacity to respectively encompass and experience the sublime of death and the grandness of Niagara ("Ode to Niagara" 95–96, "Inmortalidad," 13). Death in "Inmortalidad" is a type of parting. It is the poet's sublime escape from his body and the realization that his "soul will see the ruin of the world" because it is linked to "future's eternity" (13, 14). It is this sublime decay of the physical world, this exalted parting of the speaker's physical body, that enhances the speaker's immortality.

Heredia's image of the parting body reverberates on the *Democracia*'s printscape, resounding, although in an altered pitch, in the Afro-Cuban poet Plácido's sonnet, "En la Muerte de Jesucristo" (On the Death of Jesus Christ). Sublime death, in this poem, is Catholic redemption that quakes across a Gothicized nature. Plácido's sonnet opens with a dark and ominous natural setting:

Torva nuve [sic] que arroja escarcha fría,	Grim cloud that casts cold frost,
Rayos aborta que al mortar [sic] espantan;	A lightning bolt that frightens mortals;
De las tumbas los Muertos se levantan,	From the graves the dead rise,
Tiembla la tierra y se obscurece el día. (1–4)	The earth quakes and the day darkens.

Plácido's setting is foreboding and apocalyptic. Invoking the New Testament, the speaker depicts the supernatural scene after Christ's crucifixion, when the sky darkened, the earth quaked, and saints were resurrected.[61] In the following lines, the speaker projects this wrathful imagery onto "Las crespas ondas de la mar sombría . . . / Ni el río corre, ni las aves cantan, / Ni el sol su luz al universo envía" (The silk waves of the gloomy sea . . . / Neither the river runs, nor the birds sing, / Not even the sun sends its light to the universe) (5, 7–8). This dead landscape of inactivity contrasts with Heredia's sublime "bright and serene ether" ("Inmortalidad," 1). In Plácido's poem, the natural order of the world breaks after Christ's crucifixion, summoning a metaphysical tear in the speaker's psyche and environment.

In Matthew Pettway's structuralist study of the shaping force of African ideas of spirit and cosmos in Plácido's and Juan Manzano's spiritual poetics, he argues that Plácido produced "Janus-faced poetry that affirmed loyalty to the Catholic Church even while undermining its doctrinal premises with African-inspired ideas of spirit and cosmos."[62] Pettway posits that

> the central tenets of Plácido's poems about the Passion of the Christ were humility and self-abnegation, and they bespoke the qualities that the priesthood required of black mulatto prostyles. Plácido makes himself into a worthy subject in these poems for he performed the grace and humility the church expected of him.[63]

The biblical suffering of Christ and the consequential reverberations from God the Father in "En la Muerte de Jesucristo" reads like an allegory for Afro-Cuban suffering in Cuba, an island torn, or quaked, by slavery, colonial power, and war. At the end of the poem, the speaker reveals more vivid details of Christ's scenes of suffering and dread:

Cuando en el monte Gólgota sagrado	When on the holy mount Golgotha
Dice el Dios-Hombre con dolor profundo:	Says the God-Man with deep pain:
"Cúmplase, Padre, en mí vuestro mandado;"[64]	"Let your will be done, Father, in me;"
Y á la rabia de un pueblo furibundo,	And to the rage of a furious people,
Inocente, sangriento y enclavado	Innocent, bloody and nailed
Muere en la cruz el Salvador de mundo. (9–14)	The Savior of the World dies on the cross.

It is hard not to read parallels between Christ's death and Plácido's own martyred fate. In 1844, the Spanish authorities accused Plácido of conspiracy to incite a slave insurrection. The Spanish authorities had become suspicious of all educated non-white Cubans. Writers and artisans were targeted, and Plácido's writing and active social life made him an easy mark for the Spanish authorities. He was arrested and convicted of being the intellectual architect behind an insidious plot to eradicate the white population and abolish slavery on the island. Soon after, Plácido was sentence to death and shot in the back by a firing squad in Matanzas.[65] Plácido's death made him into a martyr and symbol of Cuba Libre.

Although Heredia's and Plácido's sonnets differ in their content and tone, "Inmortalidad" and "En la Muerte de Jesucristo" share the theme of parting. In these poems, parting figures as both a physical departure and an allegory for the cultural, spiritual, and political break from colonial Cuba. The theme of parting contextualizes the final sonnet in the *Democracia*'s series, Avellaneda's "Al Partir."

Originally published in 1841, "Al Partir" is one of Avellaneda's most reprinted poems. Like the two other poems in the *Democracia*'s series, "Al Partir" is about exile and errantry. The poem illustrates the parting of nation and nationality, the split of the body/poet from the body politic, and what it means to be deracinated from Cuba and the Caribbean. The poem depicts a scene from Avellaneda's own life when in 1836, at the age of twenty-two, she and her family left Cuba for Spain. In the opening lines, the speaker grieves over her departure from Cuba and addresses the island:

¡Perla de Mar! ¡estrella de Occidente!	Pearl of the Sea! Star of the West!
¡Hermosa Cuba! tu brillante cielo	Beautiful Cuba! Your brilliant sky
La noche cubre con su opaco velo,	Is covered by night's opaque veil,
Como cubre el dolor mi triste frente. (1–4)	As my brow is by the pain enveloping it.

In the opening lines, Cuba as the "Pearl of the Sea" invokes Avellaneda's own sobriquet of the "Pearl of the Antilles."[66] Both poet and homeland are linked by a suffering that is rooted in two forms of parting. One is the painful parting from home and the other the parting, or loss, of the self. In comparing Cuba's veiled skies to her own sad countenance, the speaker implies that both mourn their separation from each other. This somber scene moves to the ocean in the following lines, where the speaker describes her exile:

¡Voy a partir!—La chusma diligente	I am leaving! The vulgar crew
Para arrancarme del nativo suelo	Diligently raises the sails that will tear me
Las velas iza, y pronta a su desvelo	From my native land; and as they unfurl
La brisa acude de tu zona ardiente. (5–8)	Fiery breezes arise from your soul.

The speaker's parting is as much a geographical departure as it is a departure of the self. The phrase "¡Voy a partir!" has two germane translations in this context (5). It is both "I am leaving" and "I am cracking/breaking." The former implies the speaker's departing body, while the latter suggest a geographical chasm, a breaking of both the body and the nation. This line's importantly ambiguous signification indicates an internal break in the speaker and an outward break of her land, both of which are lost in the English translation.

The exile of "Al Partir" is unlike those in "Inmortalidad" and "En la Muerte de Jesucristo," which deal with literal death. Avellaneda's exile is not overtly politicized in the poem. Her exile is a gendered expulsion molded by her lack of choice as a woman in the nineteenth century. However, when we read Avellaneda's "Al Partir" alongside its paratext of Heredia's and Plácido's sonnets, its parting from Cuba acquires the anti-Spanish signification of the other poems. After all, the speaker's destination is Spain and therefore the root of her anguish. Furthermore, because Heredia's and Plácido's bylines were linked to their personal and public lives as anticolonial poets, their sonnets inform how the *Democracia*'s readers engage with the metaphysical death in "Al Partir," a parting that severs the speaker from her homeland and her national identity. Whether or not the speaker wanted to leave her "Star of the West!," the choice was not hers to make. In the final stanza, the speaker makes her final farewell:

¡Adiós! . . . . ya cruje la turgente vela,	Farewell! . . . . The swollen sails are rustling,
El ancla se alza, y el buque estremecido	The anchor is raised, the ship convulses,
Las olas corta y silencioso vuela! (12–14)	Ploughing the waves, flying silently!

The ship's swollen and convulsing body interrupts the speaker's final "Farewell" (12). Like the speaker's parting, the closing scene displaces the speaker's mournful voice. The poem concludes with a description of the ship in movement, its wind-filled sails, aweighed anchors, and a "ploughing" course away from Cuba (14).

A paratextual analysis of these sonnets narrativizes the Cuban nationalist poet as always in tension with their body/work: corpse, corpus, and nationality. In the *Democracia*'s sonnets, death and exile are one and the same. Whether by casket or ship, the speakers part/break from their bodies. Their bodies are metaphors for sublime sacrifices: Heredia's immortality, Plácido's faith, and Avellaneda's Cuba. Heredia's speaker sacrifices his body for his soul's immortality; his body slips into oblivion while his soul remains. In Plácido's poem, Christ sacrifices his body to be the "Savior of the World" ("En la Muerte de Jesucristo," 14). Tied to Plácido's own grim fate, the martyred Christ is a symbol of the supreme inhumanity of Cuba's institution of slavery. In Avellaneda's poem, the type of parting that is inflicted onto the speaker's body both deracinates her from "Pearl of the Sea! Star of the West!" and breaks ("parte") the speaker's national identity ("Al Partir," 1). This parting is a killing of the self. Together, these poems communicated to the *Democracia*'s readers that to be a Cuban poet meant to move in and out of various types of bodies in the service of liberation.

Conclusion

Soon after Avellaneda's death on February 1, 1873, her obituaries began appearing throughout the Hispanophone and Anglophone press. Newspapers devoted a significant amount of their pages to the famed author, expounding on her talents and celebrity status. In two full columns, the April 9, 1873 issue of the *Boletín*, for example, confirmed with an exclamation, "Es verdad! ¡El cuerpo de la que fue Gertrudis Gómez de Avellaneda descansa en un nicho del Cementerio de la sacramental de San Martin, de Madrid!" (It is true, the body that belonged to Gertrudis Gómez de Avellaneda rests in a niche in the San Martin Sacramental Cemetery, Madrid!).[67] The exclamation seems to answer a question and debate about where Avellaneda's body is to be buried, that is, what nation and people will lay final claim to her. The question of corporeal ownership is answered by burying her in Spain's capital city, in the grounds of the colonial power. There is an obvious parallel of dispossession between Avellaneda's literal and figurative body, that is, her corpse and corpus. For example, the phrase "the body that belonged to" tells us that she is no longer her body. This is an appropriate metaphor for her body of work if there ever was one. Yet it begs the question of this chapter: Was she ever in complete control of her body? Even in death she is quite figuratively exhumed from the colonial grounds as scholars attempt to contextualize her within a broader literary national tradition.

The *Boletín*'s obituary asks, "Quién fue la Avellaneda?" (Who was Avellaneda?), and answers its own question: "La Avellaneda, en vida, había poseído ... fuerza de atracción: talento, hermosura, riqueza, posición social; su sexo la ponía fuera del alcaneo del tiro de la opinión política, que todo envenena ... " (Avellaneda, in life, possessed ... the power of attraction: talent, beauty, wealth, social position; her sex put her outside the range of political opinion, which poisons everything ...).[68] The obituary's insistence on aligning the poet with apolitical and gendered aesthetics suggests that even in death Avellaneda posed a threat to the colonial social order. In the *Boletín*, Avellaneda's very being amounted to two mutually exclusive characteristics: her power of social attraction and her sex. The public and private spheres of colonial domination which Avellaneda threatened to dismantle in her writing are diametrically opposed in her death. Like the power of colonial Spain, the power of attraction is one-sided, vindicating the colonizer and, more importantly, complicating the colonized's affinities to the poet.

The paratext figures prominently in Avellaneda's multinational and political reputation. Puerto Rico's most popular (anti)colonial newspapers shaped a specific vision of Avellaneda for their readers. Through her poems' paratext, the editors and publishers of these papers attempted to contain and manipulate her influence and cultural capital, framing her work and reputation within agreeable discursive and rhetorical structures. Pro-Spanish newspapers in Puerto Rico depicted Avellaneda as an apolitical and anti-propagandist Spanish national poet. Aware of the threat posed by a public figure with known ties to abolitionist and liberation efforts, the colonial press contextualized Avellaneda via paratextual critiques that framed and reinforced the Spanish *status quo*. In the exile press of New York and progressive Puerto Rican newspapers, however, Avellaneda represented an anticolonial liberation movement. In these freedom-fighting newspapers, she was a symbol of Cuban independence, feminism, and abolitionism.

This chapter teaches us how Avellaneda's paratext in Puerto Rico's colonial newspapers contributed to the dispossession of her corpus and corpse. In the context of political newspapers, her individual verses are read not as single poems but as part of a larger political collective. Furthermore, the poems' paratextuality reveals the intimate relationship between politics and culture in the Hispanophone Caribbean, how a place's literary production and culture are politicized by editors and publishers. Thus, Avellaneda was not simply a poet but a shaper of the always already political culture of the Hispanophone world.

Notes

1. Carmen Bravo-Villasante, *Una vida romántica: la Avellaneda* (Madrid: Instituto de Cooperación Iberoamericana, Ediciones Cultura Hispánica, 1986), 57–58.
2. Walter Mignolo, *The Darker Side of Western Modernity: Global Futures, Decolonial Options* (Durham, NC: Duke University Press, 2011), xxvii.
3. Mignolo, *Darker Side*, 2–3.

4. Mignolo, *Darker Side*, xii.
5. Beth Miller, "Gertrude the Great: Avellaneda, Nineteenth-Century Feminist," *Women in Hispanic Literature: Icons and Fallen Idols*, ed. Beth Miller (Berkeley: University of California Press, 1982), 203.
6. Miller, "Gertrude the Great," 203.
7. Catherine Davies, "Founding-Fathers and Domestic Genealogies: Situating Gertrudis Gómez De Avellaneda," *Bulletin of Latin American Research* 22, no. 4 (2003): 423.
8. Davies, "Founding-Fathers," 423.
9. María C. Albin, Megan Corbin, and Raúl Marrero-Fente, "A Transnational Figure: Gertrudis Gómez de Avellaneda and the American Press," *Gender and the Politics of Literature: Gertrudis Gómez de Avellaneda, Hispanic Issues Online* 18 (2017): 126.
10. Albin, Corbin, and Marrero-Fente, "Transnational Figure," 68.
11. "Multiple News Items," *Daily Evening Bulletin*, July 27, 1864.
12. "A Washington," *La Verdad*, March 20, 1852; "A Washington," *El Clamor Público*, July 10, 1858. There are several references to the poem in the US press, such as in the *Omaha Daily Bee* (Nebraska) on January 15, 1899; the *Charleston Courier* (South Carolina) on October 7, 1854; and the *Daily Illinois* (a student newspaper from the University of Illinois) on July 8, 1926.
13. Albin, Corbin, and Marrero-Fente, "Transnational Figure," 75.
14. Brickhouse, *Transamerican Literary Relations*, 173.
15. Brickhouse, *Transamerican Literary Relations*, 173.
16. Davies, "Founding-Fathers," 429.
17. Davies, "Founding-Fathers," 429.
18. Davies, "Founding-Fathers," 429.
19. According to Rogelia Lily Ibarra, *La América* published the first edition of *Sab* "in nine installments, from May 15 to September 15 of 1871. The first publication of *Sab* in Cuba was printed in the magazine *El Museo*, of Havana, in serial form in 1883." Rogelia Lily Ibarra, "Gómez de Avellaneda's 'Sab': A Modernizing Project," *Hispania* 94, no. 3 (2011): 394.
20. Albin, Corbin, and Marrero-Fente, "Transnational Figure," 76.
21. Rodrigo Lazo, *Writing to Cuba: Filibustering and Cuban Exiles in the United States* (Chapel Hill: University of North Carolina Press, 2005), 117, 74.
22. Lazo, *Writing to Cuba*, 11.
23. Albin, Corbin, and Marrero-Fente, "Transnational Figure," 93.
24. Albin, Corbin, and Marrero-Fente, "Transnational Figure," 90.
25. In 1836, *La Gazeta* replaced the "z" in its title with a "c." The new title remained until *La Gaceta*'s final issue in 1902. This is the title I use my analysis.
26. "About *Gazeta de Puerto-Rico*," Chronicling America Database, Library of Congress, <https://chroniclingamerica.loc.gov/lccn/2013201074/>.
27. Original Spanish: "el matrimonio . . . [del] Sr. Sabater actual jefe político de Madrid, y la conocida y aplaudida escritora Doña Gertrudis Gómez Avellaneda." "España," *La Gaceta de Puerto-Rico*, July 28, 1846.
28. "España."
29. Gertrudis Gómez de Avellaneda, "Serenata: A su Alteza Real: la Serma. Sra. Infanta Duquesa de Montpensier: La Vispera de Su Cumpleaños," *La Gaceta de Puerto-Rico*, April 20, 1858.

30. Avellaneda, "Serenata." Original Spanish: "Esta poesía fue leída por la señora Avellaneda a los señores Duques de Montpensier con motivo del cumpleaños de S. A. D. Luisa Fernanda, y al siguiente día los Príncipes enviaron a la poetisa un rico regalo que consiste en un lindo estuche con una rica joya de brillantes perlas y rubíes de exquisito trabajo."
31. For one example, see Juan Nicasio Gallego, Introduction to *Poesías de la Señorita Da. Gertrudis Gomez de Avellaneda* (Madrid: Establecimiento Tipográfico, 1841), xiii.
32. Carolina Coronado, "Poets do not make any illusions . . . ," *La Gaceta de Puerto-Rico*, May 14, 1861.
33. Antonio S. Pedreira, *El periodismo en Puerto Rico* (Río Piedras: Universidad de Puerto Rico, 1969), 81.
34. "About *Gazeta de Puerto-Rico*."
35. See Ayendy Bonifacio, "'Se habla Español': Hispanophone-Merchant Advertisements in José Ferrer de Couto's *El Cronista* (1878)," *American Periodicals: A Journal of History & Criticism* 30, no. 2 (2020): 118–21.
36. Gruesz, *Ambassadors of Culture*, 20.
37. Original Spanish: "La única de las escritoras de la escuela analítica sentimental que tiene alguna semejanza con la Sra. Gómez de Avellaneda, es miss Mulock, porque, llevada de su instinto vigoroso, refiere los acontecimientos con desembarazado y firme estilo, comenta con sobriedad, no abusa demasiado del análisis filosófico." In 1871, this excerpt was also reprinted in *La Revista de España*. "Noticias Literarias," *El Boletín mercantil de Puerto Rico*, September 22, 1871.
38. Original Spanish: "Esta creación de la fantasía popular, hábilmente reproducida por miss Mulock, vino a nuestra memoria como delicada analogía de naturalezas femeniles, al leer La flor del ángel de la Sra. Gómez de Avellaneda, flor del Deva, muy semejante en forma a una abeja." "Noticias Literarias."
39. Original Spanish: "Las mujeres comprenden y sienten más delicada e intensamente que los hombres estas fantásticas ilusiones de la musa de las montañas, y la Sra. Gómez de Avellaneda nada tiene que envidiar en esta parte a la imaginación soñadora de las razas septentrionales." "Noticias Literarias."
40. Original Spanish: "Esta nunca prescinde de sus insanos designios sistemáticos por lo general tan inciertos, que hasta Proudhon, que no es, por cierto, escrupuloso y asustadizo en materias de audacias y de innovaciones, condene con energía y hasta con desabrimiento su encarnizado afán de emancipación femenina sin restricción y sin medida, y todas las consecuencias inevitables de esta filosofía de *vacante revelada* según la expresión violenta de Proudhon, a saber: la igualdad absoluta de ambos sexos; la libertad en el amor, la proscripción del matrimonio; o en otros términos, envidia y odio al hombre, y espontáneo envilecimiento de la mujer." "Noticias Literarias."
41. "Noticias Literarias."
42. Original Spanish: "Nada añadiremos nosotros á este tremendo juicio del crítico francés sobre una escritora." "Noticias Literarias."
43. Original Spanish: "La Sra. Gómez de Avellaneda es novelista y no propagadora de arriesgadas y ambiciosas doctrinas; no desnaturaliza la novela ni el drama, convirtiendo estos géneros literarios, destinados al culto y honesto recreo de las gentes, en órgano de trastornos y agitación moral." "Noticias Literarias."

44. "Noticias Literarias."
45. Original Spanish: "La moral de las leyendas y novelas de la Sra. Gómez de Avellaneda es franca, resuelta y sana, la cual ofrece de suyo el estudio sincero de la naturaleza humana, sin barruntos de doctrina social y sin melindres de forma." "Noticias Literarias."
46. Original Spanish: "Las mujeres . . . cultivan su entendimiento y ayudan, en las letras o en las artes, a la civilización general y al lastre de su patria." "Noticias Literarias."
47. Robert L. Scheina, *Latin America's Wars: The Age of the Caudillo, 1791–1899* (Lincoln: University of Nebraska Press, 2003), 358.
48. Cuba became a protectorate of the United States, giving the US oversight over its government and educational system. A military government was soon installed on the island headed up by General Guy Vernor Henry.
49. Ramón B. López, "The Needs of Porto Rico [sic]," *The Independent*, November 29, 1900.
50. Original Spanish: "Un diario americano, que ya da como un hecho la anexión de Cuba, publica un retrato y un bosteo biográfico de la gran poetisa Cubana doña Gertrudis Gomez de Avellaneda, a quien reputa como una de las mas brillantes gloria "americanas" . . . La palabra "americano" no se emplea hoy sino sinónimo de Yankee, y de grado o por fuerza tenemos que conformarnos, porque a decir verdad, los yankees la han ilustrado mas que nosotros, y nosotros nunca hemos, protestado contra ese monopolio, que, bien considerado, es base disimulada pero solida para la fuerza absorción de todo el continente." "Nuestras Glorias," *La correspondencia de Puerto Rico*, August 22, 1899.
51. "Nuestras Glorias."
52. "Nuestras Glorias."
53. Like "Nuestras Glorias," "La prensa americana" was likely authored by the newspaper's bilingual editor, López. It would not have been uncommon for editors to write several columns for their newspaper.
54. Stuart B. Schwartz, "The Hurricane of San Ciriaco: Disaster, Politics, and Society in Puerto Rico, 1899–1901," *Hispanic American Historical Review* 7, no. 3 (1982): 308.
55. Original Spanish: "No puedo decirse, en resumen, que haya un solo periódico en el contiene que no se haya ocupado extensamente de los destrozos causados por la tormenta, y que no excite al pueblo para que acuda a socorrer con sus suscripciones, a los necesitados." "La prensa americana," *La correspondencia de Puerto Rico*, August 22, 1899.
56. López, "Needs of Porto Rico."
57. "Nuestras Glorias."
58. Édouard Glissant, *Poetics of Relation* (Ann Arbor: University of Michigan Press, 1997), 11.
59. Glissant, *Poetics of Relation*, 13.
60. Frederick Luciani, *José María Heredia in New York, 1823–1825: An Exiled Cuban Poet in the Age of Revolution, Selected Letters and Verse* (Albany: State University of New York Press, 2020), 30.

61. Matthew 27:53, *The New Oxford Annotated Bible with the Apocryphal/Deuterocanonical Books: New Revised Standard Version*, ed. Michael D. Coogan, Marc Z. Brettler, Carol A. Newsom, and Pheme Perkins (New York: Oxford University Press, 2001).
62. Matthew Pettway, *Cuban Literature in the Age of Black Insurrection: Manzano, Plácido, and Afro-Latino Religion* (Jackson: University Press of Mississippi, 2020), 4.
63. Pettway, *Cuban Literature*, 111.
64. In Plácido's original publication, there is a stanza break following the word "mandado." The original poem concludes with two tercets. See Plácido (Gabriel de la Concepcion *Valdés*), *Poesias Completas de Plácido (Gabriel de la Concepcion Veldés)* (Paris: En Casa de Mme C. Denné Schmitz, 1856), 3; Plácido (Gabriel de la Concepcion *Valdés*), *Poesias Completas de Plácido (Gabriel de la Concepcion Veldés)* (Paris: En Casa de Mme C. Denné Schmitz, 1862), 3.
65. Pettway, *Cuban Literature*, 5.
66. Gallego, Introduction to Avellaneda, *Poesías*.
67. "Variedades," *El Boletín mercantil de Puerto Rico*, April 9, 1873.
68. "Variedades."

CODA:
"IN DEFENSE OF NEWSPAPER POETS"

On July 28, 1910, James E. Kinsella, known as "Chicago's Post Office Poet," published a short column in the *Chicago Tribune* titled "In Defense of Newspaper Poets," expressing his outrage over William Butler Yeats's lambasting comments about newspaper poets. Kinsella criticized Yeats for "cast[ing] a slur on the newspaper profession by contemptuously alluding to some paragraph writers as 'Newspaper Poets.'"[1] Kinsella asked his readers, "Are not newspaper poets better than the average magazine poets?" and answered this question by tracing the source of Yeats's discontent to a type of lost history, the disconnection between established writers and their early careers.[2] Kinsella reminded the public that popular magazine writers of the day, including Bret Harte, Rudyard Kipling, and Andrew Lang, launched their literary careers as newspaper poets. Kinsella's defense of newspaper poets came in a time when modernist conventions about publishing deemed newspaper writing out of fashion and non-reputable. By the turn of the nineteenth century, newspaper poetry was becoming a thing of the past. The high-status New England literary magazines that Nancy Glazener calls "the *Atlantic* group" controlled literary and moral standards for many writers.[3] To borrow from Edmund Clarence Stedman's term about the depreciation of poetry in the era of American Realism, "The Twilight of the [Periodical] Poets" came into its own during the first half of the twentieth century. Newspaper poets became associated with old-world Victorian norms, what George Santayana called the "genteel tradition."[4] Santayana argued that "the mediocrity of the genteel tradition" had degraded American cultural production.[5] He called for a complete rejection of these Romantic, transcendentalist, Victorian idealisms and advocated for a modern literary tradition that embraced the changing cultural climate of the US.[6] Santayana believed that a failure to do so would stifle the country's intellectual and literary growth. Such modernist ideals generated modernist canon-making methods like centralizing authorship, books, and reputation that positioned the newspaper poet outside of the realm of intellectual and aesthetic significance.

Twelve years after Kinsella's publication, a reporter named Glen Allen published a satirical cross-genre column titled "Pity the Poor Newspaper Poets!" in the *New York Times Magazine* that explored the state of newspaper poetry in the early part of the twentieth century. He opened his column by citing the British poet Richard Le Gallienne's disdain for newspaper poetry. Gallienne defined newspaper poems strictly within the parameters of class, calling this brand of verse "'the folklore of the lower middle classes' that is read in the subway."[7] For Allen, Gallienne represented an influential coterie of magazine and book writers, custodians of modernist poetics, who believed that the dying art of newspaper poetry only appealed "to low-browed businessmen who cherish in their wallets bits of verse culled from the bottom of the editorial page."[8] Gallienne and other modernists claimed that these poems catered

> to the needs of the masses, the untutored multitudes who play the concertina and still read the works of Tennyson and Longfellow: who continue artlessly to expect poetry to contain rhyme, rhythm, sentiment and other elements foreign to the work of the professional poets of today.[9]

Gallienne ridiculed readers of these poetic relics and cited Tennyson and Longfellow, two of the most popular newspaper poets of the nineteenth century, as examples of bad poetry. Newspaper poets, Gallienne posited, were out of fashion because they wrote occasional poems about current events and "burst into song . . . to all that sort of thing."[10] By comparison, professional magazine poets, or "real poets," were immune to such sentiment: "They cannot be distracted by the thrill of great events. They are absorbed in their own emotions and sensations."[11] These real poets, according to Gallienne, portrayed their emotions and sentiments in "polychromatic prose and 'new-fangled manipulations of pauses and discords'" unlike newspaper poet who emulated the form and content of a dated genteel tradition.[12]

As a way of countering modernists' condescension toward newspaper poetry, the rest of Allen's column presents a series of rebuttals to Gallienne's claims. First, Allen argues that, contrary to popular opinion, the great ancient classical poets were indeed engulfed in their cultural moment and wrote poems that were occasioned by history, asking, "Would the world's literature have been as rich today, I wonder, if the sophisticated poets of the past had been immune to the thrill of great events?"[13] Occasional verse, he claims, produced the great works of *The Iliad*, *The Odyssey*, and *The Aeneid*, which would not exist without "the thrill of great events."[14] Second, Allen claims that the newspaper is a democratic literary form that makes poems widely accessible to many readers worldwide. Thus, modernist professional writers should consider it an honor to publish in "a great daily that circles the globe: that is read in the sanctum of scholars as well as in the subway; and in the far-off palaces of Kings as well as in the New York ex-brownstone-front houses done over into two-room-and-bath apartments."[15]

In part, Allen showed his readers that modernist poets introduced their own modern expectations and biases when making sense of newspaper poets of the past and present. The article's paratext helps to satirically contextualize these modernist disappointments and expectations. For example, serving as a type of banner for the article, the *New York Times Magazine* included a satirical illustration above Allen's publication titled "Furnishing pin feathers for the wings of Pegasus" (see Figure C.1).

The illustration features two men in early twentieth-century attire who invite a sitting horse dressed as Pegasus to pull a chariot and take flight using its "pin wings." The illustration introduces the reader to an important lesson about authenticity and the artifice of forcing something to be what it is not. The horse is no Pegasus, and its pin wings will not grant it the power of flight.

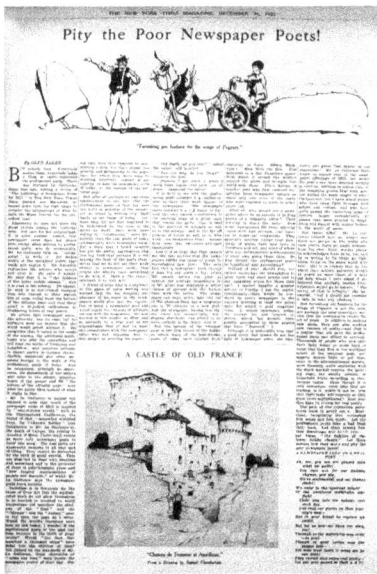

Figure C.1 *The New York Times Magazine*, December 31, 1922. Newspapers.com. Public domain.

In a similar logic, the newspaper poet is no modernist poet, and anachronistically implicating modernist convention onto these poets, as Allen writes and the illustration depicts, is at best comical.

Allen's cross-genre column appropriately concludes with a sonnet titled "A Newspaper Poet to a Real Poet", a dramatic monologue with all the stereotypical formal- and content-based characteristics of newspaper verse. The poem's speaker acts as a respondent to modernists' accusations:

> Ah, me, you are not pleased with what we write!
> You care not for our tinkling rhymes, you say,
> We're sentimental, and our themes cliché;
> We cater to the ignorant delight
> Of the untutored multitudes who fight
> Their way into the subway cars each day,
> And read our poems on their journey's way—
> But in your breast no rapture we excite.
> But let us live—we have our uses, too!
> Through us the multitudes may come—to you!
> Though at your verses now the peepul balk—
> Yet man must learn to creep ere he can walk!
> They cannot now enjoy real poetry—
> Let our poor poems be their A B C!

Like the rest of Allen's column, "A Newspaper Poet to a Real Poet" is complexly layered in irony. The poem's form, for instance, plays up modernist-generated stereotypes about newspaper poems. It is a sonnet, one of the most popular newspaper genres in the nineteenth century for its convenient length and versatile content. It is also ironic that "A Newspaper Poet to a Real Poet" follows the rhyme scheme ABBAABBACCDDEE to refute Gallienne's accusation that newspaper poets "continue artlessly to expect poetry to contain rhyme, rhythm."[16] The poem repudiates this stereotype by undermining Gallienne's very opinion, that is, by being stubbornly non-compliant to a so-called custodian of poetry. Rhyming poems, according to the speaker, serve an important purpose. They are the "A B C!" of "our poor," that is, the rhyme schemes of the poem and the readers' elementary introduction to and education in poetry (14).

The content of "A Newspaper Poet to a Real Poet" is also packed with ironic gestures. The opening line explicitly alludes to modernists' disdain for the formal traits the poem intentionally reproduces: "Ah, me, you are not pleased with what we write! / You care not for our tinkling rhymes, you say, / We're sentimental, and our themes cliché" (1–3). The speaker emulates the very stereotypes he cites, "sentimental" and full of "cliché[s]," with the poem's opening histrionic exclamation, "Ah," often used to express a range of emotions. The speaker continues this sentimental performance with the saccharine discourse used in the rest of the poem. For example, mid-way through the poem, the speaker claims that newspaper poets' impassioned themes and rhymes "excite" "no rapture" "in your breast" (8). The hyperbolic language of "rapture" and "excite" evokes uncontained feelings which Gallienne claims are artlessly over-sentimental. Perhaps the most ironic part of the poem comes from the union of its form and content, the fact that this sentimental sonnet is occasioned by Gallienne's own complaints. As scholars like Paula Bernat Bennett and Elizabeth Renker have argued, irony as a poetic trait in newspaper poetry was often disregarded and misunderstood by readers and scholars of later generations. The paratext creates a viable opportunity for scholars to refurnish newspaper poems with this important component.

The discourse and history surrounding "A Newspaper Poet to a Real Poet," which, I have argued in this book, is represented in the poem's paratext, enables us to read the poem's irony as more completely a defense of newspaper poetry. The poem appears next to an illustration of the "Chateau de Tennesue at Amailloux," titled "A Castle of Old France," by the American graphic artist Samuel Chamberlain (1895–1975) (see Figure C.1). The image is a break from the comedy and satire of Allen's column. Yet it serves as useful context for the speaker's defense of the value of non-modern themes like the sentimental, romantic, and clichéd. Next to the poem, Chamberlain's sketch represents an old-world aesthetic, the ruins of a French castle and a lone, inscrutable figure standing prominently in front of it. In juxtaposition to the grandness of the castle, the figure in the center seems small yet powerful, almost sublime. Without this figure, Chamberlain's sketch would simply be study of "A Castle of Old France." But the figure's presence enables an affective reading, allowing readers to ponder the figure's presence, lonesomeness, and purpose in that place. The image is an aesthetic item that, like the loathed newspaper poem, draws from the reader's emotions. The proximity of Allen's poem to the image allows readers to engage with the poem and article as more than a comical plea, and rather as an earnest defense of non-modern aesthetic traditions.

Allen's "A Newspaper Poet to a Real Poet'" even intertextually borrows words, phrases, and concepts from its paratext, including "untutored multitudes," "subway," and "peepul" (5, 6, 11). Both Allen and the poem's speaker arrive at similar arguments about the function that newspaper poets serve. Allen claims that newspaper poems will generate an interest in magazine poetry: "Next Year they may be crying of real poetry,"[17] while the poem's speaker posits that "we have our uses, too! / Through us the multitudes may come—to you!," that is, to the modernist poet (9–10). Even in a poem about the demise of newspaper poetry, the paratext becomes a useful site for contextualizing not just the speaker's irony but our very methods for reading and contextualizing nineteenth-century poetry.

I conclude this book with these obscure defenses of newspaper poetry because they represent a moment of reflection in the early twentieth century as writers were conceptualizing modern poetic taste and value. Kinsella and Allen feared the loss of a genre and literary tradition that belonged to the public. *Paratextuality in Anglophone and Hispanophone Poems in the US Press, 1855–1901* is not necessarily a defense of newspaper poets, like we see in Kinsella's and Allen's publications. This book is instead an attempt to return newspaper poems to their moment in time, within the discursive paratexts that occasioned them, that gave them cultural, social, and historical significance.

In this book, I have argued that the forms and material contexts of nineteenth-century poems published in newspapers inflect their meanings in a more profound way than most critics recognize. By reading newspaper poems not only historically but within the most immediate framework of their paratexts (i.e. the surrounding advertisements, notices, and (un)related stories in proximate pages of the newspaper), this book shows how certain poems spoke to ongoing events and the particular concerns of local and regional audiences. The world of newspaper poems included poets, poems, paratexts, and publics that were multilingual, existing within geopolitical spaces of an expanding US empire. It is for this reason that the Hispanophone press centers so prominently in this book. One of the book's arguments is that any comprehensive study of nineteenth-century literary production must account for the significant production of Spanish letters by American Hispanics. The paratext opens a material space from which to bridge publics of different linguistic backgrounds. Through such an approach, I hope this book expands the conventional parameters of nineteenth-century American literature.

In addition to bridging the languages that poets printed and publics consumed in newspapers, I wish to encourage print culture scholars to resist methodologies that centralize the relationship between authors and texts in order to offer a more investigative and less rigid mode of engaging with the past. As Katherine Bode reminds us, when we move away from origin narratives predicated on author-centered disciplinary infrastructures, byline-less texts present a unique framework for analyzing cultural production.[18] "Our paradoxically author-centered approach to literary anonymity and pseudonymity," she argues, overemphasizes "composite figures and bodies of work that did not exist and could not have existed in the era in which th[o]se texts were written."[19] Author-centered approaches to recovery work tend to reproduce gendered and racist systems of canon-making that more often than not centralize white men writing for the public. For instance, Jennifer Putzi argues that a reevaluation of nineteenth-century poets (particularly women writers) has taken place on an "author-by author-basis."[20] However, this mode of recovery is limited, "given that it makes very little room for the work of other women poets since scholars begin searching for poems that resemble the style of other poets."²¹ Putzi is arguing for a restructuring of our methodological approach to nineteenth-century poetry, moving beyond the conventional templates for recovering and estimating the value of nineteenth-century poets. Our author- and book-centered methodologies generate the study of writers that resemble and reproduce the canon, creating little possibility to seriously consider the works of lesser and unknown newspaper writers, women, and writers of color whose careers were not defined by a "great" book and/or their celebrity reputation. One of the major goals of this book is to generate serious inquiry into the works of these seldom sung writers and demonstrate how their poems were textually, culturally, and historically synchronized with the world of print.

Each chapter in *Paratextuality in Anglophone and Hispanophone Poems in the US Press, 1855–1901* has shown that newspaper poems were embedded in the public discourse of their publication moment, shaping and responding to the poetic demands of consumers. In Chapter 1, I looked at how the newspaper poem functioned as a celebrity-making genre in Robert E. Bonner's *New York Ledger*. Bonner's strategic publication of the authorial bylines of celebrity poetesses Lydia H. Sigourney and Alice Cary helped to build his paper's cultural legitimacy even while their poems negotiated and gave expression to anti-patriarchal poetics and complex forms of women's agency. Chapters 2–4 focused on reproduction, a process in newspaper publishing that often erases bylines through mass circulation. Chapter 2 centralized Francisco P. Ramírez's unauthorized reprints in *El Clamor Público*. Ramírez's editorship unbound many reprint poems from the nation-making artifact of the author, book, and anthology, warping and, in some cases, erasing popular poetry genres like satire and the dedication. Culled from across the Hispanophone world and reprinted in California, these verses exemplify the significance of the newspaper poem for sustaining the identity of Californios after the US–Mexico War. Chapters 3 and 4 analyzed the phenomenon of the reprint poem in circulation via the robust and uncharted archive of reprint poems occasioned by two major hemispheric crises, the Panic of 1857 and the New York cholera epidemic of 1866, respectively. In these chapters, newspaper poets participated in social and political debates. Their poems gained a sense of significance in the public through robust circulation.

Through these chapters, I hope to have made a case for how the paratext creates the possibility for scholars to rethink the value and social significance of poems beyond the strictures of modern intellectual disciplines. Nancy Glazener reminds us that "disciplinarity can routinize and standardize intellectual work in a way that merely manages intellectual questions. The imperative of innovation can lead scholars to overstate the novelty and significance of their work."²² The tendency for innovation, Glazener posits, often produces static convention in our discipline, "so that the value of something new or old gets distorted by the perpetual construction of the new-hot versus the old-tired (complicated by the ongoing discovery of the old and its repackaging as new again)."[23] A restructuring of our disciplinary focus is imperative for the flourishing of the study of American poetry, but it is exceptionally significant for the recovery work of women poets. For this reason, the final chapter in this book turned to the poems and paratext of Gertrudis Gómez de Avellaneda in Puerto Rico's colonial press. Avellaneda is seldom included in books and syllabi on nineteenth-century US poetry. Yet, as the final chapter argued, her textual presence in North America, South America, and Europe reveals a triptych image of colonial, anticolonial, and decolonial interests that links the Hispanophone Caribbean to Spain and the United States. Avellaneda's poems and paratext allow us to open up the canon of American poetry to include voices that, because of trends in how we discover new writers, have been excluded from serious intellectual inquiry. These writers are often relegated to footnotes because of the language in which they wrote, the medium in which they published, and the publics who read them. Avellaneda is one example of how broadening our field to include Hispanophone poets (as well as other non-English writers) writing for newspapers can help us to restructure and reimagine the field of American poetry in a way that reflects the demographic make-up of the US today.

I hope that readers of this book take a way an impulse to broaden the capacity of our recovery work through intersectional and interdisciplinary approaches. I invite scholars of nineteenth-century poetry to think beyond the realm of the English language when writing about the paratexts of newspaper poems, and to turn to the important interdisciplinary works of scholars who are already bridging connections between languages, publics, and discourse like Dixa Ramírez, Lorgia García Peña, Rodrigo Lazo, Marlene Daut, Carmen Lamas, Kirsten Silva Gruesz, Jesse Alemán, Bernadine M. Hernández, Karen Roybal, and many others whose work sheds light on the forgotten modernities of people whose perspectives are relegated to the margins of society.

Ultimately, reading newspaper poems through a poetics of paratextuality enables a more media- and page-based approach that engages with the arbitrariness of nineteenth-century poetic taste and value and opens the canon to works that have been excluded by modern aesthetic standards. For future study, I hope this book signals the importance of including the paratext in theorizing nineteenth-century literature (particularly poetry), not only to show that these texts are worthy of being included in the debate, but more importantly to move us toward new disciplinary traditions and conventions that centralize the textual ephemerality of our literature.

Notes

1. James E. Kinsella, "In Defense of Newspaper Poets," *Chicago Tribune*, July 28, 1910.
2. Kinsella, "In Defense of Newspaper Poets."
3. Glazener, *Reading for Realism*, 5.

4. George Santayana, "The Genteel Tradition in American Philosophy," *The Genteel Tradition: Nine Essays*, ed. Douglas L. Wilson (Cambridge, MA: Harvard University Press, 1967), 39.
5. Santayana, "Genteel Tradition," 44.
6. Santayana, "Genteel Tradition," 44.
7. Glen Allen, "Pity the Poor Newspaper Poets!," *The New York Times Magazine*, December 31, 1922.
8. Allen, "Pity the Poor Newspaper Poets!"
9. Allen, "Pity the Poor Newspaper Poets!"
10. Allen, "Pity the Poor Newspaper Poets!"
11. Allen, "Pity the Poor Newspaper Poets!"
12. Allen, "Pity the Poor Newspaper Poets!"
13. Allen, "Pity the Poor Newspaper Poets!"
14. Allen, "Pity the Poor Newspaper Poets!"
15. Allen, "Pity the Poor Newspaper Poets!"
16. Allen, "Pity the Poor Newspaper Poets!"
17. Allen, "Pity the Poor Newspaper Poets!"
18. Bode, "Thousands of Titles," 309.
19. Bode, "Thousands of Titles," 284.
20. Putzi, *Fair Copy*, 210.
21. Putzi, *Fair Copy*, 210.
22. Nancy Glazener, *Literature in the Making: A History of U.S. Literary Culture in the Long Nineteenth Century* (Oxford: Oxford University Press, 2015), 193.
23. Glazener, *Literature in the Making*, 193–94.

BIBLIOGRAPHY

"About *Anti-Slavery Bugle*." Chronicling America Database, Library of Congress. <https://www.loc.gov/item/sn83035487/>.

"About *Gazeta de Puerto-Rico*." Chronicling America Database, Library of Congress. <https://chroniclingamerica.loc.gov/lccn/2013201074/>.

"About the *Wheeling Daily Intelligencer*." Chronicling America Database, Library of Congress. <https://www.loc.gov/item/sn84026844/#:~:text=During%20this%20tumultuous%20era%2C%20the,Virginia%20on%20June%2020%2C%201863>.

Adams, Michael. *Slang: The People's Poetry*. Oxford: Oxford University Press, 2009.

Albin, María C., Megan Corbin, and Raúl Marrero-Fente. "A Transnational Figure: Gertrudis Gómez de Avellaneda and the American Press." *Gender and the Politics of Literature: Gertrudis Gómez de Avellaneda. Hispanic Issues Online* 18 (2017): 67–133.

Allen, Glen. "Pity the Poor Newspaper Poets!" *The New York Times Magazine*, December 31, 1922.

Allen, Irving Lewis. *The City in Slang: New York Life and Popular Speech*. Oxford: Oxford University Press, 1993.

Anbinder, Tyler. *Nativism and Slavery: The Northern Know Nothings and the Politics of the 1850s*. Oxford: Oxford University Press, 1992.

Andrews, Clarence A. *Michigan in Literature*. Detroit: Wayne State University Press, 1992.

Arnold, David. *The New Cambridge History of India: Science, Technology and Medicine in Colonial India*. Cambridge: Cambridge University Press, 2000.

"Assorting Brokers." *The Anti-Slavery Bugle*, October 24, 1857.

Balmaseda, Francisco Javier. *Rimas Cubanas*. Habana: Tipografía de Don Vicente de Torres, 1846.

Barr, Amelia E. *All the Days of My Life: An Autobiography*. New York: D. Appleton and Company, 1913.
Barrett, Faith. "'What witty sally': Phoebe Cary's Poetics of Parody." *A History of Nineteenth-Century American Women's Poetry*. Ed. Jennifer Putzi and Alexandra Socarides. Cambridge: Cambridge University Press, 2017.
Bataille, Gretchen M. *Native American Representations: First Encounters, Distorted Images, and Literary Appropriations*. Lincoln: University of Nebraska Press, 2001.
Baym, Nina. "Rewriting the Scribbling Women." *Legacy* 36, no. 1 (2019): 137–52.
Beckert, Sven, and Seth Rockman. "Introduction." *Slavery's Capitalism: A New History of American Economic Development*. Ed. Sven Beckert and Seth Rockman. Philadelphia: University of Pennsylvania Press, 2016.
Beecher, Henry Ward. "Lessons from the Times." *The Evening Post*, October 2, 1857.
Bennett, Emerson. "The Refugees: An Indian Tale of 1812." *The New York Ledger*, January 24, 1857.
Bennett, Paula Bernat. *Poets in the Public Sphere: The Emancipatory Project of American Women's Poetry, 1800–1900*. Princeton: Princeton University Press, 2003.
—. "Was Sigourney a Poetess? The Aesthetics of Victorian Plenitude in Lydia Sigourney's Poetry." *Comparative American Studies: An International Journal* 5, no. 3 (2007): 265–89.
Benstock, Shari. "At the Margin of Discourse: Footnotes in the Fictional Text." *PMLA* 98, no. 2 (1983): 204–25.
Blank, G. K. "Shelley's Wind of Influence." *Philological Quarterly* 64, no. 4 (1985): 475–91.
"The Board of Health and Brooklyn." *The Daily Eagle*, July 20, 1866.
Bode, Katherine. "Thousands of Titles Without Authors: Digitized Newspapers, Serial Fiction, and the Challenges of Anonymity." *Book History* 19, no. (2016): 284–316.
Bonifacio, Ayendy. "'Se habla Español': Hispanophone-Merchant Advertisements in José Ferrer de Couto's *El Cronista* (1878)." *American Periodicals: A Journal of History & Criticism* 30, no. 2 (2020): 118–21.
Bravo-Villasante, Carmen. *Una vida romántica: la Avellaneda*. Madrid: Instituto de Cooperación Iberoamericana, Ediciones Cultura Hispánica, 1986.
Brickhouse, Anna. *Transamerican Literary Relations and the Nineteenth-Century Public Sphere*. Cambridge: Cambridge University Press, 2004.
"Brooklyn and the Cholera." *The New York Times*, July 20, 1866.
Browne, Junius Henri. *The Great Metropolis: A Mirror of New York*. Hartford: American Publishing Company, 1869.
Bryant, William Cullen. *The Letters of William Cullen Bryant Volume IV, 1858–1864*. New York: Fordham University Press, 2019.
—. *Poems by William Cullen Bryant: Collected and Arranged by the Author*. New York: D. Appleton and Company, 1854.
Burnett, Alfred. *Humorous, Pathetic and Descriptive: Incidents of the War*. Cincinnati: R. W. Carroll & Co., Publishers, 1874.
Burstein, Daniel Eli. *Next to Godliness: Confronting Dirt and Despair in Progressive Era New York City*. Champaign: University of Illinois Press, 2006.
Byerly, Alison. *Realism, Representation, and the Arts in Nineteenth-Century Literature*. Cambridge: Cambridge University Press, 1997.

Calcaterra, Angela. *Literary Indians: Aesthetics and Encounter in American Literature to 1920.* Chapel Hill: University of North Carolina Press, 2018.

Calomiris, Charles W., and Larry Schweikart. "The Panic of 1857: Origins, Transmission, and Containment." *The Journal of Economic History* 51, no. 4 (1991): 807–34.

Carlyle, Jane Welsh. *Jane Welsh Carlyle: Letters to Her Family, 1839–1863.* Garden City: Double, Page & Company, 1924.

Cary, Alice. "Looking Back." *The New York Ledger*, December 27, 1856.

—. "Work." *The National Magazine*, November 1854.

—. "Work." *The New York Ledger*, January 10, 1857.

Casey, Jim, and Sarah H. Salter. "Challenges and Opportunities in Editorship Studies." *American Periodicals: A Journal of History & Criticism* 30, no. 2 (2020): 101–4.

Chávez, John R. *The Lost Land: The Chicano Image of the Southwest.* Albuquerque: University of New Mexico Press, 1984.

Child, Lydia Maria. *Looking Toward Sunset.* Boston: Ticknor and Fields, 1865.

"Cholera Report." *The New York Sun*, July 23, 1866.

Clark, Barbara R. "Tennyson Across the Atlantic." *Tennyson Research Bulletin* 5, no. 1 (1987): 1–8.

Clemmer, Mary. *The Poetical Works of Alice and Phoebe Cary: With a Memorial of Their Lives.* Boston: Houghton, Mifflin and Company, 1876.

Coeckelbergh, Mark. *New Romantic Cyborgs: Romanticism, Information Technology, and the End of the Machine.* Cambridge, MA: MIT Press, 2017.

Cohen, Michael C. *The Social Lives of Poems in Nineteenth-Century America.* Philadelphia: University of Pennsylvania Press, 2015.

"The Coming Pestilence: Ravages of the Cholera. Its Westward Progress." *The Evening Post*, August 29, 1865.

Coogan, Michael D., Marc Z. Brettler, Carol A. Newsom, and Pheme Perkins, eds. *The New Oxford Annotated Bible with the Apocryphal/Deuterocanonical Books: New Revised Standard Version.* New York: Oxford University Press, 2001.

Cordell, Ryan. "Reprinting, Circulation, and the Network Author in Antebellum Newspapers." *American Literary History* 27, no. 3 (2015): 417–445.

Coronado, Carolina. "Poets do not make any illusions . . . " *La Gaceta de Puerto-Rico*, May 14, 1861.

Coronado, Raúl. *A World Not to Come: A History of Latino Writing and Print Culture.* Cambridge, MA: Harvard University Press, 2013.

Culler, Jonathan. "Why Lyric?" *PMLA* 123, no. 1 (2008): 201–6.

D'Amore, Maura. *Suburban Plots: Men at Home in Nineteenth-Century American Print Culture.* Amherst: University of Massachusetts Press, 2014.

Davies, Catherine. "Founding-Fathers and Domestic Genealogies: Situating Gertrudis Gómez De Avellaneda." *Bulletin of Latin American Research* 22, no. 4 (2003): 423–44.

De Jong, Mary. "Lines From a Partly Published Drama: The Romance of Frances Sargent Osgood and Edgar Allan Poe." *Patrons and Protégées: Gender, Friendship, and Writing in Nineteenth-Century America.* New Brunswick: Rutgers University Press, 1988.

Derby, James Cephas. *Fifty Years Authors, Books and Publishers.* New York: G. W. Carleton & Co., Publishers, 1884.

Dietrich, Lucas. "Charles W. Chesnutt, Houghton Mifflin, and the Racial Paratext." *MELUS* 41, no. 4 (2016): 166–95.
"Discredited Bank Notes." *Summit County Beacon*, September 2, 1857.
"The Districts Where the Cholera Raged in 1849." *New York Herald*, July 23, 1866.
Domett, Alfred. *Poems*. London: Henry Leggatt, 1833.
Donawerth, Jane. "Hannah More, Lydia Sigourney, and the Creation of a Women's Tradition of Rhetoric." *Rhetoric, the Polis, and the Global Village*. Ed. C. Jan Swearingen. Mahwah, NJ: Lawrence Erlbaum Associates, Publishers, 1999.
Douglass, Ann. *The Feminization of American Culture*. New York: Straus and Giroux, 1977.
Duffy, John. *A History of Public Health in New York City 1625–1866*. Hartford: Russell Sage Foundation, 1968.
Duncan, James S., and David R. Lambert. "Landscape, Aesthetics, and Power." *American Space/American Place: Geographies of the Contemporary United States*. Ed. John A. Agnew and Jonathan M. Smith. New York: Routledge, 2002.
Effron, Malcah. "On the Borders of the Page, on the Borders of Genre: Artificial Paratexts in Golden Age Detective Fiction." *Narrative* 18, no. 2 (2010): 199–219.
Eisenstadt, Peter. *The Encyclopedia of New York State*. Syracuse: Syracuse University Press, 2005.
"Epidemic Cholera: Pathological Conclusions. The 'Propositions' of the Famous Dr. James Johnson." *New-York Daily Tribune*, January 27, 1866.
Errett, Isaac. "The Newspaper and Periodical Press." *The Christian Quarterly* 2 (January 1870): 56–65.
"España." *La Gaceta de Puerto-Rico*, July 28, 1846.
Fatima Raza Kolb, Anjula. *Epidemic Empire: Colonialism, Contagion, and Terror, 1817–2020*. Chicago: University of Chicago Press, 2021.
Ferber, Michael. *A Dictionary of Literary Symbols*. Cambridge: Cambridge University Press, 1999.
Ferme, Charles, *A Logical Analysis of the Epistle of Paul to the Romans, by Charles Ferme, Translated from the Latin By William Skae, A.M.; and A Commentary on the Same Epistle, by Andrew Melville in the Original Latin*. Ed. William Lindsay Alexander, D.D. Edinburgh: Woodrow Society, 1801.
Fern, Fanny. "The Hard Times." *The New York Ledger*, November 7, 1857.
Finnerty, Páraic. "Women's Transatlantic Poetic Network." *A History of Nineteenth-Century American Women's Poetry*. Ed. Jennifer Putzi and Alexandra Socarides. Cambridge: Cambridge University Press, 2017.
Finney, Henry Anson. *Accounting Principles and Bookkeeping Methods, Volume 1*. New York: H. Holt and Co., 1924.
"Front Page." *Plattsburgh Republican*, October 31, 1857.
Fuller, Margaret. *Art, Literature, and the Drama*. Boston: Brown, Taggard, and Chase, 1860.
Gallego, Juan Nicasio. Introduction to *Poesías de la Señorita Da. Gertrudis Gomez de Avellaneda*. Madrid: Establecimiento Tipográfico, 1841.
Ganster, Mary T. "Fact, Fiction, and the Industry of Violence: Newspapers and Advertisements in 'Clotel.'" *African American Review* 48, no. 4 (2015): 431–44.

Gardner, Jared. *The Rise and Fall of Early American Magazine Culture*. Champaign: University of Illinois Press, 2012.

Garvey, Ellen Gruber. *Writing with Scissors: American Scrapbooks from the Civil War to the Harlem Renaissance*. Oxford: Oxford University Press, 2012.

Genette, Gérard. *Paratexts: Thresholds of Interpretation*. Cambridge: Cambridge University Press, 1987.

—, and Marie Maclean. "Introduction to the Paratext." *New Literary History* 22, no. 2 (1991): 261–72.

Glazener, Nancy. *Literature in the Making: A History of U.S. Literary Culture in the Long Nineteenth Century*. Oxford: Oxford University Press, 2015.

—. *Reading for Realism: The History of a U.S. Literary Institution, 1850–1910*. Durham, NC: Duke University Press, 1997.

Glissant, Édouard. *Poetics of Relation*. Ann Arbor: University of Michigan Press, 1997.

Gómez de Avellaneda, Gertrudis. "Serenata: A su Alteza Real: la Serma. Sra. Infanta Duquesa de Montpensier: La Vispera de Su Cumpleaños." *La Gaceta de Puerto-Rico*, April 20, 1858.

Grafton, Anthony. *The Footnote: A Curious History*. Cambridge, MA: Harvard University Press, 1997.

Gray, Paul Bryan. *A Clamor for Equality: Emergence and Exile of Californio Activist Francisco P. Ramírez*. Lubbock: Texas Tech University Press, 2012.

—. "Francisco P. Ramirez: A Short Biography." *California History* 84, no. 2 (2006): 20–38.

Griswold del Castillo, Richard. *Los Angeles Barrio, 1850–1890: A Social History*. Berkeley: University of California Press, 1979.

Gruesz, Kirsten Silva. *Ambassadors of Culture: The Transamerican Origins of Latino Writing*. Princeton: Princeton University Press, 2002.

Hale, Will T. "Authors and the Mighty Dollar." *Christian Advocate*, July 20, 1913.

Halpine, Charles G. *The Poetical Works of Charles G. Halpine (Miles O'Reilly)*. Ed. Robert B. Roosevelt. New York: Harper & Brothers Publishers, 1869.

"Hard Times." *Edgefield Advertiser*, October 14, 1857.

"Hard Times and the Shoemaker." *Edgefield Advertiser*, August 12, 1857.

Hedrick, Joan D. *Harriet Beecher Stowe: A Life*. Oxford: Oxford University Press, 1995.

Hermans, Tobias. "Poetics of the Periodical Paratext: Editorial Footnotes and Reader Agency in Robert Schumann's *Davidsbund* Writings." *Colloquia Germanica* 49, no. 2/3 (2016): 157–76.

Hershberger, Mary. "Mobilizing Women's Abolition: The Struggle Against Indian Removal in the 1830s." *Journal of American History* 86, no. 1 (1999): 15–40.

Hollander, John. "The West Wind and the Mingled Measure." *Daedalus* 111, no. 3 (1982): 131–48.

Hughes, Linda K. "What the 'Wellesley Index' Left Out: Why Poetry Matters to Periodical Studies." *Victorian Periodicals Review* 40, no. 2. (2007): 91–125.

Huston, James L. *The Panic of 1857 and the Coming of the Civil War*. Baton Rouge: Louisiana State University Press, 1999.

Hutcheon, Linda. *A Theory of Parody: The Teachings of Twentieth-Century Art Forms*. Champaign: University of Illinois Press, 2000.

Ibarra, Rogelia Lily. "Gómez de Avellaneda's 'Sab': A Modernizing Project." *Hispania* 94, no. 3 (2011): 385–95.
Ingraham, Caroline. "Sarah Percival; or the Bride of 'The House of Gold,'" *The New York Ledger*, January 3, 1857.
Irmscher, Christoph. *Longfellow Redux*. Champaign: University of Illinois Press, 2006.
Jackson, Virginia. *Dickinson's Misery: A Theory of Lyric Reading*. Princeton: Princeton University Press, 2005.
Jameson, James. *Report on the epidemick cholera morbus, as it visited the territories subject to the Presidency of Bengal, in the years 1817, 1818, and 1819 / drawn up by order of the Government, under the superintendence of the Medical Board*. Calcutta: Government Gazette Press, 1820.
Jay, William. *The Works of the Rev. William Jay, of Argyle Chapel, Bath: Comprising Matter not Heretofore Presented to the American Public in Three Volumes, Vol. 3*. New York: Harper & Brothers Publishers, 1852.
Johnson, Wendy Dasler. *Antebellum American Women's Poetry: A Rhetoric of Sentiment*. Carbondale: Southern Illinois University Press, 2016.
Kaminski, Nicola, Nora Ramtke, and Carsten Zelle. "Zeitschriftenliteratur/Fortsetzungsliteratur: Problemaufriß." *Zeitschriftenliteratur/Fortsetzungsliteratur*. Ed. Nicola Kaminski, Nora Ramtke, and Carsten Zelle. Hanover: Wehrhahn, 2014.
Kanellos, Nicolás. "*El Clamor Público*: Resisting the American Empire." *California History* 84, no. 2 (2006): 10–18.
Kelly, Gary. Introduction to *Lydia Sigourney: Selected Poetry and Prose*. Ontario: Broadview Editions, 2008.
Kete, Mary Louise. *Sentimental Collaborations: Mourning and Middle-Class Identity in Nineteenth-Century America*. Durham, NC: Duke University Press, 2000.
—, and Elizabeth Petrino, *Lydia Sigourney: Critical Essays and Cultural Views*. Boston: University of Massachusetts Press, 2018.
Kilcup, Karen L. *Fallen Forests: Emotion, Embodiment, and Ethics in American Women's Environmental Writing, 1781–1924*. Athens: University of Georgia Press, 2013.
"King Cholera." *Mrs. Grundy*, August 26, 1865.
Kinsella, James E. "In Defense of Newspaper Poets." *Chicago Tribune*, July 28, 1910.
Kreitz, Kelley. "Network." *American Periodicals: A Journal of History & Criticism* 30, no. 1 (2020): 5–8.
"La prensa americana." *La correspondencia de Puerto Rico*, August 22, 1899.
Last, John M. *A Dictionary of Public Health*. Oxford: Oxford University Press, 2007.
Lazo, Rodrigo. "Introduction: Historical Latinidades and Archival Encounters." *The Latino Nineteenth Century*. Ed. Rodrigo Lazo and Jesse Alemán. New York: New York University Press, 2016.
—. *Writing to Cuba: Filibustering and Cuban Exiles in the United States*. Chapel Hill: University of North Carolina Press, 2005.
Leal, Luis. "Pre-Chicano Literature: Process and Meaning (1539–1959)." *Handbook of Hispanic Cultures in the United States: Literature and Art*. Ed. Francisco Lomelí. General eds. Nicolás Kanellos and Claudio Esteva-Fabregat. Houston: Arte Público Press, 1993.

—. "Truth-Telling Tongues: Early Chicano Poetry." *Recovering the U S. Hispanic Literary Heritage.* Ed. Ramón Gutiérrez and Genaro Padilla. Houston: Arte Público Press, 1993.

Ledbetter, Kathryn. "Bonnets and Rebellions: Imperialism in 'The Lady's Newspaper.'" *Victorian Periodicals Review* 37, no. 3 (2004): 252–72.

"Life." *The New York Ledger*, December 27, 1856.

Llona, Numa P. *Cantos Americanos: Coleccion de Poesias de D. Numa P. Llona.* Paris: P.-A. Bourdier, 1866.

"Localities Where the Pestilence First Appeared in 1832 and 1849." *New York Herald*, July 23, 1866.

"The Locomotive Engineers in Council." *Brotherhood of Locomotive Engineer Monthly Journal* 3, no. 1 (January 1869): 498.

Longfellow, Henry Wadsworth. *The Letters of Henry Wadsworth Longfellow, Volume V: 1866–1874.* Cambridge, MA: Harvard University Press, 1982.

—. *The Poetical Works of Henry Wadsworth Longfellow: Volume III.* Boston: Houghton, Mifflin and Company, 1886.

Looby, Christopher. "Southworth and Seriality." *Nineteenth-Century Literature* 59, no. 2 (2004): 179–211.

Lopate, Phillip, ed. *Writing New York: A Literary Anthology.* New York: Washington Square Press, 1998.

López, Ramón B. "The Needs of Porto Rico [sic]." *The Independent*, November 29, 1900.

Lozano, Rosina. *An American Language: The History of Spanish in the United States.* Oakland: University of California Press, 2018.

Luciani, Frederick. *José María Heredia in New York, 1823–1825: An Exiled Cuban Poet in the Age of Revolution, Selected Letters and Verse.* Albany: State University of New York Press, 2020.

McCoy, Beth A. "Race and the (Para)Textual Condition." *PMLA* 121, no. 1 (2006): 156–69.

McGill, Meredith. *The Traffic in Poems: Nineteenth-Century Poetry and Transatlantic Exchange.* New Brunswick: Rutgers University Press, 2008.

—. *American Literature and the Culture of Reprinting, 1834–1853.* Philadelphia: University of Pennsylvania Press, 2007.

Marx, Leo. *The Machine in the Garden: Technology and the Pastoral Ideal in America.* Oxford: Oxford University Press, 1964.

Melosi, Martin V. *The Sanitary City: Environmental Services in Urban America from Colonial Times to the Present*, abridged edition. Pittsburgh: University of Pittsburgh Press, 2008.

Meltzer, Allan H. *A History of the Federal Reserve, Volume 1: 1913–1951.* Chicago: University of Chicago Press, 2003.

Mercer, Lloyd J. *Railroads and Land Grant Policy: A Study in Government Intervention.* New York: Academic Press, 1982.

Mignolo, Walter. *The Darker Side of Western Modernity: Global Futures, Decolonial Options.* Durham, NC: Duke University Press, 2011.

Miles, Tiya. "'Circular Reasoning': Recentering Cherokee Women in the Antiremoval Campaigns." *American Quarterly* 61, no. 2 (2009): 221–43.

Miller, Beth. "Gertrude the Great: Avellaneda, Nineteenth-Century Feminist." *Women in Hispanic Literature: Icons and Fallen Idols*. Ed. Beth Miller. Berkeley: University of California Press, 1982.
Moran, Joe. *Star Authors: Literary Celebrity in America*. London: Pluto Press, 2000.
Mott, Frank Luther. *American Journalism*. New York: The Macmillan Company, 1941.
—. *A History of American Magazines, 1741–1850*. Cambridge, MA: Harvard University Press, 1966.
Muller, Gilbert H. *William Cullen Bryant: Author of America*. Albany: State University of New York Press, 2008.
"Multiple News Items." *Daily Evening Bulletin*, July 27, 1864.
Nelson, Scott Reynolds. *A Nation of Deadbeats: An Uncommon History of America's Financial Disasters*. New York: Random House, 2012.
Noonan, Mark. "Printscape." *American Periodicals: A Journal of History & Criticism* 30, no. 1 (2020), 9–11.
"Notes [to the Articles within This Issue]." *California History* 84, no. 2 (2006): 69–74.
"Noticias Literarias." *El Boletín mercantil de Puerto Rico*, September 22, 1871.
"Nuestras Glorias." *La correspondencia de Puerto Rico*, August 22, 1899.
Nunn, Suzanne. "A Court for King Cholera." *Popular Narrative Media* 2, no. 1 (2009): 5–21.
O'Connor, Erin. *Raw Material: Producing Pathology in Victorian Culture*. Durham, NC: Duke University Press, 2000.
O'Neill, Bonnie Carr. *Literary Celebrity and Public Life in the Nineteenth-Century United States*. Athens: University of Georgia Press, 2017.
O'Neill, Michael. *The Cambridge History of English Poetry*. Cambridge: Cambridge University Press, 2010.
"Our Albany Correspondence." *The Brooklyn Daily Eagle*, February 19, 1866.
Ovalle Perez, Vanessa. "Voicing a Transnational Latina Poetics: The Dedication Poems of Amelia Denis and Carlota Gutierrez." *J19: The Journal of Nineteenth-Century Americanists* 8, no. 2 (2020): 295–319.
"Panic Poetry." *Plattsburgh Republican*, October 31, 1857.
Parton, James. *The Life of Horace Greeley, Editor of the New-York Tribune*. New York: Derby and Miller, 1868.
"Passing Down the Avenue." *Evening Star*, January 1, 1857.
Pedreira, Antonio S. *El periodismo en Puerto Rico*. Río Piedras: Universidad de Puerto Rico, 1969.
Pettway, Matthew. *Cuban Literature in the Age of Black Insurrection: Manzano, Plácido, and Afro-Latino Religion*. Jackson: University Press of Mississippi, 2020.
Pierpont, John. *The American First-Class Book; or, Exercises in Reading and Religion*, revised and improved edition. Philadelphia: J. B. Lippincott & Co., 1856.
Plácido (Gabriel de la Concepcion Valdés). *Poesias Completas de Plácido (Gabriel de la Concepcion Veldés)*. Paris: En Casa de Mme C. Denné Schmitz, 1856.
—. *Poesias Completas de Plácido (Gabriel de la Concepcion Veldés)*. Paris: En Casa de Mme C. Denné Schmitz, 1862.
Poe, Edgar Allan. "Review of *Poems*, by Frances S. Osgood." *Broadway Journal* 2, no. 23 (December 13, 1845).

"Poets don't get your hopes up." *La Gaceta de Puerto-Rico*, May 14, 1861.

"Preparations for the Cholera." *The Brooklyn Daily Eagle*, November 13, 1865.

"Previous Ravages of the Cholera in New York." *New York Daily Herald*, November 5, 1865.

Prideaux, W. F. "Domett and Browning." *Notes and Queries: A Medium of Intercommunication for Literary Men, General Readers*, Seventh Series, vol. 12. London, 1891.

"The Pulpit and Sanitary Reform." *New York Times*, March 10, 1865.

Putzi, Jennifer. *Fair Copy: Relational Poetics and Antebellum American Women's Poetry*. Philadelphia: University of Pennsylvania Press, 2021.

Ramírez, Francisco P. *El Clamor Público*, April 7, 1855.

Ratner, Joshua, "Paratexts." *Early American Studies: An Interdisciplinary Journal* 16, no. 4 (2018): 733–40.

Renker, Elizabeth. *Realist Poetics in American Culture, 1866–1900*. Oxford: Oxford University Press, 2018.

Richards, Eliza. *Gender and the Poetics of Reception in Poe's Circle*. Cambridge: Cambridge University Press, 2004.

Rosenberg, Charles E. *The Cholera Years: The United States in 1832, 1849, and 1866*. Chicago: University of Chicago Press, 1962.

Ruiz, Ricardo Navas. *El Romanticismo Español*. Madrid: Cátedra, 1982.

Said, Edward. *Orientalism*. New York: Pantheon Books, 1978.

Santayana, George. "The Genteel Tradition in American Philosophy." *The Genteel Tradition: Nine Essays*. Ed. Douglas L. Wilson. Cambridge, MA: Harvard University Press, 1967.

Scheina, Robert L. *Latin America's Wars: The Age of the Caudillo, 1791–1899*. Lincoln: University of Nebraska Press, 2003.

Schneirov, Matthew. *The Dream of a New Social Order: Popular Magazines in America 1893–1914*. New York: Columbia University Press, 1994.

Schwartz, Stuart B. "The Hurricane of San Ciriaco: Disaster, Politics, and Society in Puerto Rico, 1899–1901." *Hispanic American Historical Review* 7, no. 3 (1982): 303-34.

"Second Stock of Fall and Winter Goods." *The Wheeling Daily Intelligencer*, November 3, 1857.

Senchyne, Jonathan. *The Intimacy of Paper in Early and Nineteenth-Century American Literature*. Boston: University of Massachusetts Press, 2020.

Senior, Emily. *The Caribbean and the Medical Imagination, 1764—1834: Slavery, Disease and Colonial Modernity*. Cambridge: Cambridge University Press, 2018.

"September Birthdays." *Journal of Education*, August 26, 1897.

Sexton, Jay. *Debtor Diplomacy: Finance and American Foreign Relations in the Civil War Era 1837–1873*. Oxford: Oxford University Press, 2005.

Shakespeare, William. *A Midsummer Night's Dream: The Oxford Shakespeare*. Ed. Peter Holland. Oxford: Oxford University Press, 1994.

Sigourney, Lydia H. "The Best Investment." *The New York Ledger*, February 21, 1857.

—. *The Daily Counsellor*. Hartford: Brown and Gross, Publishers, 1858.

—. "Fair Traffic." *The New York Ledger*, January 24, 1857.

—. "Leave Time and Place to God." *The New York Ledger*, January 3, 1857.

—. *Letters of Life*. New York: D. Appleton and Company, 1867.
—. *Letters to my Pupil*. New York: Robert Carter & Brothers, 1851.
—. *Letters to Young Ladies*. Hartford: P. Canfield, 1833.
Sinche, Bryan. "Lydia Sigourney's Sailors and the Limits of Sentiment." *Legacy: A Journal of American Women Writers* 29, no. 1 (2012): 62–85.
Siskind, Mariano. *Cosmopolitan Desires: Global Modernity and World Literature in Latin America*. Evanston, IL: Northwestern University Press, 2014.
Smith, Erin A. "Religion and Popular Print Culture." *The Oxford History of Popular Print Culture, Volume Six: US Popular Print Culture 1860–1920*. Ed. Christine Bold. New York: Oxford University Press, 2012.
Smith, Harry B. *A Sentimental Library: Comprising Books Formerly Owned By Famous Writers, Presentation Copies, Manuscripts, and Drawings*. Privately Printed, 1914.
Soares, Rebecca D. "Material Spirits and Immaterial Forms: The Immaterial Materiality of Elizabeth Barrett Browning's Abolitionist Poetry." *Victorian Poetry* 53, no. 4 (2015): 353–74.
Sorby, Angela. *Schoolroom Poets: Childhood, Performance, and the Place of American Poetry, 1865–1917*. Durham, NH: University of New Hampshire Press, 2005.
Stanitzek, Georg. "Texts and Paratexts in Media." *Critical Inquiry* 32, no. 1 (2005): 27–42.
Stark, Robert. *Ezra Pound's Early Verse and Lyric Tradition: A Jargoner's Apprenticeship*. Edinburgh: Edinburgh University Press, 2012.
"The State Capital." *New York Herald*, January 31, 1866.
Stokes, Claudia. *The Altar at Home: Sentimental Literature and Nineteenth-Century American Religion*. Philadelphia: University of Pennsylvania Press, 2014.
—. *Old Style: Unoriginality and Its Uses in Nineteenth-Century U.S. Literature*. Philadelphia: University of Pennsylvania Press, 2021.
Stormonth, Rev. James. *Etymological and Pronouncing Dictionary of the English Language*. Edinburgh: William Blackwood and Sons, 1881.
"Thurlow Weed Defines His Position." *The Brooklyn Daily Eagle*, October 9, 1866.
"Variedades." *El Boletín mercantil de Puerto Rico*, April 9, 1873.
Venable, William Henry. *Beginnings of Literary Culture in the Ohio Valley: Historical and Biographical Sketches*. Cincinnati: Robert Clarke & Co., 1891.
"The Voice of the Pestilence." *Daily National Intelligencer*, August 25, 1865.
Walker, Cheryl. *American Women Poets of the Nineteenth Century*. New Brunswick: Rutgers University Press, 1992.
Warner, Michael. *The Letters of the Republic: Publication and the Public Sphere in Eighteenth-Century America*. Cambridge, MA: Harvard University Press, 1990.
—. *Publics and Counterpublics*. Brooklyn: Zone Books, 2002.
Warren, Joyce W. *Fanny Fern: An Independent Woman*. New Brunswick: Rutgers University Press, 1992.
Washington, Margaret. "Frances Ellen Watkins: Family Legacy and Antebellum Activism." *The Journal of African American History* 100, no. 1 (2015): 59–86.
Whitman, Walt. "Slang in America." *Prose Works 1892*. Ed. Floyd Stovall. New York: New York University Press, 1964.
"Who is Partisan." *New York Tribune*, February 14, 1866.

Wolosky, Shira. *Feminist Theory Across Disciplines: Feminist Community and American Women's Poetry*. New York: Routledge, 2013.

—. *Poetry and Public Discourse in Nineteenth-Century America*. New York: Palgrave, 2010.

Woods, James Playsted. *The Story of Advertising*. New York: The Ronald Press Company, 1958.

INDEX

Note: page numbers in *italic* indicate illustrations.

'A Aquella', 78–9
'A la Vírgen' (Avellaneda), 161–2
'A Mi Amigo Don Juan Arguedas' (Pompilio Llona), 80
'A Mi Maria Antonia' (Ramírez), 80–4
'A Sabater' (Avellaneda), 161–2
'A Washington' (Avellaneda), 158, 159, 161–2, 164
abolitionist papers, 106–9
Adams, Michael, 96
advertisements, 5, 97–9
Aeolian harp poetry, 129
aesthetic practice: originality/unoriginality, 12
African American literature, 5
'Al Céfiro: Oda Sáfica' (Villegas), 78–9
'Al Partir' (Avellaneda), 159, 169–71, *170,* 173–5
Albin, María C., 157
Album de Momo (anthology), 75–6
Allen, Glen, 182–4, 186
   'A Newspaper Poet to a Real Poet', 184–5
   'Pity the Poor Newspaper Poets!', 182–4, *183*

Allen, Irving Lewis, 96
Allo, Lorenzo de, 159
América, La (later *La América Ilustrada*), 159
American First-Class Book; or, Exercises in Reading and Religion, The (Pierpont), 131
Ames, Mary Clemmer, 50
Anti-Slavery Bugle, 106, *107*
Armas, Juan Ignacio de, 159
Arnold, David, 133
Atlantic group, 21
Atlantic Monthly, The, 21
Avellaneda, Gertrudis Gómez de, 7, 19, 20, 149, 154–76, 188
   'A la Vírgen', 161–2
   'A Sabater', 161–2
   'A Washington', 158, 159, 161–2, 164
   'Al Partir', 159, 169–71, *170,* 173–5
   obituaries, 175–6
   Obras Literarias de la Señora Doña Gertrudis Gomez de Avellaneda, 160–1, 164
   paratextual context, 176

Avellaneda, Gertrudis Gómez de (*cont.*)
   in Puerto Rican anticolonial press,
     166–9
   in Puerto Rican conservative press,
     159–66
   Sab, 158–9, 164
   'Serenata: A su Alteza Real: la
     Serma. Sra. Infanta Duquesa de
     Montpensier', 160–1
   sonnets in *La Democracia*, 169–70
   in US periodical press, 157–9
Avellaneda, Manuel Gómez de, 154
Avila, Petra, 68

Balmaseda, Francisco Javier, 76–7, 85
Barr, Amelia E., 31
Barrett, Faith, 103
Barrett Browning, Elizabeth, 55
Bataille, Gretchen, 44, 62n76
'Battle of Life, The', 93
Baym, Nina, 10
'Becerro de Oro, El', 80
Beckert, Sven, 106, 109
Beecher, Henry Ward, 59n5, 97
Belmont Chronicle, 93
Belvis, Segundo Ruiz, 166–7
Bennett, Emerson, 48
   The Refugees: An Indian Tale of 1812,
     41–4, *43*, 47
Bennett, James Gordon, 144
Bennett, Paula Bernat, 10–11, 27, 185
'Best Investment, The' (Sigourney),
   45–7, *46*, 48
Betances, Ramón Emeterio, 166–7
Blank, G. K., 150n19
Bobbett, Alfred, 42–4, *43*, *46*, 47, 48
Bode, Katherine, 74
Boletín mercantil de Puerto Rico, El, 7,
   160, 163–4, 175–6
Boletín Popular, El (San Francisco), 67
Bolívar, Simón, 166
Bonner, Robert Edwin, 9, 16–17, 21, 25,
   26–7, 28, 29, 30–1, 36, 37–8, 42,
   45, 48, 187
   collaboration with Cary, 54–5

Booth, Samuel, 147
Borges, Jorge Luis, 2–3
Bretón de los Herreros, Manuel, 162–3
Brickhouse, Anna, 69, 158
Brontë, Emily, 128
Brooklyn Daily Eagle, 142–3, 145, 146,
   147
Brown, William Wells, 5
Browning, Robert, 130
Bryant, William Cullen, 31, 59n5, 128–9
Burnett, Alfred 'Alf' F., 110–15
   'Hard Times', 18, 20, 91, 92, 110–15
   'The Sexton's Spade', 121n69
Burstein, Daniel Eli, 127, 150n15
Butler University: Sigourney Society, 33
Byerly, Alison, 129

Calcaterra, Angela, 44–5
'Calendario en Verso, El' (Balmaseda),
   76–7
Californio: definition of, 65
Calomiris, Charles W., 112–13, 117n11
'Canción' (Zorrilla), 77–8
Cantos Americanos (Pompilio Llona), 80
'Captain's Well' (Whittier), 31
Carlyle, Jane Welsh, 27
Carroll Free Press, 110
Cary, Alice, 16–17, 19, 26, 27–8, 31–2,
   48
   advice columns, 51
   collaboration with Bonner, 54–5
   cross-genre pastoralism, 49–57, 58
   'Homesick', 54
   idleness, 55–6
   'Looking Back', 51–3, 57
   'Nobility', 54
   The Poems of Alice and Phoebe Cary,
     49
   'Work', 54–6, 57
Cary, Elmina, 49
Cary, Phoebe, 49–50
Cary, Robert and Elizabeth, 49
Casey, Jim, 54–5
'Castle of Old France, A' (Chamberlain),
   185

censorship, 19
Century Magazine, The, 21
Chamberlain, Samuel, 185
Chávez, John R., 66
Chesnutt, Charles W., 5
Child, Lydia Maria, 53–4
cholera, 18, 124–5, 126–7, 134
cholera poems, 18, 124–49
   'The Health Bill: A Talk Between Two Repubs at Albany', 18, 125, 129–35, 143–8
   'King Cholera', 18, 125, 129, 135–43, 148
   'The Voice of the Pestilence', 18, 125, 129–35, 143–8
Christian Quarterly, 25
Cincinnati Dollar Times, 110, 111–12
Citizens' Association of New-York, 143
Clamor Público, El, 2, 7, 17, 19, 65, 84–6, 158, 187
   dedication poems, 79, 85–6
   reprint poems, 67, 69–80, 73, 84–5
   satire in, 75–7, 85
Clotel: The President's Daughter (Brown), 5
'Cloud, The' (Shelley), 128, 130
Coeckelbergh, Mark, 50–1
Cohen, Michael C., 11, 74, 76, 109
Coleridge, Samuel Taylor, 56
colonial subjectivity, 161
coloniality: Mignolo's definition of, 155
Comercio de Lima (newspaper), 80
Comité Revolucionario de Puerto Rico, 166–7
'Confesión, La' (Villergas), 75–6
'Confidence and Credit', 93
'Constellations, The' (Bryant), 59n5
'Contestacion de las Mugeres' (Balmaseda), 76–7
Corbin, Megan, 157
Cordell, Ryan, 72, 91, 99, 113–14
Coronado, Carolina, 162–3, *162*
Coronado, Raúl, 71
correspondencia de Puerto Rico, La, 7, 166, 167–9

'Court for King Cholera, A' (Leech), 136–7, *137*
Covert, Bernard, 40
cross-genres (hybrid genres), 48–57, 182–4
   cross-genre pastoralism, 49–57, 58
Cuba, 166–7
Cueto, Leopoldo Augusto de, 164–6
Culler, Jonathan, 13

Daily Counsellor, The (Sigourney), 48
Daily Evening Bulletin, San Francisco, 157–8
D'Amore, Maura, 50
Dana, Charles A., 9, 30
Darnton, Robert, 5
Davies, Catherine, 157, 159
De Jong, Mary, 28
dedication poems, 79–80, 85–6
Democracia, La, 166
   Cuban sonnets in, 169–75
Derby, James Cephas, 27–8
'Devil and Tom Walker, The' (Irving), 146
Dickens, Charles, 59n5, 112
Dietrich, Lucas, 5
Domett, Alfred, 129
Donawerth, Jane, 61n53
Douglass, Ann, 32
Duncan, James S., 51

Edgefield Advertiser, 113–14, *114, 115*
Effron, Malcah, 4
Emerson, Ralph Waldo, 57
'En la Muerte de Jesucristo' (Valdés), 169–71, *170,* 172–3, *174,* 175
'England and America in 1782' (Tennyson), 31
epitexts, 3, 18
   Genette's definition of, 126
   'The Health Bill: A Talk Between Two Repubs at Albany,' 125, 129, 143–8
   'King Cholera', 125, 129, 135–43
   'The Voice of the Pestilence', 125, 129–35

Errett, Isaac, 25, 32
Evening Post, The, New York, 99–100
   on cholera, 134
   fire insurance ads, 97–9
   'The Lay of the Directors', 93–9, *94, 98*
   'Lines by Buster', 102–6
'Excelsior' (Longfellow), 118n17
exile press, 8

'Fair Traffic' (Sigourney), 40–4, 48
Fayetteville Weekly Observer, 113
Fenton, Reuben, 147
Ferber, Michael, 150n24
Fern, Fanny, 26, 116
Field and Fireside, 153n61
financial depressions, 117n6
Finnerty, Páraic, 27
Finney, Henry Anson, 121n59
fire insurance ads, 97–9
Foucault, Michel, 74
Frank Leslie's Illustrated Newspaper, New York, 157–8
Franklin Female College, 33
Fuller, Margaret, 9, 30

Gaceta de Puerto-Rico, La, 160, 161–2, *162,* 163
Gallienne, Richard Le, 182, 184, 185
Ganster, Mary T., 5
Gardner, Jared, 116n1
Garrison, William Lloyd, 108–9
Garvey, Ellen Gruber, 14, 90–1
Genette, Gérard, 5, 6, 29, 105
   definition of epitext, 126
   on paratext, 2–3
   on poem titles, 77, 78
'Gesang der Geister über den Wassern' (Goethe), 127–8
'Give Me the People', 93
'Give me the Splendid Silent Sun' (Whitman), 57
Glazener, Nancy, 21, 181, 187–8
Glissant, Édouard, 170–1
Godey's Lady's Book, 21

Goethe, Johann Wolfgang von, 127–8
Goldsmith, Oliver, 103–4
Graham's Magazine, 21, 28
Gray, Paul Bryan, 66, 68, 69
Greeley, Horace, 9, 30, 49, 144–5, 146, 147
Greenville Enterprise, 110
Griswold del Castillo, Richard, 71, 82, 83
Gruesz, Kirsten Silva, 29, 84, 163
Guadalupe Hidalgo, Treaty of, 66–7
Gutiérrez, Juan María, 74

Habermas, Jürgen, 11
Hale, Sarah Joseph, 33
Halpine, Charles G., 18, 125, 129–35, 143–8
'Hanging of the Crane, The' (Longfellow), 31, 59n5
'Hard Times, The' (Fern), 116
'Hard Times' (Burnett), 18, 20, 91, 92, 110–15
   paratextual context, 113
   reprint life, 112–15, *114, 115*
Hard Times (Dickens), 112
Harper's Weekly, 42
Harte, Bret, 96
Hartford Courant, 32, 44
'Health Bill: A Talk Between Two Repubs at Albany, The' (Halpine), 18
   epitexts, 125, 129–35, 143–8
Hedrick, Joan D., 132
Hemans, Felicia, 32
Heredia, José María, 154
   'Inmortalidad', 169–71, *170*, 173, 174, 175
   'Ode to Niagara', 129, 171
Hermans, Tobias, 3, 4
hermeneutic poems, 35–49, 57–8
Hershberger, Mary, 45
Hidden Hand (Southworth), 59n6
Hijar y Jaro, Juan B., 67
Hispanophone press, 67
Hollander, John, 129
'Hombres Y Mugeres' (Balmaseda), 76–7

'Homesick' (Cary), 54
Houghton, Mifflin and Company, 5
Household Book of Poetry (Dana), 9, 30
Hughes, Linda K., 29
'Hunted Down' (Dickens), 59n5
Huston, James L., 104, 113
hybrid genres (cross-genres), 48–57, 182–4

'In Defense of Newspaper Poets' (Kinsella), 181
'Indian Girl's Burial' (Sigourney), 45
'Indian Names' (Sigourney), 45
Ingraham, Caroline, 37–40, 48, 51–3
'Inmortalidad' (Heredia), 169–71, *170*, 173, 174, 175
Irmscher, Christoph, 118n17
irony, 76, 103, 184–5
Irving, Washington, 146
'Italy', 31
iteration, culture of, 116n1

Jackson, Virginia, 12–13, 35–6
Jameson, James, 133, 134, 151n36
'Jamie's On the Stormy Sea' (Covert), 40
Jay, William, 62n68
Johnson, James, 133

Kaminski, Nicola, 3
Kanellos, Nicolás, 66, 70
Kelly, Gary, 33
Kete, Mary Louise, 32–3
Kilcup, Karen L., 44, 51, 57
'King Cholera', 18, 148
  epitexts, 125, 129, 135–43
Kinsella, James E., 181, 186
Kircher, Athanasius, 150n24
Know-Nothing Party, 71
Kolb, Anjuli Fatima Raza, 131, 134
Kreitz, Kelley, 15

Lady's Newspaper, 47
Lambert, David R., 51
Latin American Wars for Independence, 166

'Lay of the Directors, The' (anon), 18, 91, 92, 93–102, *94*
  paratextual context, 97–9, *98*
  reprint afterlife, 99–102, *100*
Lazo, Rodrigo, 17, 159
Le Gallienne, Richard *see* Gallienne, Richard Le
Leal, Luis, 66, 68, 69
'Leave Time and Place to God' (Sigourney), 36–8, 39, 40, 48
Leaves of Grass (Whitman), 13
Ledbetter, Kathryn, 5, 47
Leech, John, 136–7, *137*
Leeds Mercury, 153n61
Lejeune, Philippe, 3
'Lessons from the Times' (Beecher), 97
Letters of Life (Sigourney), 34, 35
Letters to My Pupil (Sigourney), 61n50
Letters to Young Ladies (Sigourney), 61n50
Liberator, The, 93, 106, 108–10, *108*
'Life' (column), 52
'Lines by Buster' (anon), 18, 91, 92, 93, 102–9
  in abolitionist papers, 106–9
  paratextual context, 102–3, 105–6
  parody, 102–5
  reprint poems, 105
'Lines Written on the back of a Protested Note', 109–10
Longfellow, Henry Wadsworth, 59n5, 31, 118n17
Looby, Christopher, 59n6
'Looking Back' (Cary), 51–4, 57
Looking Toward Sunset (Child), 53–4
López, Ramón B., 167–8, 169
Los Angeles Star, 68
Lozano, Rosina, 67
Luciani, Frederick, 171

McCoy, Beth A., 5
McGill, Meredith, 10, 29, 69, 86, 90
McLean's Monthly, 135, *135*
Manzano, Juan, 172

Maria Christina of the Two Sicilies, 160–1
Marrero-Fente, Raúl, 157
Martí, José, 156
Marx, Leo, 50
Matthews, Brander, 118n22
Melosi, Martin V., 125, 127, 137, 141
Meltzer, Allan H., 103
Memorial of Alice and Phoebe Cary, A (Ames), 50
Metropolitan Health Bill, New York (1866), 143–8
miasma theory, 125, 126–7, 130, 133
Midsummer Night's Dream, A (Shakespeare), 105–6, *105*
Mignolo, Walter, 155
Miles, Tiya, 45
Miller, Beth, 157
Monroe, Harriet, 21
Moran, Joe, 28
Moss and Brother (Philadelphia publisher), 49
Mott, Frank Luther, 9–10
Mrs. Grundy (weekly humor magazine), 136
Muller, Gilbert H., 129
Mulock, Dinah Maria (Dinah Maria Craik), 164

National Magazine, 54–5
Nelson, Scott Reynold, 92
networks, 15
New-York Citizen, 143
New-York Daily Tribune, 117n11, 133, 144–5
New York Herald, 139–40, *140*, 142, 144–5
New York Ledger, 17, 19, 25–7, 29–32, 116, 187
  Cary's cross-genre pastoralism, 49–57
  hermeneutic poems, 57–8
  poetry in, role of, 29–32
  printscape, 47–8
  Sigourney's hermeneutic poems, 35–49, *43*

New York Sun, 140–1
New York Times, 134, 141–2, 147–8
New York Times Magazine, 183, *183*
'Newspaper Poet to a Real Poet, A' (Allen), 184–5
newspaper poets: attacks on/defence of, 181–6
'Night-Wind, The ' (Brontë), 128
'Nobility' (Cary), 54
Noonan, Mark, 15
Northern Mexico, 66–7
Norwood (Beecher), 59n5
'Nuestra Glorias', 167
Nuevo Mexicano, El (New Mexico), 67
Nuevo Mundo, El (San Francisco), 67
Nunn, Suzanne, 136–7

Obras Literarias de la Señora Doña Gertrudis Gomez de Avellaneda (Avellaneda), 160–1, 164
O'Connor, Erin, 153n61
'Ode to Niagara' (Heredia), 129, 171
'Ode to the West Wind' (Shelley), 128, 150n19
Ohio American Anti-Slavery Society (later Western Anti-Slavery Society), 106
Ohio Life Insurance and Trust Company, 92
'On the Mode of Communication of Cholera' (Snow), 125
O'Neill, Bonnie Carr, 27
O'Neill, Michael, 128
O'Reilly, Miles *see* Halpine, Charles G.
Osgood, Frances Sargent, 28
Ovalle Perez, Vanessa, 79, 82, 83

Panic of 1837, 20
Panic of 1857, 17–18, 90, 91–3, 104, 109
  railroad industry, 91–2
  and reprint poems, 92
panic poetry, 17–18, 20, 90–116
  'Hard Times' (Burnett), 18, 20, 91, 92, 110–15

INDEX

'Lay of the Directors, The' (anon), 18, 91, 92, 93–102, *94*
'Lines by Buster' (anon), 18, 91, 92, 93, 102–9
paratextuality, 149
  advice columns, 49
  biblical epigraphs, 35, 36
  definition of 'paratext', 2
  poetics of, 2–6, 7
  sensational tales and illustrations, 36
  serials, 49
Parlor Magazine, The, 54
parody, 102–5
Partido Conservador (later Partido Incondicional Español), 163
pastoral Romanticism, 51
pastoralism, 49–57
patriarchal Romanticism, 52–4, 57
Pedreira, Antonio S., 163
Peninsular War, 166
peritexts, 3, 18
Petrino, Elizabeth, 33
Pettway, Matthew, 172
Pierpont, John, 131
Pittsburgh Daily Commercial, 134
'Pity the Poor Newspaper Poets!' (Allen), 182–4, *183*
Plácido *see* Valdés, Gabriel de la Concepción (Plácido)
Plattsburgh Republican, 93, 105–6, *105*
'Pobre Hombres!', 76–7
Poe, Edgar Allan, 28
Poems of Alice and Phoebe Cary, The (Cary), 49
poetess: definitions of, 27
Poetical Works of Charles G. Halpine, The (ed. Roosevelt), 143–4
poetics
  of paratextuality, 2–6, 7
  relational poetics, 12
Poetry Magazine, 21
political reportage, 19
Pompilio Llona, Numa, 80, 85
'Preparations for the Cholera', 142
Prideaux, W. F., 130

printscapes, 15–16, 21, 47–8
'Prisionero, El' (reprint poem), 77–8
Proudhon, Pierre-Joseph, 165
public health system, New York, 143
Puerto Rico, 18–19, 166–7
Punch Magazine, 136–7, *137*
Putzi, Jennifer, 12, 13, 32, 33, 186–7

railroad bonds, 92
railroad industry, 91–2
Ramírez, Francisco P., 7, 17, 19, 187
  'A Mi Maria Antonia', 80–4
  biographical details, 68–9
  reprint practices, 65–6, 74
  writing style, 80–3
Ramírez, Juan M., 68
Ramtke, Nora, 3
Ratner, Joshua, 3, 4, 72
reading practices, 12–13, 28
Reed, Enos B., 111
Refugees: An Indian Tale of 1812, The (Bennett), 41–4, *43*, 47
relational poetics, 12
Renker, Elizabeth, 12, 185
reprint poems, 14–15, 17–18, 20
  'A Aquella', 78–9
  anthologies, 75–6
  Anti-Slavery Bugle, 106–10
  'El Becerro de Oro', 80
  in *El Clamor Público*, 67, 69–80, *73*, 84–5
  'La Confesión' (Villergas), 75–6
  digital map, *73*
  'The Lay of the Directors' (anon), 99–102
  'Lines by Buster' (anon), 105
  and Panic of 1857, 92
  paratextual context, 101–2, 106–8, *107*
  'Pobre Hombres!', 76–7
  'El Prisionero', 77–8
Ribera, José Rómulo, 67
Richards, Eliza, 28, 33, 35

207

Riley, James Whitcomb, 96
Rimas Cubanas (Balmaseda), 76–7
Robinson, Marius R., 106
Rockman, Seth, 106, 109
Rojo, Manuel Clemente, 68
Romanticism, 50–1, 166
   pastoral Romanticism, 51
   patriarchal Romanticism, 52–4, 57
   Romantic poetry, 127–9
Roosevelt, Robert B., 143–4
Rosenberg, Charles E., 124, 127
Rossetti, Christina, 128

Sab (Avellaneda), 158–9, 164
Said, Edward, 130–1
Salter, Sarah H., 54–5
San Ciriaco hurricane, 168–9
Sand, George, 165
Santayana, Jorge/George, 12, 181–2
Sarah Percival; or the Bride of 'The House of Gold (Ingraham), 37–40, 48, 51–3
Sarmiente, Domingo Faustino, 74
satire, 75–7, 85
Schweikart, Larry, 112–13, 117n11
scrapbooks, 14
Senchyne, Jonathan, 104
Senior, Emily, 132
'Serenata: A su Alteza Real: la Serma. Sra. Infanta Duquesa de Montpensier' (Avellaneda), 160–1
Seward, William Henry, 146
Sexton, Jay, 92
'Sexton's Spade, The' (Burnett), 121n69
Seymour, Robert, 135, *135*
Shakespeare, William, 105–6, *105*
Shelley, Percy Bysshe
   'The Cloud', 128, 130
   'Ode to the West Wind', 128, 150n19
   'To a Skylark', 128
Sigourney, Lydia Huntley, 16–17, 19, 26, 27, 31, 32–49, 57–8
   'The Best Investment', 45–7, *46*, 48
   biblical epigraphs, 35, 36
   The Daily Counsellor, 48

'Fair Traffic', 40–4, 48
gendered rhetorical theory, 61n53
hermeneutic poems, 35–49, *43*, 57–8
'Indian Girl's Burial', 45
'Indian Names', 45
knitting, 34
'Leave Time and Place to God', 36–8, 39, 40, 48
Letters of Life, 34, 35
Letters to My Pupil, 61n50
Letters to Young Ladies, 61n50
Traits of the Aborigines of America, 44–5
Sigourney Society, Butler University, 33
Sinche, Bryan, 33
Siskind, Mariano, 84
slavery
   abolitionist papers, 106–9
   anti-slavery fiction, 158
   in 'The Voice of the Pestilence', 132
Smith, Erin A., 59n5
Smith, Harry B., 130
Snow, John, 125
Soares, Rebecca, 4
Sorby, Angela, 96
Southworth, E. D. E. N., 59n6
Spanish-language press, 6–7
Stanitzek, Georg, 5, 6, 77
Stedman, Edmund Clarence, 181
Stokes, Claudia, 12, 96
story papers, 21; *see also New York Ledger*
Strong, George Templeton, 117n11
'Summer Wind' (Bryant), 128–9
Summit County Beacon, 109

Tennyson, Alfred, Lord Tennyson, 31
Thoreau, Henry David, 57, 129
'Times, The', 93
'To a Skylark' (Shelley), 128
Tolón, Miguel T., 159
Torres, Luis A., 67
Traits of the Aborigines of America (Sigourney), 44–5
transcendentalism, 51

Trial of Tears, 45
Trumbull, Lyman, 147
'Two Rivers' (Emerson), 57

Union Magazine, 9–10

Valdés, Gabriel de la Concepción (Plácido), 156
  'En la Muerte de Jesucristo', 169–71, *170,* 172–3, 174, 175
Verdad, La, New York, 158, 159
Vigil, J. M., 67
Vignes, Jean-Louis, 68–9
Villaverde, Cirilo, 159
Villegas, Esteban Manuel de, 78–9
Villergas, Juan Martínez, 74–6, 85
'Voice of the Pestilence, The', 18, 143–8
  authorship of, 129–30
  biblical connotations, 132
  epitexts, 125, 129–35
  slavery, 132

Waite, James S., 68
Walden (Thoreau), 57
Walker, Cheryl, 33

Warner, Michael, 13–14, 116n1
Warren, Joyce W., 26
Weed, Thurlow, 145, 146
Western Anti-Slavery Society (previously Ohio American Anti-Slavery Society), 106
Western Review, 9
Wheeling Daily Intelligencer, 99–101, *100, 101*
'When Lovely Woman Stoops to Folly' (Goldsmith), 103–4
Whitman, Walt, 13, 57, 96, 118n21
Whittier, John Greenleaf, 31
'Who Has Seen the Wind?' (Rossetti), 128
wind poetry, 127–9
Wolosky, Shira, 10, 11, 91, 125
'Work' (Cary), 54–6, 57
'Work Without Hope' (Coleridge), 56

Yeats, William Butler, 181
yellow journalism, 21
Yorkville Enquirer, 113

Zelle, Carsten, 3
Zorrilla, José, 77–8, 85, 154

EU representative:
Easy Access System Europe
Mustamäe tee 50, 10621 Tallinn, Estonia
Gpsr.requests@easproject.com